Mountain Biking
North
Carolina

Timm Muth

FALCON®

Guilford, Connecticut

An imprint of The Globe Pequot Press

A FALCON GUIDE®

Cover photo by Bob Allen.

All black-and-white photos by the author unless otherwise noted.

Library of Congress Cataloging-in-Publication Data
Muth, Timm, 1961-
    Mountain biking North Carolina/by Timm Muth.
    p.   cm. — (A FalconGuide)
ISBN 1-56044-809-1
1. All terrain cycling—North Carolina—Guidebooks. 2. North Carolina—Guidebooks. I. Falcon guide.

GV1045.5.N752 M87 2000
796.6'3'09756—dc21   99-055393
                                                                CIP

 Text pages printed on recycled paper.

Manufactured in the United States of America
First Edition/Second Printing

CAUTION
Outdoor recreational activities are by their very nature potentially hazardous. All participants in such activities must assume the responsibility for their own actions and safety. The information contained in this guidebook cannot replace sound judgment and good decision-making skills, which help reduce risk exposure, nor does the scope of this book allow for disclosure of all the potential hazards and risks involved in such activities.

Learn as much as possible about the outdoor recreational activities in which you participate, prepare for the unexpected, and be cautious. The reward will be a safer and more enjoyable experience.

For Bill Scarborough, who left us doing what he enjoyed best: riding with his son.

Acknowledgments

This book was nothing at all like a solo effort. On every trip I had the company of one or more of my crew, someone to share the adventure with me. Their energy often made the difference between thrashing and crashing, between a cool, fun ride and a painful, heartbreaking one. It's their book too. My thanks then to Ned, David T, Jeffrey, Daniel the Excitable Boy, Brian Beatty, and my intrepid bud Curt-o, who would ride his bike downhill in a hurricane and just call it "slick and fast." A special thanks to the Grand Ambassadors of Pisgah, Butchie and Tony Landolfi, who opened their hearts and their home to us, offered us fine singletrack and cold beer, and taught us what it really means to be young. Other riding compadres included Bruce, Matt, Susan Balfor and the NC FATS crew, Debra, Rob (buy a sleeping bag, son!), Tom, Joy, John Grout, Kelly and Mike, Kim, Brian Plaster, and the rest of the trail monkeys whose names temporarily escape me.

Thanks to all the folks who gifted me with new paths to ride, and then gladly showed me the way. Some I know by name, and others were just friendly spirits along the path. These folks include Jason of Chain Reaction, Gina Elrod of Biltmore Estate, Hopeann of Paul's Schwinn, "Bear," JT and Robin, Mike of Magic Cycles, Tom at Epic Cycles, Mike at the Outdoor Ed Center, Adam and Todd Hancock, Mike Green at Beech Mountain, Mike and Rob, the folks at Ski Country, and Tracy at Fontana Village.

I couldn't have ridden the first mile without a tight-running bike. For that, my humble thanks to Bob at The Clean Machine and Fred at Cycle Center. Night or day, whatever it took, these guys kept me rolling. They also taught me the fine art of un-tacoing a tire. Thanks to Scott, Art, Todd, Mark, and the rest of the crew at The Clean Machine for always believing my stories (*really, I didn't even hardly crash!*), and hooking me up with warranty returns, repairs, and replacements. Thanks to Chris Kuhlkin at Cannondale for a supreme hook-up and kudos to Cannondale, for making one helluva tough machine.

Thanks from riders everywhere, to the landowners and managers who've allowed us to build, maintain, and enjoy bike trails all across the state. Thank you for your foresight and consideration and for sharing your forests and woodlands with us.

Thanks to Mom, Dan, Sue, Roo, Rich, Lori, and Alli, my extended family, for calmly seeing me through various stages of book production and body repair.

Thanks, of course, to Falcon Publishing and particularly to my editor, Peggy O'Neill-McLeod, for making this adventure a possibility.

And all the thanks in my heart to the Creator, for blessing us with such a beautiful world, for granting me strong limbs and lungs to venture out in it, and for these wonderful machines we call bicycles.

Contents

Map Legend

Interstate	(90)	Campground	▲
U.S. Highway	(12)	Picnic Area	🛏
State or Other Principal Road	(22) (222)	Buildings	🏠 or ☐
Forest Road	444	Peak/Elevation	⛰ 4,507 ft.
Interstate Highway	〰	Bridge/Pass	) (
Paved Road	〰	Gate	⊸
Gravel Road	〰	Parking Area	Ⓟ
Unimproved Road	⋯	Boardwalk/Pier	▰
Trail (singletrack)	⋯	Railroad Track	┼┼┼
Trailhead	⓪	Power Lines	•—•—•
Trail Marker	⓪	Park Boundary	⌐_⌐
Waterway	〰	Map Orientation	N ↑
Lake/Reservoir	⬭		
Marsh/Swamp	⊻	Scale	0 0.5 1 MILES

Locator

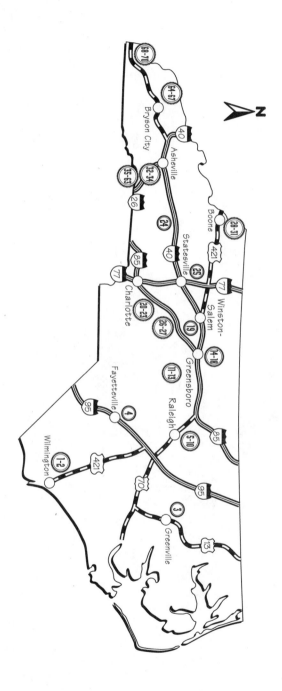

Introduction

Between these pages lies a treasure map of singletrack gems tucked away across the Tar Heel State, from the beach to the Smoky Mountains. Anything you could want in a mountain bike ride you can find here somewhere: roots, rocks, twisty sylvan highways, mudholes, tortuous climbs, jagged descents, breathtaking scenery, and lakes of adrenaline. We generally didn't include greenways or other commuter paths and avoided riding on roads (graveled, paved, or otherwise) when at all possible. This book is about singletrack: twisty hardpack, slaloming through trees and roots and rocks, rising through heartbreaking climbs, and descending in sometimes frightening fashion. That's what we came to ride; that's what it's all about.

Roughly half of the book is dedicated to rides about town, for the "I've got a 2-hour window and I want to ride now" crew. While I expected to find lots of lame, mulched footpaths, instead wherever we went we discovered kicking little trails tucked away in all sorts of places. Buffed, rolling cruisers, root and rock thrashers, big logs and big drops. They grow in small county and city parks, municipal properties or right-of-ways, on university and watershed property, and on private land.

The remainder of the book pays homage to our own bits of singletrack heaven. Pisgah and Nantahala National Forests hold some of the most beautiful singletrack anywhere in the world. Rides out here are longer, steeper, faster, and rougher than most other places you've probably ridden. You can cruise along the buffed berms of Tsali for miles and miles. And you can get lost in the depths of Pisgah Forest for days. You can climb for hours to a hidden gap, then return on a long ridgeline run, or maybe just turn and plummet through 2,000 feet of vertical in 2 miles. It's the big leagues of riding, and you'll come back humbled. But you'll keep coming back.

We rode a lot of trails in the course of this book. For every two trails we found, we had to discard a third because it was off-limits by someone's count. Most trails we rode at least twice; one we rode five times trying to get it right (and then had the bloody thing get posted!). Some trails we fell in love with, only to watch as they were dozed a month later. So I apologize to any trails I missed or wasn't able to pull together in time. If you've got some legal track, please share. I promise to get it into the next revision.

How to Use This Guide

We tried to give you enough information to find your way easily through the trails, and allow more time to simply ride and enjoy yourself.

MAPS

Every effort was taken to ensure the accuracy of the maps and the directions. Some of the trails required several rides to figure out the layout and to find the best run. But have no (or at least little) fear: Most of these places are easy to navigate through. While the maps may not show every twist and turn of the trail, we tried to include enough landmarks to keep you on your way. Just remember that back in the big woods, old roads can disappear, new paths can spring up, and everything takes longer than you think.

ELEVATION PROFILES

The elevation profiles give you an idea of what gravity has in store for you on a ride. Gravity in one direction usually means speed, adrenaline, and air potential. Gravity in the other direction usually means pain. The profiles show trail elevation (in feet) up the side, and distance in miles along the bottom. While small changes in grade aren't shown, they are usually mentioned in the write-up. Recognize that the profiles were compressed to fit them on the page, so the slopes may look steeper than they feel—and then again, they may not.

Technical ratings are given for each section of trail, with major obstacles noted along the way. The profile also shows changes in the tread surface.

TRAIL INFORMATION

Ride name and number: The rides in this book are numbered roughly east to west as they appear across the state. Use these numbers to locate trails on the state map or in the ride index. Names of the trails were taken from posted signs when possible and local lore when necessary.

Location: Approximate location and driving time from the nearest major metro area.

Distance: The ride's total length, in miles. Out-and-backs are measured out and back.

Time: A range of average riding time for the trail, listed from advanced riders to novices. Times include a normal complement of stops along the way, if warranted. Base your time estimates on distance *and* technical requirements, because 5 miles can take you 3 hours if it's brutal enough.

Tread: Types of surfaces you'll be riding across, and approximate distances for each.

Aerobic level: This is the physical, cardiopulmonary challenge of the ride. Though this usually means elevation change, it can also be affected by distance, speed, technical requirements, and adrenaline level. Trails are rated easy, moderate, or strenuous.

Easy: Mostly flat, generally smooth rides. Ride might include some short, rolling hills.

Moderate: Many climbs; some may be steep and/or rocky. You'll have gasping lungs and burning legs at several points along the ride, and may even push in a spot or two.

Strenuous: By the time you finish one of these, you're done for the day. Serious fatigue and lactic burn, and probably some form of bloody trail offering along the way. Rides may have significant or continuous elevation change. They may be long grinders that last for days, endless hike-a-bikes, or a constant assault of steep drops and climbs. Remember that tough technical moves and anaerobic sprints definitely up the ante here.

Technical difficulty: This scale of 1 to 5 gives you an idea of what it takes in terms of balance, body English, and technical skills to survive the trail and have a good time. Everyone's scale is a little different, so ride a few of the trails and see how your skills match the ratings. Note that the trails located in the mountains generally rank an order of magnitude higher in difficulty than their flatland cousins.

Tech 1: Smooth, buff track, flat or slightly rolling, with little or no technical challenges. There are no tech 1 trails in Pisgah.

Tech 2: Mostly clear track, with small rocks, roots, and other obstacles that are fairly easy to avoid or roll over.

Tech 3: More serious obstacles: small boulders, breaching roots, erosion gullies, patches of loose chicken heads, 1- to 2-foot logs. Steep descents may add a point to the rating. Opportunities for a nasty biff begin to appear.

Tech 4: Continual assault of major technical moves, most of which carry a serious penalty in case of failure. Things like 3-foot water bars, large boulders and rock slabs, waist-high logs, long nasty root carpets, gaping erosion gullies, and dragon-toothed descents. Extreme steeps in either direction may add to the fray.

Tech 5: All-or-nothing moves that you either ride or talk about at the ER. May include large boulder and staircase descents, vertical drops, lethal landing zones, high bridges, sketchy, narrow track with long fall lines, and other things that can hurt you bad. Luckily, these monsters thrive only up in Pisgah.

Highlights: In short, this is what to expect along the trail: types of obstacles, elevation changes, sites of interest, or any particular fun or sketchy spots.

Land status: Tells who owns/manages that piece of prime singletrack you're about to nab: city or county park, national forest, watershed, or private land. Also lists any entrance fee, when required.

Contacts for trails are listed in Appendix B.

Maps: Lists other maps available of the area and trails. May include U.S. Geological Survey topographic maps, USDA Forest Service maps, trailhead signs, Internet sketches, or third-party trail maps.

Access: How to get there and where to find the trailhead. Most directions take you in from the closest metro area or interstate.

Notes on the trail: Here's the soul of the trail—thoughts of the ride, distilled to reveal its dirt-encrusted essence. It includes remembrances of climbs conquered, of technical battles both won and lost. You may also find philosophical musings on the transcendence of weightlessness, the sublime arch of a long carved berm, and the joy found astride our two-wheeled steeds.

The Ride: This is a point-by-point description of the ride, with all major turns, obstacles, and other features noted and marked. Most of these notes were recorded during the ride itself, so it gives you a pretty good feel for the rhythm of the ride. Realize that different bike computers rarely measure exactly the same, so take all distances as approximate.

High tech minus batteries equals junk. DAVID TOLLERTON PHOTO

How to Ride

To retain the trails we treasure and to hold promise for new trails in the future, everyone needs to ride responsibly. Obey all trail rules (even if you don't always agree with them), help anyone who seems to need it, use the proper safety equipment, ride only when weather permits, take care of the trail, and just generally don't mess the place up.

TRAIL CONDITIONS

Some trails can suffer considerable damage if ridden in wet conditions, as can the relationship with said trail's owners. Soft loamy surfaces can stay fragile for several days after a good rain. Other trails, often those on steeper hills, drain very quickly and can be ridden in just about all conditions. The simplest rule of thumb is, don't tear the trail up and respect all trail closure signs.

TRAIL MAINTENANCE

If you really want to help out on a trail, join the local club or group that maintains the trail. They'll show you the best construction techniques. Remember that nothing enrages a trail builder more than to find that some bonehead has cut through a log or moved a boulder or bypassed a root that other riders were obviously managing. Here are a few guidelines for making adjustments to the trail:

- Remove any loose limbs that threaten to catch spokes or derailleurs.
- Do not remove any logs, rocks, or other obstacles from the trail. If it looks like anyone has even tried to make it, then be assured that it's ridable. Leave it alone, find a way around, and try it again another day.

Streams can occasionally get dammed or rerouted by fallen limbs or rocks, washing out an existing trail. Five minutes spent rerouting things will not only transport you back to childhood but will leave a better trail for the next rider.

Mention any serious trail problems to the club or individuals who manage or maintain the trails.

COMPANIONS

Nothing makes a ride more enjoyable than good riding companions. Someone to laugh with, laugh at, swap stories and sketchy lines, someone to cheer your successes and haul your broken body to the hospital if need be. Riding buddies make the trip safer just by being there, which—by some thinking—frees you to push things just a little harder than you would alone. With a crew to ride with, you've always got the right tool, an extra Cliffy, and enough energy to make it to the top.

It's cool to ride with folks who can suck you up long grinders in their wake, or who can show you the one threadline of safety through a nasty rock garden. But the best buds are those who simply enjoy riding as much as you do. Try to match up with riders of similar ability levels to maximize your fun.

CONTROL

Try to maintain control of your bike at all times, since being out of control often directly precedes a major biff. Crazy, bombing descents are a blast, but crashing big—or worse, running someone down—will really dampen the entire riding experience. Unless you know the trail is clear ahead, use extra caution where sight is limited. And always, always hang on to your bike.

TRASH

There's just one rule: Don't Leave Trash Behind! If that tube or Power Bar wrapper didn't weigh too much to carry in, it certainly doesn't weigh too much to carry out. And that goes for the Clif Shots too: They're not biodegradable, you know. The worst violators of this rule seem to be racers, who can't afford the extra second to stash their trash. Come on folks: It's not only disrespectful to the earth, but it points the finger at us as surely as an empty can of Vienna sausages says "Bubba was here." Let's continue the widely accepted consensus that mountain bikers are the least intrusive users of the forest.

RIDING ETIQUETTE

Besides the following IMBA rules, here are a few other suggestions that will make other people enjoy riding with you more.
- Tell someone which side you plan to pass them on: "Track right!"
- Help folks with directions, mechanicals, water, or first aid, whether they're riders or not.
- Make sure your friends (particularly the wobbly ones) make it safely past the nasty sections.
- Yield the right-of-way whenever you can.
- Let someone in the group know if you're stopping or bailing for home. Nothing's worse than searching the woods for 3 hours for some guy who's already home watching TV.

IMBA Rules of the Trail

Thousands of miles of dirt trails have been closed to mountain bicyclists. The irresponsible riding habits of a few riders have been a factor. Do your part to maintain trail access by observing the following rules of the trail, formulated by the International Mountain Bicycling Association (IMBA). IMBA's mission is to promote environmentally sound and socially responsible mountain biking.

1. Ride on open trails only. Respect trail and road closures (ask if not sure), avoid possible trespass on private land, and obtain permits and authorization as may be required. Federal wilderness areas are closed to bicycles and all other mechanized and motorized equipment. The way you ride will influence trail management decisions and policies.

2. Zero impact. Be sensitive to the dirt beneath you. Even on open (legal) trails, you should not ride under conditions where you will leave evidence of your passing, such as on certain soils after a rain. Recognize different types of soils and trail construction; practice low-impact cycling. This also means staying on existing trails and not creating new ones. Be sure to pack out at least as much as you pack in. Some of the rides feature optional side hikes into wilderness areas. Be a low-impact hiker also.

3. Control your bicycle! Inattention for even a second can cause problems. Obey all bicycle speed regulations and recommendations.

4. Always yield trail. Make known your approach well in advance. A friendly greeting (or bell) is considerate and works well; don't startle others. Show your respect when passing by slowing to a walking pace or stopping. Anticipate other trail users at corners and blind spots.

5. Never spook animals. All animals are startled by an unannounced approach, a sudden movement, or a loud noise. This can be dangerous for you, others, and the animals. Give animals extra room and time to adjust to you. When passing horses use special care and follow directions from the horseback riders (dismount and ask if uncertain). Chasing cattle and disturbing wildlife is a serious offense. Leave gates as you found them or as marked.

6. Plan ahead. Know your equipment, your ability, and the area in which you are riding—and prepare accordingly. Be self-sufficient at all times, keep your equipment in good repair, and carry necessary supplies for changes in weather or other conditions. A well-executed trip is a satisfaction to you and not a burden to others. Always wear a helmet.

Keep trails open by setting a good example of environmentally sound and socially responsible off-road cycling.

Getting Ready to Ride

Most important, take a good attitude. Things happen in the woods: Bikes break, riders biff, trails end, the weather turns, and people get lost. Some days you ride well, and some days you suck. It's just all part of the adventure, so relax and remember to enjoy yourself. The things listed below will help you to maintain this good attitude and will keep you riding longer.

SAFETY EQUIPMENT

Some riders, both novices and advanced, will stand there almost naked on the trail and tell you, "Oh, I don't need a helmet/glasses/gloves. I'm not going to fall down or get poked in the eye." This is a bigger myth than the Easter Bunny. If you ride, you will fall down. Hit a single rock wrong, and even the tamest green path can slap you down and chew on you for a while. Busting in some of the nasty stuff could make you wish you'd been in a car wreck instead.

In short, this safety gear works, and it's a whole lot cheaper than brain surgery. Get it and wear it.

At a minimum, use the following:

- Helmet—no excuse. Get one that fits right, and wear it properly.
- Riding glasses (since eyeballs are fragile things—two per customer).
- Gloves (unless you really don't like skin on the palms of your hands).
- Arm guards (optional). Lately though, this has been my personal armor of faith.

FIRST AID

Crashing is usually not as bad as you think it'll be, but it's seldom a lot of fun. Just think of it as the coin we have to pay for such enjoyment. Puts it all in perspective.

To really know how to fix busted people on the trail, take the appropriate rescue courses. For the rest of us, when you crash, be calm and take your time. First, assess the injuries. If it's really serious, of course, just stop any major bleeding and get some help. But for most biffs and endos, get up out of the dirt and get yourself and your bike out of the trail (getting run over won't help your day any). Try to wash any crud out of your cuts and scrapes with water from your bottle or backpack. You can try to medicate and bandage yourself on the trail, but a little light bleeding helps to flush the wound, and it lets everyone know you're really enjoying the ride. Clean things out good when you get home, and use some Possum Grease or your favorite healing salve. Better yet, let your significant other do it, and get some sympathy in the process. Obviously, if things still look bad, go see a doctor.

Remember that everyone's comfort level and pain tolerance are different. Some riders I know will stitch up their own leg, then continue pedaling. Others are ready to bail after the first round with the dirt monkeys. Here's a good rule to help determine whether you turn back or keep riding after a big bust: Is the crash victim still having a good time? If not, then call it a day and head home. But if that victim's still grinning, still hungry for adventure, then ride on, brave soul.

TOOLS AND SPARES

Some folks like to ride light with no tools or spares, then just hike back to the car and drive to the shop when things break. If you'd rather ride than push, carry and know how to use these items, and you can fix 90 percent of your breakdowns on the trail.

- spare tube
- tube patches
- tire patch (milk-jug strip, dollar bill, or bar wrapper)
- 10 mm wrench
- 4, 5, and 6 mm Allen wrench set
- air pump or cartridges
- small screwdriver
- spoke wrench
- several sizes of zip ties
- chain breaker

FOOD AND WATER

Be sure to take enough water for your ride. Dehydration makes for a lousy time; so does intestinal infestation. Drinking from local streams, even high in the mountains, is risky at best. When in doubt, take more than you'll need. In hot weather, an extra bottle to squirt over your head is the hook for lowering your body temp.

I hope I brought enough tubes.

While you can do without extra food on short rides, nothing will help you kick it on the end of that 5-hour death ride like some power food. Trail mix, fig bars, or any of the many bars or goops, it's all good. Just take enough for that friend of yours who always forgets his.

WEATHER

North Carolina is a wide state, and the weather can really vary from one end to the other on any given day. But except for the mountains up near Boone, you can generally plan on riding year-round. Winter temperatures are mild with some unexpected short-sleeve days in the middle of February. High temperatures and humidity can be a problem in the summer, unless you like air the consistency of hot chicken soup.

Be aware that thunderstorms can crop up suddenly over the mountains. Pouring rain and a sudden 30-degree drop in air temperature is a good recipe for hypothermia, so carry rain gear or keep moving. It's always an excellent idea to keep a dry change of clothes waiting at your vehicle.

TERRAIN

The terrain gradually steepens as you travel west across North Carolina: flat in the beaches to the Sandhills, rolling hills from Raleigh through the rest of the Piedmont, then climbing into the emerald embrace of the Blue Ridge Mountains. Pisgah National Forest stretches in wide strokes from Boone down past Asheville to the Cradle of Forestry, encompassing the highest peaks east of the Mississippi. Travel farther west and you drop into Nantahala National Forest, a temperate rain forest of lush, dark mountains. Entering these hills always feels like venturing into Mother Earth's womb. It's a welcome return to home.

The rides in this book can be divided between urban/suburban rides and mountain rides. The urban/suburban rides are those in the Sandhills and Coast area; the Triangle area; the Triad area; and the Charlotte, Statesville, and Morganton area.

Mountain rides are those in the Uhwarrie National Forest; the Boone area; the Pisgah National Forest; and the Nantahala National Forest.

Sandhills and Coast

North Carolina gets awfully flat once you move east past Raleigh. Although you might grab your surfboard heading that direction, you probably wouldn't think to grab your bike as well—and you'd miss out, my friend. Here are four excellent rides, and none with more than 20 feet elevation gain, if that. Nab UNCW or Blue Clay the next time you're heading to Wilmington and the beach. If your rounds take you anywhere near Greenville, be sure to check out the Bicycle Post Trail. And if orders condemn you to living in Fayetteville, Smith Lake will at least put a smile on your face.

UNCW

Location: University of North Carolina, Wilmington campus.

Distance: 6.4-mile loop.

Time: 45 minutes to 1.5 hours.

Tread: Sand singletrack and doubletrack. Most of it is surprisingly hardpacked. Crossing the loose fire roads will have you sinking and flailing at times, though.

Aerobic level: Easy. Very, very flat terrain. Too twisty to push it very fast. Nice spinning trail.

Technical difficulty: Tech 1 +. Smooth easy track for the most part with a number of cool, knee-high humps. Some tech 2 roots and several tech 3 logs.

Highlights: Logs, pyramids, lots of humps, tight cruising.

Land status: University property.

Maps: USGS Wilmington.

Access: Take Interstate 40 East to Wilmington. As it enters town, the freeway ends and turns into College Road. Turn left at Randall Avenue into UNCW campus. Follow this road to the dining hall parking lot. Ride your bike around the dining hall to the left until you get to the dormitory known as Madeline Suites. Look for a small wooden bridge to your left. The trail clearly begins just across the bridge.

Notes on the trail

This trail is open to riders of all ability levels. There's no elevation gain, but hey, you're at the beach; what do you expect. The many humps are lots of fun, and the logs are big enough to require some attention and effort. There's a maze of trails in here, but the blue arrows mark the loop fairly well.

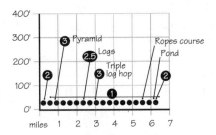

The Ride

0.0 From the bridge, trail begins as tech 1+, fairly hardpacked, sand and pine needle singletrack. Ride over a series of humps and through some tech 2 roots.

0.3 Trail drops out onto Rose Avenue (paved). Turn left, run the track on the edge of the road for 30 feet, then left again back into the singletrack.

0.4 Turn right and follow the blue arrows.

0.7 Bear right at this Y, following the blue arrows.

0.9 Cross a log pyramid, then turn left to follow the arrows.

1.0 Turn right just before a wide sandy fire road and follow the blue arrows.

1.2 Bear right at this Y and follow the blue arrows. Trail skirts the edge of an old burnt section of woods.

1.5 Turn right at first Y, then left at second Y, following the arrows. Track dumps you into an old sandy doubletrack.

2.1 Turn left as doubletrack ends at a private nursery, which puts you on a very loose sandy road. Take the immediate left onto very obscure track; look closely for the arrows. Trail opens up again as soon as you get back into the trees.

2.2 Turn left, following arrows.

2.4 Go over two respectable log hops, then cross a deep, sandy wash.

2.5 Follow the arrows, turning left, left, right, left in close succession. It's not nearly as confusing as it sounds.

3.0 Take three solid, tech 3 log hops in a row.

3.3 Turn left just before you hit the east-west fire road, following the arrows.

3.5 Cross a small bridge of broken cinderblocks.

3.6 Cross the north-south fire road. This is a chance for you to figure out how to ride in deep sand.

3.9 Turn left and follow the blue arrows. Small, sandy berms follow.

4.2 Trail hops a respectable log, then turns around and hops it the other direction.

4.4 Turn right and follow the blue arrows. Then bear left as trail starts to parallel the paved road in front of the dining hall. More of those fun sandy humps.

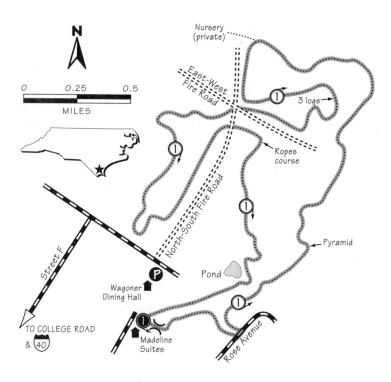

N

0   0.25   0.5

MILES

Nursery
(private)

East-West
Fire Road

3 logs

Ropes
course

North-South Fire Road

Pyramid

Pond

TO COLLEGE ROAD
& 40

Street F

Wagoner
Dining Hall

P

Madeline
Suites

Rose Avenue

5.0 Turn left just before you hit the north-south fire road, and start heading away from campus again. Lots more humps.

5.4 Turn right just before you hit the intersection of the north-south and the east-west fire roads. Cross the north-south fire road and pick up the track on the other side. Watch for the arrows.

5.5 Turn right and follow the blue arrows past the ropes course. Then take a quick left, just before a waist-high log walk (part of the ropes course). Take another left, this time at a Y. Follow the arrows and run through a fern glen.

5.9 Turn right at the T.

6.0 Turn left at the Y.

6.1 Turn right onto this hardpacked dirt road.

6.2 Come up on a small pond. Follow the bank around the left of the pond and drop out the other side past some gravel piles. Trail ducks into a tight little forested tunnel.

6.4 Return to the trailhead, although on the other side of the bridge.

Blue Clay

Location: 10 minutes west of Wilmington.

Distance: 3.1-mile loop.

Time: 30 minutes to 1 hour.

Tread: 2.7 miles of sandy and hardpacked singletrack; 0.4 mile of grassy doubletrack.

Aerobic level: Easy. No long stretches or climbs. Too easy? Try dropping your seat and standing for the whole ride.

Technical difficulty: Tech 2+ overall. Some smooth track with lots of tech 3 logs and pyramids; tons of steep, little drops and climbs; serious tech 4 log bridge. Trials area for anyone feeling really cocky.

Highlights: Liberally sprinkled with logs; nice roller-coaster action; trials area by entrance.

Land status: New Hanover County Park.

Maps: Flyer and map available at local bike shops.

Access: Take Interstate 40 East toward Wilmington. Exit onto North Carolina Highway 132 North (Exit 420). Drive roughly 3.5 miles, then turn right onto Juvenile Center Road. Drive to the end of the pavement and park in the grassy field under power lines.

Notes on the trail

Excellent little technical gem, particularly for an area that's mostly swamp, pine groves, and sand dunes in some combination. The logs and pyramids just keep coming, and the big creek crossing will give even the most foolhardy a moment's pause. This is a good test of balance, handling, and unclipping skills. The trail is well laid out, making good use of the terrain and natural obstacles. A trials area near the parking lot is continually under development and offers an even higher level of skill.

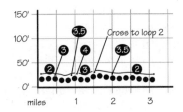

Blue Clay

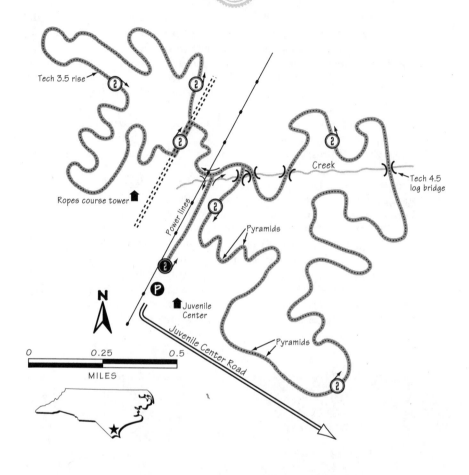

Tech 3.5 rise

Ropes course tower

Power lines

Creek

Tech 4.5 log bridge

Pyramids

Pyramids

Juvenile Center

Juvenile Center Road

N

0   0.25   0.5

MILES

The Ride

0.0 Start from grassy area at end of Juvenile Center Road. Follow power lines past trials area and pick up grassy doubletrack in middle of field.

0.1 Cross wide, muddy stream and turn right to follow singletrack into woods.

0.2 6-foot climb as you enter woods, immediately dropping down to a choice of bridges. Follow track over the right bridge.

0.4 Two respectable log pyramids in an otherwise flat, smooth, twisty piece of track. Muddy section is a quagmire after rain.

0.8 Tech 3+ log crossing with another pair of pyramids.

1.1 Stream crossing over long, single, split-log bridge. Twelve-inch-wide log sits 4 feet or so above a skanky creek. It's certainly wide enough to ride, but the run-in sucks and the exit isn't much better; call it a tech 4 move to clean it all. Penalty for failure would be high on this one.

1.3 Lots of little drops and uphill lunges as you cross back and forth over little ridges. Drop from the ridge to cross one wooden bridge, then a second bridge, before finishing this loop and shooting back out to the power line clearing.

1.4 Ride back across power lines toward muddy stream crossing, but follow singletrack into opposite woods instead of turning to cross stream. Second loop starts with a pair of bridges, a short but steep tech 3 climb, and a tough uphill switchback.

1.5 Log bridge. This one is a walker pending further construction. A legion of ridable log crossings still awaits.

1.7 Turn right onto grassy doubletrack at the T. Ropes course tower is back to the left.

1.8 Turn left onto sandy singletrack. Track is a little unclear at first, but look for orange flags and know that it opens up quickly. Starts with a sweet little 2-foot drop-in; extremely fun riding with track like a sandy roller coaster. Much smoother and less twisty than first loop.

2.0 Series of tough humps leads to a sharp turn up a 3-foot, root-laced riser. Call it a tech 3+ move; I was denied both tries. Remember though: A trail that you don't master the first time out is a trail that you'll ride again.

2.2 Trail runs into clearing. Hug right side of clearing to pick up track. Track begins to cross and recross a pair of parallel ditches, yielding a dozen or more trippy little humps, dips, and sharp cut-backs in a row.

Crossing a dicey bridge at Blue Clay.

2.4 Singletrack gradually turns into a wide, sandy doubletrack, which dashes through some small pine groves. **Warning:** The mudholes are a lot deeper than you think—believe me.

2.7 Complete loop and return to intersection near tower. Turn left into woods to follow track back to the beginning.

3.0 Three big humps and a sketchy bridge for a little parting adrenaline shot just before you leave the woods. Return to the power line field and turn right across the muddy stream crossing.

3.2 Return to parking area.

Bicycle Post

Location: 15 minutes west of Greenville.

Distance: 8.6-mile loop.

Time: 1 to 1.5 hours.

Tread: Singletrack—nothing but singletrack (well, except for two minuscule pieces of doubletrack that don't even count).

Aerobic level: Easy to moderate. Although the course is mostly flat, what few hills there are, are liberally laced with roots. You can really crank it through here if you want to work harder.

Technical difficulty: Tech 2. Mostly smooth, tech 1+ cruising track; however, there are lots of hops, dips, humps, logs, and pyramids (tech 3 to 3.5 stuff) thrown into the mix, more than enough to keep it from ever getting boring. The toughest stream crossing borders on a tech 4 move.

Highlights: Fast flatland cruising; logs; pyramids; stream crossings; berms; dips.

Land status: Private land, managed by the Bicycle Post for the exclusive use of mountain bikers.

Maps: USGS Greenville NW.

Access: Since this is a private trail, and the folks at the Bicycle Post have to pay for the lease and insurance, it isn't fair to give directions here so that anyone can go and poach it. Stop by either of the Bicycle Post shops in Greenville for directions, map, and membership fees. To get to the Bicycle Post from points west, come into town on U.S. Highway 264. Turn right onto Memorial Boulevard, then left onto Arlington Boulevard. The shop is on the left side of the street, next to the Buccaneer Theater.

Notes on the trail

This is the best trail we've seen east of Raleigh so far. It's safe for newbies, and still fun for advanced riders. It's fast and fun, with plenty of room to stretch your legs and spin, and plenty of obstacles to keep your attention. Whoever laid this out knew what they were doing, 'cause the trail swoops and twists with just enough room through the trees to let you keep your speed up. The many pyramids and berms are all very well constructed for your increased riding pleasure. There's a good bit of everything thrown in— except for any monumental climbs, that is.

While it can get to feel like a bit of a maze in here, it's not too tough to find your way through. We tried to follow the clearest track and the red flags, whenever possible.

"Oh yeah, definitely, definitely a fun ride. Yeah." —Rainman

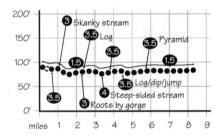

The Ride

0.0 Although there is a trail entrance right next to the Bicycle Post sign, it looked to me like most riders end here. Turn right and ride up the side of the field 200 feet or so, then break left into the woods at the next entrance. Trail starts off as smooth, flat, wide-open, tech 1 singletrack.

0.2 First of many log pyramids, a respectable tech 3 number. Then turn right at the T, following the arrows. Some small logs and another pyramid to follow.

0.4 Trail pops back out of the woods, not far from where you put in. Turn left and follow the dirt doubletrack as it hugs the edge of the field.

0.5 Trail turns left to slip back into the woods and starts to parallel the hardtop road. Watch for an 8-foot rooty drop (tech 3+), then lots of droppin' and poppin' as the track dives in and out of an old roadbed. Most of the trail is still a clear, tech 1+ run.

1.2 Skanky stream crossing—a slippery and gooey tech 3 move that you don't want to watch too closely from behind.

1.3 Bear right at the Y and hop an old log that's obviously been ridden a lot. Believe it or not, shortly after you even get a bit of a zippy downhill, quick running with well-packed sandy berms.

1.9 Continue straight past the (blue-flagged) turn. Then some short drops and climbs, a little back-and-forth gully action, and a short wooden bridge.

Bicycle Post

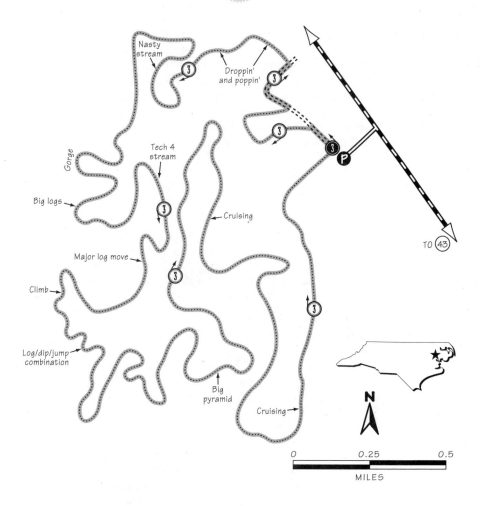

2.3 Small gorge down to the right with that dark, unsettling look of the snake-infested, tech 3 roots along the lip threatening to toss you down into its depths if you blow it.

2.5 Tech 3+ log hop, then shortly after a dip/log/dip combination for another tech 3+ move. Long, flat, tech 1 cruising track follows.

3.2 Another muddy stream crossing with rooty banks on either side. Tech 3+ to tech 4, depending on the severity and depth of the slime. Then more flat cruising with fast, solid berms in the turns.

3.7 Nice 4-foot drop, backed by a 20-inch log hop; another tech 3+ move. Trails start converging from all sides at this point, and it's easy to get turned around. Try to follow the clearest line, which jags right then left.

4.4 A surprise climb, with some tech 3 roots along the way. Turn right at the top.

4.5 6-foot drop, in and out; then a tough, tech 3+ log/dip/jump combo.

4.9 Excellent whoop-dee-doos, followed by another short but steep rooty climb. Some off-camber logs and nice dips to follow keep you hopping.

5.7 Massive, 3-to 4-foot-tall pyramid, then a pair of 18-inch logs.

6.3 Continue straight, following the main track. Excellent fast, twisty track through the trees. Curves and berms are laid perfectly to allow you to just *crank* through here.

7.5 Turn right on this branch, following the red flags.

8.6 Trail ends and pops out right by the Bicycle Post sign.

Smith Lake

Location: Smith Lake Park, Fort Bragg.

Distance: 7.9 miles, total for all three loops.

Time: 1 to 2 hours.

Tread: 7.5 miles of well-packed, sandy singletrack; 0.4 mile of mushy sandy road.

Aerobic level: Easy. This is a prime cruising trail, with basically no change in elevation. You could ride this puppy on a big, fat beach bike.

Technical difficulty: Tech 1 overall. Lots of jumps, both small and large, almost all perfectly smooth. A few tech 3 root drops and some nice, high log pyramids add a little spice.

Highlights: Fast, easy cruising; lots of berms and bunny hops; natural half-pipe; large jumps (or humps, if you prefer).

Land status: U.S. military base; recreation facility.

Maps: USGS Vander.

Access: From Interstate 95, take Exit 56 and follow U.S. Highway 301 into Fayetteville. At the first light, turn right onto North Carolina Highway 24 West. Go to the third light, and turn right onto Ramsey Street, which you'll follow for about 3 miles, then turn left onto McArther Road. Go to the second light, and turn left onto Honeycutt Road. After 0.7 mile, turn left onto an unmarked gravel road. The trailhead is 1 mile down on the left. Trails start from the information board.

Notes on the trail

Smith Lake is an excellent introductory trail—a good place to take friends you want to show a good time and where they won't biff. The track is most often smooth and flawless, and if you're expecting lots of loose sand here in the Sandhills, think again. The pine needles and sand pack down like pavement between the trees, leaving smooth berms and dozens of perfect bunny hop opportunities. The trail is broken into three loops (Green, Blue, and Black), but just about all riders will be able to negotiate the entire thing. The local bike club and trail gurus continue to add new sections to the trails, so check the bulletin board at the trailhead for any map updates.

The fee for riding is $5 a day or $20 per year, payable at the park office, which is farther down the gravel road by Smith Lake.

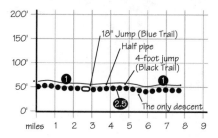

The Ride

0.0 Turn right past the bulletin board onto the Green Trail, which starts off right away with smooth, flawless tech 1 sandy singletrack, twisting through the trees. Nice berms and perfectly formed 6-inch bunny hop shots.

0.5 Cross several old roads. Just follow the clear track and the green blazes on the trees, and enjoy the ride.

2.4 Return to the trailhead. Turn right on the gravel entrance road, and follow it up to the start of the Blue Trail.

2.8 Go under some power lines, then turn left. Entrance to Blue Trail is clearly signed. Nice 18-inch jump at the beginning, then more perfect track.

3.7 As the trail crosses an old roadbed, it forms a cool, if shallow, half-pipe that you can drop and hop to your heart's content.

3.9 Trail runs along an old fire road for a bit, then cuts a sharp left back into the woods. Keep an eye out for it; if you go under the power lines again, you went too far. After that, you'll pass through the edge of paintball area.

4.6 Cross another fire road and enter the Black Trail. And, as if to justify its rank, Black throws up a sumo-sized roller of a jump, about 4 feet high. This was the whole crew's favorite spot on the trail.

5.5 Excellent, 3-foot-tall log pyramid. Like everything in here, it's well-constructed and fun to ride. Cool triple drop afterward, then a small downhill surfing through the rare loose sand.

Smith Lake

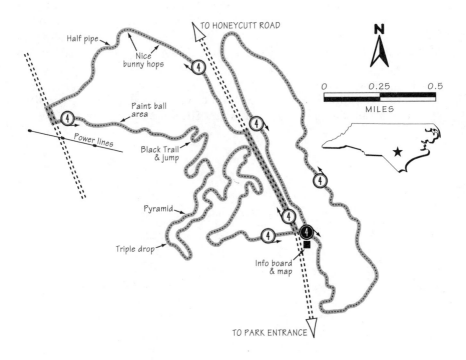

6.8 Trail T's into a fire road. Turn right, then right again immediately back into the woods.

7.3 Bear left. Track straight ahead is signed "Off Limits." Remember, this is a military base. Don't be an idiot and go wandering into a bombing range somewhere.

7.9 Return to the trailhead.

Triangle

For such a large metro area, the Raleigh/Durham/Chapel Hill Triangle is limited as far as long and *legal* rides go. Lake Crabtree offers some good introductory riding, together with the gravel roads at Umstead Park. Tiny Chapel Hill actually offers the best rides with two short technical beauties as well as a small beginner loop. The fire roads through Duke Forest in Durham are okay for spinning but don't really measure up. Ask around about other nonsanctioned trails in the area.

Lake Johnson

Location: Lake Johnson Nature Park, southwest edge of Raleigh.

Distance: 4.9-mile loop.

Time: 30 minutes to 1 hour.

Tread: 2.4 miles of singletrack; 1.3 miles of doubletrack; 1.2 miles of paved greenway.

Aerobic level: Easy to moderate. Greenway and doubletrack are mostly flat, smooth, and easy to spin along. Between the roots and the constant up and down though, the singletrack can easily get you puffing.

Technical difficulty: Greenway and doubletrack are tech 1; singletrack is a constant tech 3 root garden, spiked with a tech 4 climb and an optional tech 4 stream crossing.

Highlights: Excellent test of root-crossing skills; greenway provides fun option for those not fond of dirt and falling. Overlook gives nice viewpoint of lake. Lake abounds with birds, turtles, and even a few beavers.

Land status: City park.

Maps: USGS Raleigh West.

Access: From Interstate 440 (the Raleigh Beltline), take Western Boulevard into Raleigh. At about 3 miles turn right onto Avent Ferry Road at the light by Mission Valley shopping center. Follow Avent Ferry for another 3 miles, then turn left into the entrance for Lake Johnson Park, just before you go over the lake.

Notes on the trail

This is another excellent in-town Raleigh ride, one that can be linked with Centennial Campus via greenways and a short bit of road riding. Ridden in either direction, you get a decent warm-up before hitting the root extravaganza waiting in the woods. Beginners can try a bit of the track, with an easy bailout option if the learning curve proves too steep or painful, because the greenway is always circling just uphill of the singletrack. Intermediate riders will push the limits of their slow-speed balance and navigation skills, and even more advanced folks will be pressed by some of the dicey root moves and the big stream crossing. When in doubt at any trail branching, pick the track that runs closest to the lakeshore.

The point on the backside of the lake looks over the breeding grounds of some gorgeous geese, swans, herons, kingfishers, and a variety of ducks. And I guess to be fair, I should mention the proliferation of turtles sunning along the walkway and lakeside sections, for those of you who like your critters cold-blooded.

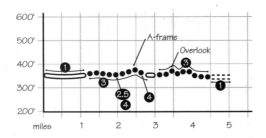

The Ride

0.0 Starting from Lake Johnson parking area, follow the paved greenway path.

0.8 Greenway splits. Turn right to continue clockwise around lake.

0.9 Cross lake dam and wooden bridge over spillway. Again, bear right when greenway splits to continue around lake.

1.0 Short sections of singletrack drop off from greenway to run along the lake edge a bit before popping back onto paved path. Okay to jump on just for the warm-up.

1.2 As paved path enters area of obvious storm damage and moves uphill a bit, watch closely for singletrack down to the right that runs along the lake's edge, showing green blazes. Hardpack track begins with immediate tech 2+ root barrage, filled with stubbies, root interlaces, and small dips. If terrain is not to your liking at this point, best bail out now, 'cause this is a good sampling of the track to follow.

1.6 Tech 3 root interlace in middle of short, steep climb. Rooty descent afterward. Constant up and down; not much flat running to be found.

1.8 Tech 3 rooty descent.

Lake Johnson

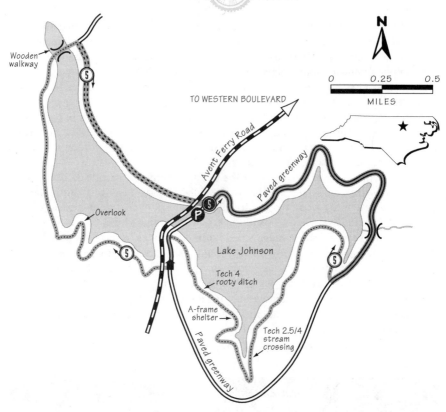

Wooden walkway

TO WESTERN BOULEVARD

Avent Ferry Road

Paved greenway

N

0   0.25   0.5

MILES

Overlook

P S

Lake Johnson

Tech 4 rooty ditch

A-frame shelter →

Paved greenway

Tech 2.5/4 stream crossing

2.0 Tricky, off-camber roots as you descend to large stream. Lower stream crossing is tech 2+ with a steep entry. Crossing higher up is a tech 4 move, requiring a very tight line through a gap in the large rocks on the far side. To make this move, swing high upstream, then double back and drop into the stream at an angle to line up with the gap. Blow this move, and you're either wet or in need of a new derailleur.

2.1 Three-way fork; turn right and follow green blazes. Immediately after, hit another fork; turn left (uphill) this time and work up a steep, rooty climb.

2.3 Trail follows stream up away from lake, then curves back for an easy crossing.

2.4 A-frame shelter at top of rooty climb is good resting and viewpoint. Trail crosses paved path and drops down other side. Descent is ugly, steep, rooty, and washed out—tech 3+. I've never been able to climb this section when riding the other direction. Try it if you don't believe me. Watch for rooty ditches at bottom.

2.6 Deep, root-filled, tech 4 ditch to cross. Novices and intermediates should walk this, as it's a bad faceplant zone. Swing high up if you try to ride it, or go lower if you've got trials skills.

2.7 Trail drops you back onto the paved greenway. Turn left to continue to other side of lake. Right returns you to parking area via a long, wooden walkway across the lake.

2.8 Pavement splits; turn right.

2.9 At edge of parking area, make immediate right to cross Avent Ferry Road and resume singletrack. Choice of tracks; follow either one to wooden bridge at the bottom.

3.0 Cross another short wooden bridge. Ignore faint track immediately to the right; follow main track up to the left for a tough climb and a fun descent. Use brakes judiciously here, as the combination of root interlace and front brake application can yield a big endo. Green blazes still evident on trees.

3.3 Track splits. Turn right and continue following track along lake edge.

3.5 Three-way fork; continue straight to ride up to overlook. Nice view out over lake; good spot to meditate on the world and your bike's place in it. Leaving overlook, follow track and green blazes back down to lake's edge. Ignore track back to left; it was just a bypass for those too busy to sit at the overlook and contemplate Nature's goodness.

3.6 Cross stream, then get ready for the toughest climb of the ride. Loose surface, laced with roots, and sprinkled with chicken heads. After this climb, the trail drops you onto a wide woodchip and hardpacked tech 1 doubletrack to catch your breath. Bear right to continue around the edge of the lake.

3.8 Tech 3 stream crossing: steep sided with loose rocks in the bottom.

4.0 Rooty descent down to long wooden walkway; tech 3 move to negotiate the roots and hop up the steps. Walkway crosses a wide swampy area; good spot for spotting various wildlife and for trying to decipher the animal tracks in the mud.

4.2 Turn right off walkway onto wide, dirt doubletrack.

4.8 Cross over Avent Ferry Road again. **Warning:** Watch for cars, as they come around the blind corner to the left very quickly.

4.9 Return to Lake Johnson parking lot.

Be sure to bring extra food for your hungry buddies.

Lake Crabtree

Location: Lake Crabtree Park, 5 minutes west of Raleigh.
Distance: 3.9-mile loop.
Time: 25 minutes to 1 hour.
Tread: 3.9 miles of singletrack.
Aerobic level: Easy. What few hills exist are pretty moderate, and the length isn't enough to get you too worked up.
Technical difficulty: Tech 1 +. No serious technical challenges, but not exactly a greenway either; there are enough roots to make sure you pay attention.
Highlights: Tight cruising; bridges; water bars; easy access to Black Creek Greenway and fire roads in Umstead Park.
Land status: County park.
Maps: USGS Raleigh West; park map available at office.
Access: From Interstate 40 near the Raleight-Durham airport, take Exit 285, Aviation Parkway, south. Turn left at the Lake Crabtree Park entrance, just 200 yards down the road. Turn right off the entrance road into a gravel parking area. The trailhead is just across the entrance road, clearly marked by a small wooden bridge, a trail conditions sign, and an information kiosk.

Notes on the trail

This is an excellent beginner trail where I send any novices looking for rides in the area. It's smooth and safe with just enough roots and humps to keep it interesting. The park management and NC FATS deserve a big round of applause for their foresight in constructing the only legal singletrack in Wake County. Be careful of heavy bike traffic and idiots without helmets on the weekends. The park also offers picnic shelters, boating, volleyball, fishing, and playgrounds for the rest of the family.

For ease of navigation, this route goes in on entrance 1, then takes mostly lefts to work its way around all three loops.

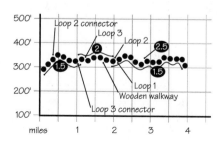

Lake Crabtree

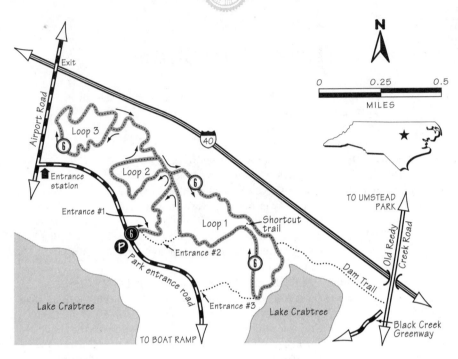

The Ride

0.0 Start off at entrance 1 by the wooden bridge and information kiosk. Trail starts off with smooth, tech 1+ hardpacked singletrack.

0.1 Bear left at this Y. Either way will take you up to the loops, but the maps and mileage were made using the left branch.

0.3 Trail drops you onto the lower section of Loop 1. Turn left, go across the opening for the gas line easement, and immediately hit the intersection with Loop 2. Turn left onto Loop 2. Sign points left and right for Loop 2 and right for Loop 3.

0.8 Turn left onto the Loop 3 Connector Trail (red blazes). Sign points left for Loop 3 and right for return to Loop 1.

1.1 Turn left onto Loop 3 (yellow blazes).

1.2 Multiple switchbacks. Small bridge and some tech 2 roots.

1.7 20-foot-long wooden walkway.

1.8 Return to Loop 3 Connector Trail. Turn left, following the red blazes.

2.1 Intersection with Loop 2. Turn left, following the yellow blazes. After about 100 yards, turn left again at intersection with Loop 2 Connector Trail.

2.2 Cross the opening for the gas easement again, then take an immediate left onto Loop 1 with yellow blazes; clearly signed. Flat running, then fun descent over seven or eight small water bars.

2.6 Bear left to continue on Loop 1. Shortcut trail cuts off to the right.

2.7 Tall, tech 2+ root with a sharp right turn just after. Here's a spot for beginners to test themselves. Turn right at signed intersection to continue on Loop 1. Sign points left for access to Umstead Park, Black Creek Greenway, and dam.

3.0 Continue straight on Loop 1. Entrance 3 breaks off left and heads toward the boat ramps.

3.2 Continue straight on Loop 1. Shortcut trail cuts right.

3.4 Old homesite on left. Immediately after, entrance 2 is on your left by green "Entrance" sign. Continue straight to complete the loop or bail out here; either choice is okay.

3.6 Turn left onto entrance 1 by green sign.

3.9 Return to trailhead.

Umstead Park

Location: Umstead State Park; 5 minutes west of Raleigh.

Distance: 16.6-mile loop.

Time: 1.5 to 2.5 hours.

Tread: 13.9 miles of doubletrack; 2.2 miles of paved road (no traffic though); 0.5 mile of hardpacked roadside path (you just can't call it singletrack).

Aerobic level: Easy to moderate—depends on the pace you set. What hills there are out here tend to be very long and can wind you if you push it. Generally though, things are flat enough for anyone. Just gauge your distances well.

Technical difficulty: A true tech 1, in every sense of the word. No real technical challenges. Descent to causeway is a tech 2 for speed, erosion, and water bars. Causeway can vary from a tech 2 ankle-drencher to an impassable moat.

Highlights: Flat cruising; view of airport; old cemetery; lake views; access to Crabtree Lake trails.

Land status: North Carolina state park.

Maps: USGS Raleigh West; park map available at office.

Access: From Raleigh, take Interstate 40 West and exit at Harrison Avenue, Exit 287. Turn north (away from Cary), and follow the signs into Umstead Park, Reedy Creek Entrance. Park anywhere in the parking lot.

Notes on the trail

If you want to get outside, be surrounded by trees, and just *spin*, then this is your place. Umstead Park offers clear, well-maintained gravel Forest Service roads throughout this thick patch of woods. This is a great aerobic workout within easy distance of downtown Raleigh, though it rates on the bottom of the adventure scale. It's also a very good ride for someone who hasn't been on a bike in a long time. Umstead makes a good addition to Lake Crabtree if you want to spin after you do some singletracking.

Remember that Umstead is a state park, which means no singletrack allowed, anywhere. They really mean business, so resist the temptation. Maybe one day they'll see the light.

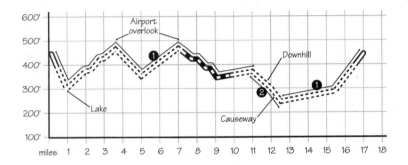

The Ride

0.0 From the parking lot, head back out toward the entrance.

0.2 Turn left onto a small paved road signed "Whispering Pines."

0.4 Continue straight. Gated road on right leads to campsite.

0.6 Turn right onto gravel road (sign: "To Reedy Creek Lake") just before several park offices. Maps usually available on the side of one office building.

1.2 Cross a wide, wooden bridge by the lake, and turn left at the T.

1.3 Cross another wooden bridge, this one across a picturesque stream. A long climb afterward.

2.1 Continue straight past gravel road to right. You'll be back for this later.

2.2 Continue straight again past a second gravel road to the right. You'll come out here later.

2.9 Old cemetery and nature area on the right.

3.1 Continue straight past gravel road to the right. Very welcome water spigot located here.

3.5 Airport overlook on the right. Picnic and rest area on the left.

4.8 Pass a gate and a ranger's residence. Tread turns into old paved roadway.

5.1 Cross over I-40 on a no-cars overpass and turn around for the return trip. By the way, you're at the back entrance to Lake Crabtree and the beginning of the Black Creek Greenway. Follow the track down to the right to get to Crabtree for some true (if mild) singletrack.

Umstead Park

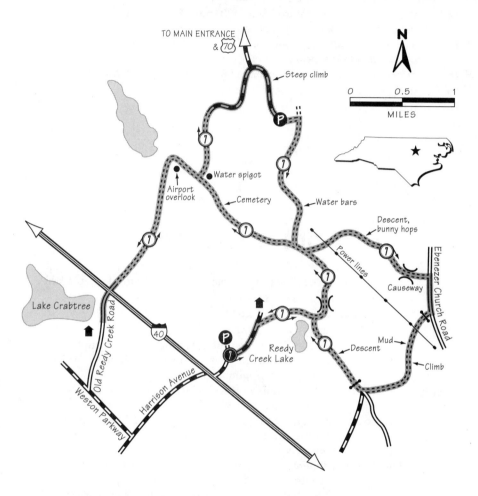

TO MAIN ENTRANCE & 70

N

Steep climb

P

0   0.5   1
MILES

Water spigot

Airport overlook

Cemetery

Water bars

Descent, bunny hops

Power lines

Ebenezer Church Road

Causeway

Lake Crabtree

Old Reedy Creek Road

40

P

Reedy Creek Lake

Descent

Mud

Climb

Harrison Avenue

Weston Parkway

7.1 Pass the airport overlook and turn left onto the gated gravel road by the water spigot. Gravel road eventually turns to pavement as it enters main park areas.

8.8 Turn right at sign, "Maple View Lodge and Bridle and Bike path."

9.5 Continue through a circular parking area and pick up the trail at back side. Quick left at T and sign, "Bridle and Bike Path."

10.9 Turn left as track T's back into main trail. I mentioned you'd come out this way.

11.0 A quick left off the main trail onto another gravel road. This tread quickly changes to hardpacked dirt doubletrack and leads down a fast, slightly eroded downhill, with a couple of enjoyable whoop-dee-doos planted along the way. The only tech 2 section of the trail.

12.6 Cross a wide causeway, which is usually flooded. Water depth can range from 2 inches to 4 feet. Either bomb down the hill and just hit it, or find a log to cross on.

12.7 Pass gate and turn right onto track alongside Ebenezer Church Road. Follow this track for 100 yards or so, until you see the turnoff.

13.2 Turn right away from road onto clear bridle path. Tread is still dirt doubletrack with even a mudhole or three.

14.3 Bear right as trail hits intersection of Trenton Road and Reedy Creek Road. Tread changes back to gravel Forest Service road.

15.3 Long, fast downhill brings you back to Reedy Creek Lake. Turn left and cross wide, wooden bridge again.

16.0 Turn left onto paved road after final climb back up to the park offices.

16.4 Turn right onto paved road back to parking lot.

16.6 Return to parking area.

Forest Theater

Location: At the edge of UNC campus, in the heart of Chapel Hill.

Distance: 4 miles out and back.

Time: 30 minutes to 1 hour

Tread: 4 miles of singletrack.

Aerobic level: Easy. Although the trail does drop 150 feet from the amphitheater to the community center, it never feels like you do any real climbing.

Technical difficulty: Tech 2 overall, with several tech 3 root-and-rock combinations, wicked stairs, and some tricky maneuvering from bridge to bridge. The technical challenges won't impress advanced riders, but novices will probably have their hands full.

Highlights: Numerous streambed crossings; tight, twisty, rooty singletrack; lots of bridges, steps, and landscaping timbers. The run down from the amphitheater can get fast at times, across loose rocks and roots. Excellent nonpaved commuter path from campus to northeastern edge of town.

Land status: University property and Chapel Hill town easement.

Maps: USGS Chapel Hill.

Access: From the U.S. Highway 15/501 bypass in Chapel Hill, take South Raleigh Road to the first light and turn right onto Country Club Road. You'll pass the amphitheater to your right in the woods. Hang a sharp right onto Boundary Street. You can park in the small amphitheater lot on your right on weekends or continue on a little farther to a public lot.

Notes on the trail

This is an excellent in-town trail that winds through some gorgeous woods with several options for different ability levels. The doubletrack is ridable by novices, though they might find some of the uphills a bit rocky. Various sections of singletrack offer up slick, off-camber roots, boulder-heading opportunities, and connecting bridges that will test your low-speed handling skills. While it seems like there are a lot of turns on this route, it's just the clearest track to navigate. Pick almost any line you want, follow the stream,

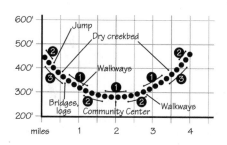

and you can't get lost. Take an easy ride over to the UNC Outdoor Education Center Trail for some more singletracking.

Note that this trail sees a *lot* of pedestrian use, particularly on the weekends. Drop your speed on the curves, and watch for family mobs festooned with strollers, poodles, and scampering bikers-to-be.

The Ride

0.0 Start at parking lot behind amphitheater stage. Follow track up around amphitheater to the left, which brings you out at the top by picnic tables and Country Club Road.

0.1 From picnic tables, look for a clear, wide tech 1 doubletrack off to the left leading back down into the woods. Smooth doubletrack gains speed quickly; watch for serious jump on left side of trail, for those who want to try out their wings early in the day. After jump, tread changes to hardpack with small roots and tech 2 washouts.

0.3 Follow singletrack as it branches off and drops down to the left. Short, tech 2 + rocky and rooty descent may have newbies wondering if they've bitten off more than they can chew. Turn right immediately after a short, gap-toothed bridge. Singletrack crosses doubletrack; continue straight on singletrack. Watch for short drop through rooty, tech 3 rock garden.

0.7 Trail branches right, down across bridge. Cross bridge, then immediately turn left. Note that a right turn after the bridge is a dead end, but it leads over two good, knee-high logs with plenty of run-out for some fun technical practice.

0.8 Turn left onto long, wooden walkways, past "Sugarberry Road/Community Center Park" sign. Transitions on and off walkways can be pretty severe, with some tight turning required.

0.9 Signs: "Sandy Creek Trail/Greenwood Road" pointing right, and "Sugarberry Road" pointing left. Turn left, travel across another bridge, through a little tunnel, and past another sign.

Forest Theater

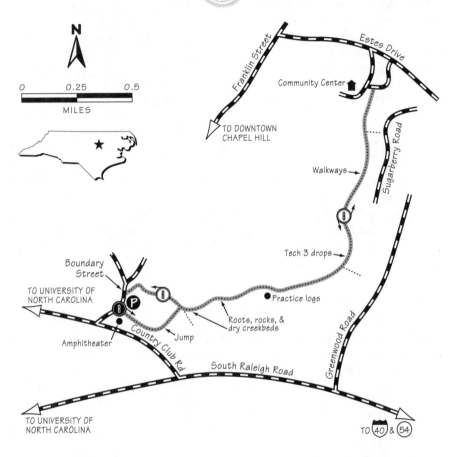

1.1 Off-camber, rooty climb, followed by a drop over a long set of washed-out, landscaping timber steps. Keep your weight off the front wheel here or pay the dentist bill. Shortly after, there is another series of walkways, all at 90-degree angles. Tough slow-motion moves.

1.3 Turn right as singletrack follows stream, tech 3 roots, rocks, and drop-offs.

1.4 Turn right at sign for Sugarberry Road.

1.5 Turn left, following sign "To Community Center Park." Shortly after, trail pops out onto paved road (Shepherd's Lane) behind apartment buildings. Turn left again, follow the sidewalk a short bit, then left again over a small bridge, to head to the community center.

1.8 At the community center parking lot, turn around and head back the way you came. Follow the gravel path back around the maintenance building, cross the bridge, and turn right on the sidewalk.

2.1 Entrance to trail is signed "Battle Branch Trail." Take an immediate left at first T.

2.9 Go straight past branching and sign for UNC campus.

3.4 Bear left across a (normally) dry creekbed, for a short, tech 3 boulder-head section. Some grassy doubletrack follows, then some tech 3 root and rock combo and another streambed.

3.6 Continue straight on the doubletrack, as the original entrance singletrack cuts across your path.

3.8 Trail drops you out at the edge of Park Place Road. Turn left to follow a track beside the road, then a left again at Boundary Street.

4.0 Return to the theater parking lot.

UNC Outdoor Education Center

Location: Outdoor Education Center, University of North Carolina, Chapel Hill.

Distance: 2.5-mile loop.

Time: 30 to 45 minutes.

Tread: 1.7 miles of singletrack; 0.8 mile of dirt and grassy doubletrack.

Aerobic level: Moderate. The opening section's constant up and down will have you anaerobic almost the whole way. Then easy cruising around the golf course and some tamer singletrack. The return climb back up to the parking lot may be the toughest part of the ride.

Technical difficulty: Tech 3+ for the Chutes and Ladders section; tech 2 overall for the rest.

Highlights: Extremely steep drops and climbs; big logs; creek crossings; lots of spinning and some big air along the golf course.

Land status: University property.

Maps: USGS Chapel Hill.

Access: From the U.S. Highway 15/501 bypass in Chapel Hill, take South Raleigh Road to the first light and turn left onto Country Club Road. Look for a big green box by the second turn to the right. Follow the driveway down to the Outdoor Education Center and the parking area. From the parking lot, take the paved path that drops down past the tennis courts toward a rope course area. **Caution:** Watch for a cable gate across the path at some point. As the paved path ends, bear right along the edge of the woods, around the ropes course, ignoring the first sets of arrows. Just as the path narrows, look for the entrance trail and sign (and possibly more blue arrows) in the woods up to the left. The trail starts and ends here.

UNC Outdoor Education Center

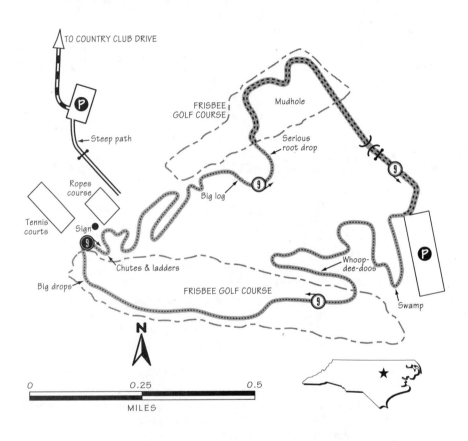

To COUNTRY CLUB DRIVE

FRISBEE
GOLF COURSE

Mudhole

Steep path

Serious
root drop

Ropes
course

Big log

Tennis
courts

Sign

Chutes & ladders

Whoop-
dee-doos

Big drops

FRISBEE GOLF COURSE

Swamp

N

0   0.25   0.5

MILES

Notes on the trail

If you come here expecting to cruise an easy 2.5 miles without dabbing or breaking a sweat, you're in for some disappointment. From the humbling of the opening climb to the last hairy drop out of the woods, you'll be challenged. The back section of singletrack is a good bit friendlier with lots of easy whoop-dee-doos and drops. The final section of grassy track across the golf course ends with two big, 20- and 30-foot drops that you can roll or just sail down.

"It was a humbling experience." —Daniel, the Excitable Boy

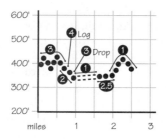

The Ride

0.0 No mercy to start. Trail begins with an imposing climb: off-camber, extremely steep, and set with a couple massive roots. It's got to be a tech 4+ move. I never made it.

0.1 Trail doubles back and pops you suddenly over the edge of a 6-foot drop, out by the ropes course. Hang a quick U-turn and dash back in between two arrowed posts for a short, steep climb.

0.2 Déjà vu—the trail doubles again, only this time sending you down an 8-foot drop. U-turn again and back in the woods once more. Cross a pair of bridges, then hit some solid tech 3 roots, rocks, logs, and whatnot.

0.5 Tech 3+ log hop, a 2-foot concrete ledge drop, then some long tech 2 contouring and stream crossings.

0.8 Tech 4 log move, this one angled and slightly off-camber.

Daniel takes the last jump on the UNC Outdoor Education Center Trail.

1.0 Trail makes a dive downslope toward the golf course. A smooth but daunting 2-foot log drop crosses the entire trail. It's an easy move at speed, but it's just plain scary. Ride it or walk it, 'cause the bust is bad. Turn right when you hit the golf course, following a grassy doubletrack.

1.2 Track bears right, following edge of woods. There's often a major mudhole here.

1.4 Caution! Just after you pass under a bridge, watch carefully for a chain strung across trail. It's really difficult to see, and it'd be a nasty surprise.

1.5 Look for sign (MTB Trail) and singletrack on the right, just as the track reaches a small parking lot. Tech 3 stream crossing, then some cool pyramids, logs, and mud.

2.0 Drop a long section of tight whoop-dee-doos, then pop out onto the golf course again. Turn right and head toward the only obvious opening up the hill.

2.4 The last section of track descends in two big waves down toward good old pin 14. With little effort, you can sail the crests of these slopes.

2.5 Bear right through the opening at the bottom of the slopes, and return to the trailhead.

Southern Park

Location: Southern Village community, just on the south edge of Chapel Hill and Carrboro.

Distance: 1.7-mile loop.

Time: 15 to 30 minutes.

Tread: 1.7 miles of singletrack.

Aerobic level: Easy to moderate. Fairly flat track most of the time with a few small climbs.

Technical difficulty: Tech 1+. Mostly smooth hardpacked track with some roots. Series of 6-inch logs at the far end gives you a chance to start and end with a little technical work.

Highlights: Pretty little trail within an easy bike ride of downtown and several new apartment complexes. Nice initial offering for first-timers.

Land status: City park.

Maps: Trail map available from Chapel Hill Parks and Recreation Department.

Access: From Chapel Hill, take South Columbia Street south out of town, which becomes U.S. Highway 15/501 South when it crosses the North Carolina Highway 54 bypass. In about 0.5 mile, turn right into the entrance for Southern Village. Drive to the leftmost parking lot and look for a trailhead and sign at the back of the lot.

Notes on the trail

For such a short trail, this track sure makes you feel like you're really mountain biking. You'll enjoy slipping through the trees, working on nice, smooth turns. This is an excellent introductory trail for your novice friend, and right at the edge of town. For more of a workout, drop your seat, stand the whole way, and lap it five or six times.

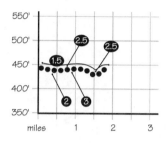

The Ride

0.0 From the Southern Village parking lot, enter past the trail sign. Turn left to start the loop. Twisty, smooth track with some small roots.

0.4 Cross Dogwood Acres Road, then hit a testy tech 2 root section and more humps.

0.5 Pass under power lines.

0.7 Respectable 12-inch log crossing. Good place for beginners to challenge themselves (and maybe develop some falling skills).

0.8 Continue straight for the loop. The spur left darts out to Merritt Drive, crossing a number of 6-inch logs, including a tough double-log combo. It's a tech 3 move to clear all of them.

0.9 Fairly flat, tech 1 track with a few little humps and twists.

1.0 Tricky little rooty downhill, followed by a small stream crossing and a rooty climb.

1.1 Go straight under power lines. Signs clearly mark where trail picks up.

1.2 Straight across Dogwood Acres Road again. Signs clearly mark where trail picks up. From here, trail hits a few small whoop-dee-doos, runs through a little mud, and twists back and forth through the pines.

1.7 Turn left and roll back out at the trailhead.

Southern Park

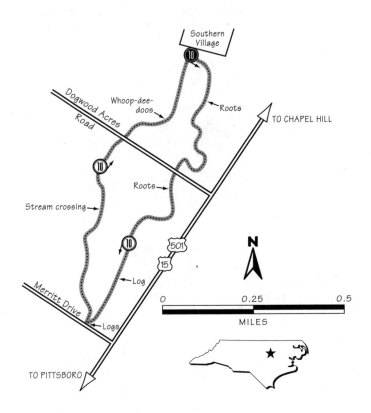

Southern Village

Whoop-dee-doos

Roots

Dogwood Acres Road

TO CHAPEL HILL

Roots

Stream crossing

501

15

Log

N

Merritt Drive

Logs

0   0.25   0.5

MILES

TO PITTSBORO

San-Lee Park

Location: San-Lee Park, 10 minutes from downtown Sanford, 35 minutes from Raleigh.

Distance: 4.6-mile loop.

Time: 45 minutes to 1 hour.

Tread: 4.3 miles of prime Piedmont singletrack; 0.2 mile of pavement; 0.1 mile of gravel road.

Aerobic level: Moderate. No huge elevation gains, but the constant up and down on a trail liberally sprinkled with roots and rocks will get you puffing in no time. Excellent training ride for racers.

Technical difficulty: Tech 2 overall. Lots of small rocks and roots force you to pay attention, but the track is generally clear and always easy to follow. Occasional tough, rocky switchbacks push it to tech 3 in places.

Highlights: Primo singletrack; roller-coaster rides down across the numerous bridges and back up; extremely high fun factor.

Land status: County park. Winter hours 8 A.M. to 5 P.M.; summer hours 8 A.M. to 8 P.M.

Maps: USGS Sanford.

Access: From Raleigh, take U.S. Highway 1 South to Sanford; from Durham–Chapel Hill, take US 15/501 South to Sanford. At the intersection of US 1 and US 15/501, go straight on Business Route 1 (Hawkins Avenue) into the center of town. At the light, turn left on Charlotte Avenue (this is the main drag in town; note that Fit to Be Tried bike shop is one block to the right, in case you need last-minute supplies). Follow this road to the fourth light and bear right onto San-Lee Drive. Go 2 miles and turn right onto Pumping Station Road (look for Harrington Farms strawberry farm on the corner). San-Lee Park is 1 mile up on the right. Park in the gravel lot.

Notes on the trail

This may well be the finest piece of legal singletrack within 1 hour of Raleigh. Another creation by the crew of Sanford Area Mountain Biking Association (SAMBA), this track uses every bit of available terrain for a joyous ride full of swooping turns, roller-coaster drops, unexpected switchbacks, and mad dashes through the woods. Every rider, from newbies to experts, will enjoy this trail. Reversing it at the end totals almost 10 miles, providing a serious workout. Nice shaded stream to relax beside after the ride. Lake provides opportunities for fishing and boating.

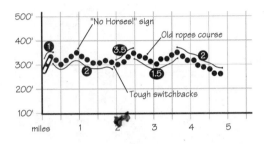

The Ride

0.0 From parking lot, take the steep paved road uphill toward the RV camping area. You'll come out at a small parking area, with the lake and a dock down to the right. Straight ahead is a chained gravel road, with a sign for RV campground and bike trail. This is the way, obviously.

0.3 As you enter the RV camping area, look for the trailhead sign and a mailbox on your right, just by the first RV parking spot. Sign your name on the sign-in sheet stashed in the mailbox, so we can prove just how often the trail is used. Now get set for some fun, as a bounty of singletrack awaits you!

0.4 First of many brakes-free zones down across small wooden bridge. Note that every bridge on this trail has a smooth transition on both sides. The drop in may be steep, but stay away from that brake lever and you'll really enjoy yourself.

0.9 Turn right as singletrack dumps you onto old doubletrack with sign that says "No Horses!" This starts a nice, zippy little speed zone that drops you down across another bridge, short switchback climb, another bridge, then a tougher steep climb. Lots of small rocks and roots mixed with speed for boatloads of fun.

1.6 Bridge crossing. Rocks after bridge can be tricky at speed (tech 2 +).

2.1 Mondo downhill switchback section (three in a row), with big roots and big rocks; call it a tech 3 to clean it.

2.2 Second open-water stream crossing, then a long gooey patch for some serious mud-dogging. Be first in line here, or be ready to eat some mud pie.

2.3 Toughest climb on the trail: steep, extremely tight and rocky switchbacks that keep coming and coming. Very tough to pick a clean line. Even advanced riders may dab here. Solid tech 3 + to clean.

2.5 At the top of this painful climb, you'll turn right onto an old doubletrack. This is a good place to stop and cheer/harass those still working the climb. Plus, you'll want to recharge here for the nice long downhill that awaits.

2.8 Watch for singletrack that peels off to right. If you suddenly find yourself busting through limbs and bushes on the doubletrack, you probably need to back up.

San-Lee Park

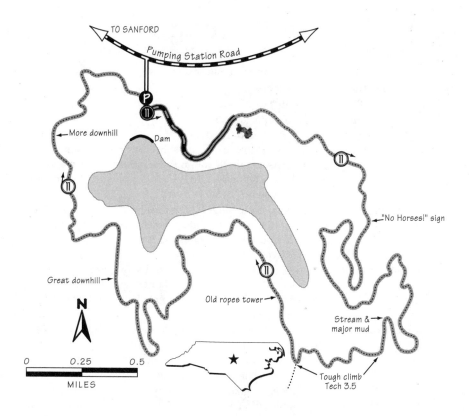

TO SANFORD

Pumping Station Road

←More downhill

Dam

←"No Horses!" sign

Great downhill→

Old ropes tower→

Stream &→
major mud

N

Tough climb
Tech 3.5

0   0.25   0.5

MILES

2.9 Cruising downhill continues. Watch for a pillow-sized rock in center of trail: excellent launch site for the vertically inclined. Pass old, rotten ropes course and tower. Note: Stay *off* the tower, as it's a deathtrap, no fooling. And one idiot killing himself here could close the whole trail, so look but don't touch!

3.5 Long, fast downhill turns into doubletrack as it passes under power lines. Continue straight on track under lines, back into woods and more singletrack. Watch for sharp left turn at bottom.

4.1 Sweet singletrack laid on old doubletrack drops for quick speed, with another sudden left at bottom. If you get carried away here, you'll be picking yourself out of the bushes.

4.6 Exit trail, crossing wide stream over long wooden-and-steel bridge. Drop onto grass for breather, return to vehicle, or turn around and go back in for a second helping.

Devil's Ridge

Location: 15 minutes west of Sanford.

Distance: 3.6-mile loop.

Time: 30 minutes to 1 hour.

Tread: Clean, hardpacked singletrack.

Aerobic level: Easy to moderate. As always, depends on how hard you push it. All climbs are quite short, but rough track and sharp turns can force you to work some to gain the top. Though the course isn't that long, charging it at race pace can wear you out in short order.

Technical difficulty: Tech 1+ overall. Toughest technical move is the tech 3+ climb up to the clearing near the end. A few tech 2+ root sections. Otherwise, most of the trail is very clean, if awfully twisty.

Highlights: Lots of roots, twists and turns, and short surprising climbs. Serious mud after a rain. As a bonus, on many Sundays you get to watch the motocrossers show you what "huge air" really means.

Land status: Private land but very friendly to mountain bikers. Track is always open to ride, except during motorcycle races and hunting season.

Maps: USGS White Hill (for topo details only; no trails shown).

Access: From Raleigh, take U.S. Highway 1 South to Sanford. Seven miles after US 1 and US 15/501 merge, turn right at the light (just past Food Lion shopping center) onto Center Church Road (sign: "Devil's Ridge Motocross"). Go 0.5 mile and turn right onto Henley Road; go 2 miles and turn right onto Dycus Road. Drive 1 mile and turn right onto Blackstone Road, then after another 0.3 mile turn left onto Kings Farm Road. The course is 1 mile up on the right and is well marked; just pull in and park. If the gate is closed, it's okay to park on the road and ride in.

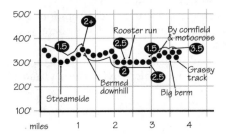

Notes on the trail

The operators of Devil's Ridge have spent a lot of time building and polishing this trail, and it really shows. The berms and bridges are solid, the signage is excellent, and the trail always seems freshly raked with little or no debris or litter. You can crank through this entire course and never catch so much as a stick in your wheel. It's smooth, fast, and not too technical—a perfect spot for introducing new riders or practicing for the next race. Beware that this place can be a serious mudfest after a rain, and a puddle that looks 2 inches deep can swallow you and your bike whole.

Note that two separate courses share the woods here: the mountain bike course and a motorcycle hare scramble course, which do not share any tracks, though they do cross numerous times. The scramble course is much deeper and wider and has obviously been dug by motorcycles. While this place can seem like a bit of a maze, the two courses generally cross at 90-degree angles, so when in doubt, go straight and keep following the orange arrows. If you're supposed to turn, it's clearly marked. The owners ask that bike riders stay completely off the motocross course located up top.

The Ride

0.0 Start from just inside the entrance gate. Look left for a clear singletrack diving into the woods alongside the road, marked with orange arrows. Tread is dirt hardpack and starts off zipping through the trees with some quick berms and little drops.

0.2 Continue straight across the motorcycle track, following the orange arrows.

0.3 Cross small wooden bridge. Continue straight through intersection of three trails, following orange arrows.

0.5 Continue straight on trail alongside the stream, following orange arrows. Note that motorcycle track cuts uphill and is marked sporadically with hollow red arrows. Just keep straight.

0.7 to 1.5 Several intersections through here, just continue straight at each one, following orange arrows.

1.7 Trail breaks out into opening near the top. Follow track as it bears left and dives back into the woods.

2.0 Cross small wooden bridge. Track bears right over a small knoll, then drops for a fast, fun, snaky descent that's over way too quickly.

2.2 Cross a pair of wooden bridges with some fun tech 2+ roots in between.

2.8 Tricky tech 2+ descent, filled with sudden twists and snaky roots. Watch for the racing rooster in this section; I''ve had him outrun me twice along here.

3.0 Rocky downhill, followed by a stream crossing. Climb up the other side, which has a 5-foot-high hump at the top just to see if you're planning ahead.

3.2 Trail leaves woods runs alongside a small cornfield as it heads up toward the motocross starting gate. When you hit the clearing at the top, follow the orange arrows straight ahead back into the woods. Serious fun, as you drop over some big whoop-dee-doos and fly around a long berm: tech 3 at speed.

Devil's Ridge

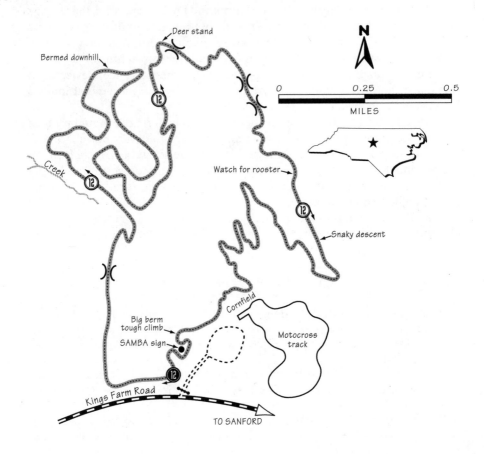

Deer stand

Bermed downhill

N

0   0.25   0.5

MILES

Creek

Watch for rooster

Snaky descent

Cornfield

Big berm
tough climb

Motocross
track

SAMBA sign

Kings Farm Road

TO SANFORD

3.4 Trail turns back up to the left for a short but steep tech 3+ climb. Pop back out into the top clearing, behind the red barn. Continue straight past the SAMBA sign, following the ever-present orange arrows. Trail dips back into the woods one last time, then pops back out and runs across the grass.

3.6 Return to starting point by entrance gate.

Launching at Devil's Ridge.

Governor's Creek

Location: 15 minutes west of Sanford.
Distance: 3.9-mile loop.
Time: 30 minutes to 1 hour.
Tread: 100 percent singletrack.
Aerobic level: Easy to moderate. Only 50 feet of elevation change at most, but it goes up and down a lot.
Technical difficulty: Tech 1+ for the regular trail; tech 4 for the Challenge Loop.
Highlights: Short, quick humps and dips for lots of little air; fast slaloming; huge pyramid; rock slabs.
Land status: Popular mountain bike race course. Open to the public to use at your own risk.
Maps: USGS White Hill.
Access: From Raleigh, take U.S. Highway 1 South to Sanford. Seven miles after US 1 and US 15/501 merge, turn right at the light (just past Food Lion shopping center) onto Center Church Road (sign: "Devil's Ridge Motocross"). Follow this to the end, then turn left onto South Plank Road. Take a quick right onto Stanton Hill Road, then another quick right onto Underwood Road. The trailhead and parking area are 0.5 mile ahead on the right. Occasional signs for Mountain Bike Park are along the way.

Notes on the trail

Mostly easy spinning around smooth berms and over rounded humps. Some short, rocky climbs and a couple of fast drops in the downhill. Nothing in here over a tech 2+. On the short Challenge Loop though, you'll find some big rock drops and the mother of all ramps for a long tech 4 section. The climb back out is a bruising tech 3.

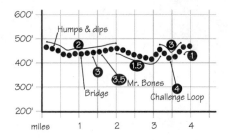

Governor's Creek

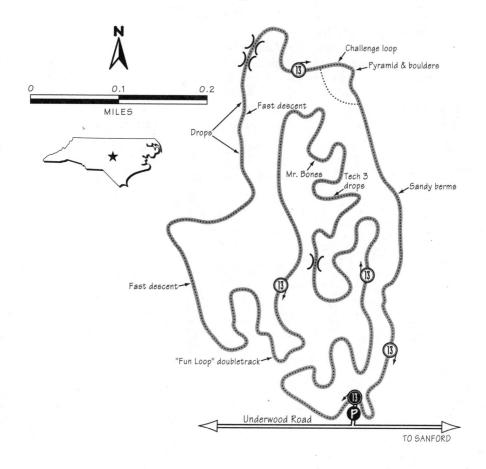

N

0   0.1   0.2
MILES

Challenge loop

Pyramid & boulders

⑬

Fast descent

Drops

Mr. Bones

Tech 3 drops

Sandy berms

⑬

⑬

Fast descent

⑬

"Fun Loop" doubletrack

⑬

⑬
Ⓟ

Underwood Road

TO SANFORD

The Ride

0.0 Trail enters the woods across the parking area, near the edge of the road. Sandy, tech 1 track.

0.2 Choice of two loops. Turn right for the Race Loop (straight is the Fun Loop). Trail turns to hardpack with some excellent berms and lots of humps and jumps. Fairly fast track, zipping through the trees.

0.8 Continuous change of terrain: tough, rooty uphill; flat; rooty; mud; rocks; bridge; uphill; and another berm, all in a half mile.

1.0 Cross a short bridge.

1.3 Bear right as singletrack T's into a clear doubletrack, the Fun Loop. Fast downhilling, over some good drops and through a few long berms.

1.6 Pass Mr. Bones hanging in the tree. He's there to warn you of the rocky drop into a stream crossing, with some more tech 3 rocks on the exit.

1.8 Another fun, fast, downhill. Cross another bridge, hug some contours, then climb.

2.3 Twisty, narrow hardpack turns to wide-open XXL singletrack.

3.0 Cross a pair of bridges, then climb.

3.3 Continue straight onto the Challenge Loop for a cool tech 4 section. You get a quick run over some small drops, a switchback into a monstrous 4-foot pyramid, then a couple of small boulder drops. Return climb is rocky and steep, a painful tech 3. (Main trail bypasses all this madness to the right.)

3.5 Turn left as you return to the main trail.

3.9 Track turns back to sand, and drops you back at the parking area.

Triad

The Triad of Greensboro, Winston-Salem, and High Point dishes out a wide variety of trails. Smooth cruising at Hagen Stone Park, rootier track through the watershed and Country Park, and respectable technical challenges at Hobby Park.

Hagen Stone Park

Location: 15 minutes south of Greensboro.

Distance: 4-mile loop.

Time: 20 minutes to 1 hour.

Tread: Mostly wide doubletrack covered with pine bark chips. Short section of hardpacked dirt singletrack.

Aerobic level: Easy (unless you're cranking it in mid-June at midday). Very small elevation changes. Flat, smooth, and wide open.

Technical difficulty: Tech 1 overall, with some tech 2 roots and a few tech 3 rock sections. One huge, tech 4+ suspended log.

Highlights: Fast cruising; creek crossings; old buildings; wildlife; small rockfield; lakes.

Land status: County park.

Maps: Wooden map posted by park office.

Access: From Interstate 40 in Greensboro, take Exit 126, and turn right onto U.S. Highway 421 South. Go 5 miles, then turn right on Hagen Stone Park Road (brown park sign posted as well). After another 2.5 miles, turn right into the park entrance. Parking area and trailhead are immediately to the left.

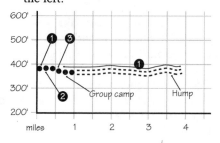

Hagen Stone Park

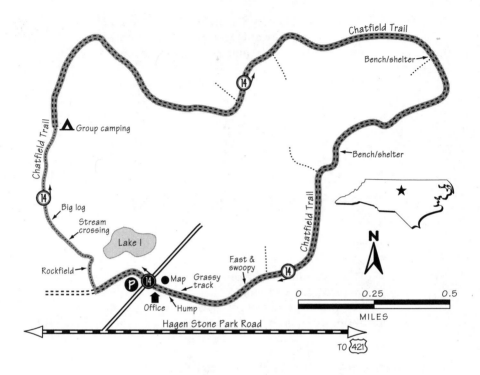

Notes on the trail

This is a fine beginner trail, lots of easy cruising with just a hint of true, rocky singletrack. More advanced riders can just soar along the whole length. One tough stream and a huge log to keep you humble.

The Ride

0.0 From the parking lot, bear left past the lake and the red boathouse (sign: "Chatfield Hiking Trail"). Tread is pine bark doubletrack.

0.2 Turn right to follow Chatfield Trail. Tread changes to hardpacked singletrack, with several short tech 2 and 3 rockfields.

0.3 Cross wooden bridge, then a short, rooty (tech 2) uphill.

0.5 A triple treat: a tough, tech 3 stream crossing; a respectable tech 3+ log with roots on the backside; and then a mondo suspended log, topping a good 3 feet off the ground, for a big tech 4+ move.

0.7 Turn right into Group Camping Area 2. Take an immediate left past campsite to continue on Chatfield Trail.

1.4 Continue straight on Chatfield Trail. Draper Trail joins in from the left. From here on, just follow the main track and ignore any side trails. Almost continuous pine bark doubletrack. Fast and easy cruising.

2.0 Bear left at the next five Y's. Fun, fast, swoopy track. Some small berms starting to develop.

3.6 Tread changes to grassy doubletrack.

3.8 Steep, 8-foot-tall hump. If you've been cranking all along, this move could push you suddenly anaerobic.

4.0 Exit the trail past the park office (the restored log cabin) and the park map, and return to the parking lot.

Owl's Roost

Location: Along Lake Brandt, on the north side of Greensboro.

Distance: 9.3-mile lariat.

Time: 1.5 to 2.5 hours, depending on whether the woods thrashes you.

Tread: 7.6 miles of singletrack; 1.7 miles of doubletrack.

Aerobic level: Moderate. Although the climbs are steep and numerous, none of them is very long. The constant pounding of roots ups the ante a bit. Returning on the doubletrack lets you cruise past some of the nasties.

Technical difficulty: Tech 3 overall. Initial drop to the lake is a tech 2, but many difficult root sections later on; some as high as tech 4. Gully drop is only a 3, but it takes commitment. Major pyramid near the end of the loop is a tall, tech 4 monster. Dabbing somewhere is almost a certainty.

Highlights: Roots, sneaky and snaky; huge log pyramid; big mud; 25-foot gully drop, lots of bunny hops; logs.

Land status: Greensboro watershed property.

Maps: USGS Lake Brandt.

Access: From Interstate 40 in Greensboro, take Exit 127 onto U.S. Highway 220 North. As you progress through town, this turns into Battleground Avenue. Turn right onto Old Battleground Avenue, then go another 0.3 mile to the Bur-Mill Park entrance on your left. The trail starts at the back of the parking lot. If you drive over the lake, you missed Old Battleground.

Notes on the trail

Owl's Roost is by far the most serious of all the watershed trails. While this track starts innocently enough, serious technical challenges lurk along the lake's edge. Lots and lots of roots, often downhill, and often laced together into long, gnarly, off-camber welcome mats. A slick, 25-foot, smooth-bellied gully waits after the worst of the roots for a weightless roller-coaster drop—you'll need to do it several times. Then a monstrous log pyramid, on an uphill no less, squatting at the top of the last hill. After all that, you can return on a fast grassy doubletrack to bypass some of the rougher terrain.

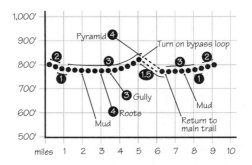

The Ride

0.0 Begin from parking area at Bur-Mill Park. Trail dives into woods near the road, immediately hitting a cool, hopping slalom run through the trees.

0.6 Trail flattens and starts to parallel the lake.

1.3 Turn right as trail hits a wide doubletrack. Track to left crosses lake over long walkway.

1.6 Turn left onto singletrack as it breaks up over the bank. Immediate tough series of humps, dips, and roots.

2.0 Mud. Thick, goopy, nasty, black mud. Sometimes the walkboards across are complete, and sometimes they're not. After you climb up from the mud pit, it's roots and more roots.

3.0 Continue straight, as the return trail branches in from the right. Shortly after, watch for a deadly, tech 4 rooty descent that's often filled with slick mud. This one will slam you.

3.3 Trail branches right, just as you hit a large gully. While the main trail has a decent bridge at the bottom, the branch right leads to an excellent roller-coaster drop. Trail hits the lip, plunges 25 feet to the bottom, and zips up the far side. Just pedal like crazy and have a blast.

3.6 Continue straight. Alternate bypass trail branches right.

4.9 A burning, uphill switchback leads you to the feet of a log pyramid that must be 5 feet tall. Up and over is a doable tech 4 with a lot of speed and a big lunge.

Owl's Roost

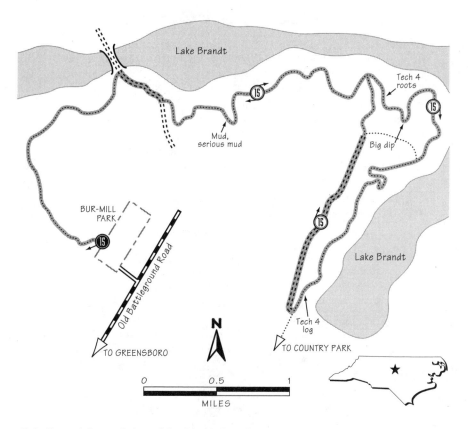

5.0 Turn right at choice of doubletrack trails. Fast, smooth return run, though the pine needles are slippery in the corners.

6.1 Continue straight as tread changes to singletrack. Trail right leads back to the lakeside trail, just in case you need to hit the Big Dip on the back.

6.3 Turn left as you T back into the main trail. Get ready for the roots again.

7.3 Cross the Black Swamp once again.

7.7 Turn right as the trail ends onto the service road.

8.0 Turn left onto singletrack, just before you reach the long walkway over Lake Brandt. Follow the track across the bridge if you want to take the road ride to either Bald Eagle or Reedy Fork Trail.

8.7 Some jumps available along the bottom of the trail. Then starts a bit of climbing to take you back to the trailhead.

9.3 Return to the trailhead.

Reedy Fork

Location: Along Lake Brandt, on the north side of Greensboro.
Distance: 6.8 miles out and back.
Time: 45 minutes to 1.5 hours.
Tread: 6.8 miles of singletrack.
Aerobic level: Easy. Very little elevation change. Cool, easy ride.
Technical difficulty: Tech 1.5 overall. Some tougher roots and a tech 3 drop onto a bridge that'll make you pay attention.
Highlights: Bridges; logs; some fun hops and drops; stream crossings; beaver construction.
Land status: Greensboro watershed property.
Maps: USGS Lake Brandt.
Access: From Interstate 40 in Greensboro, take Exit 127 onto U.S. Highway 220 North. As you progress through town, this turns into Battleground Avenue. Follow US 220 past Lake Higgins. Turn right onto North Carolina Highway 150, then right onto Lake Brandt Road. Look for parking area and trailhead on your left just as you approach the Lake Brandt dam.

To reach Reedy Fork from the Owl's Roost Trail, take Strawberry Road to Alley Road to Lunsfords Road to Lake Brandt Road.

Notes on the trail

An easy, fun ride that anyone will enjoy; good introduction trail. Mostly smooth, level cranking with enough roots and other drops to make you pay attention. You'll at least see the beavers' handiwork, if not the fat little buggers themselves.

A short tale: While resting at the far end of the trail, we chanced upon a litter of puppies that someone had dumped there to die. The four starving little guys devoured all my Clif bars. Since we couldn't leave them, we made a sack out of a sweatshirt and stuck them inside, then finished the ride back. By the time we reached the truck, we had found homes for all four of them with fellow riders.

Score: mountain bikers—4; irresponsible jerks who leave puppies to starve (and for whom a special hell is reserved)—0.

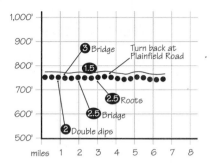

The Ride

0.0 Trail starts out as smooth, tech 1+ hardpack, running beside a wide, slow-moving stream. Trail gradually gets muddier.

0.3 More mud, then a bit of a swamp ride. Scary, tech 3 bridge to cross.

0.5 Bear right, following red arrows. Tread back to hardpack.

1.0 Trail lays out a cool double dip for you. Just after, a short alternate loop branches back to the left.

1.2 Twisty drop down to a narrow bridge: tech 3+. Then bear left following arrows.

1.4 Begin the only bit of real climbing. Other end of alternate loop branches in from left.

2.1 Another narrow bridge, flanked by rooty banks: tech 2+.

2.3 Turn right and cross a small bridge. Trail gets swampy again.

You never know what you'll find on the trail at Reedy Fork.

Reedy Fork

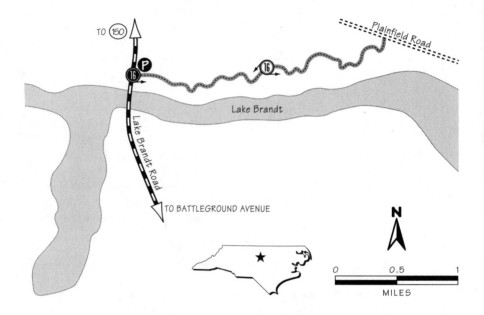

2.9 Tech 2+ roots. Sign posted for the other direction: "Reedy Fork Trail."

3.2 Cross an old, overgrown road and bear right to pick up the singletrack again.

3.4 Trail ends at Plainfield Road. Drink, check the woods for puppies, then head back.

4.5 Cross bridge, then turn left.

4.7 Cross another bridge, then a bit of fast contouring.

5.8 Double dips.

6.3 Bear left at this Y.

6.8 Return to parking area.

Bald Eagle

Location: Along Lake Higgins, on the north side of Greensboro.

Distance: 6.8 miles out and back.

Time: 30 minutes to 1 hour.

Tread: 6.8 miles of singletrack.

Aerobic level: Easy. Almost no elevation change; just twists along the contours. Good cardio trail; nice speed without being boring.

Technical difficulty: Tech 2. Lots of bunny hops, small logs, and narrow creek crossings. A few short, off-camber rooty climbs provide a little tech 3 action. Dab-free ride very possible.

Highlights: Fast singletrack cruising; bunny hops; small logs; lake views.

Land status: Greensboro watershed property.

Maps: USGS Summerfield.

Access: From Interstate 40 in Greensboro, take Exit 127 onto U.S. Highway 220 North. As you progress through town, this turns into Battleground Avenue. Follow US 220 past Lake Higgins. Just after crossing Lake Higgins, turn left on Hamburg Mill Road. Turn left shortly into the second parking area for the marina. The trailhead is clearly signed at the edge of the parking lot.

Notes on the trail

A fine, flat cruising trail, slaloming through the trees, hitting the hops, and running the streams. It's a warm-up for either of the other trails in Bur-Mill, and an excellent intro ride for beginners. Just tool along, or get in the big ring and crank, whichever you want.

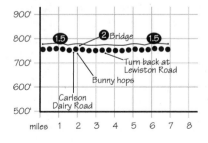

Bald Eagle

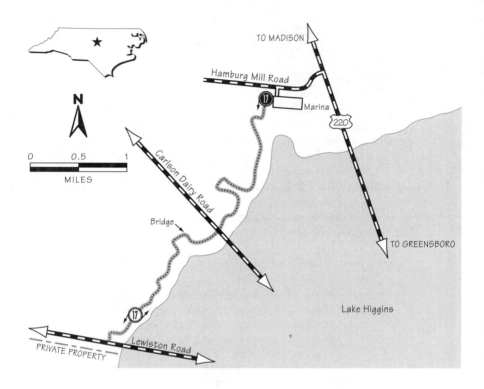

The Ride

0.0 Leave from the marina parking lot. Trail entrance clearly signed and starts right off with some fine, tech 1+ track that twists and turns through the trees. Flat contour running. Multiple creek crossings are bridged or lined with corduroy.

0.8 Cross an opening, which is a gas line right-of-way.

1.6 Cross Carlson Dairy Road. Watch for fast traffic. Trail clearly picks up on other side with more of the same fun, easy track.

2.0 Cross over a long wooden bridge. Bunny hop opportunities abound.

3.4 Trail hits Lewiston Road (paved). Turn around at this point. At the time of writing, the trail across the road was private property and closed to bikes. Look for updated signs.

5.2 Cross Carlson Dairy Road.

6.8 Return to parking area.

Country Park

Location: Jaycee Park, on the north side of Greensboro.
Distance: 4-mile loop.
Time: 45 minutes to 1.5 hours.
Tread: 3.6 miles of singletrack; 0.4 mile of dirt doubletrack.
Aerobic level: Easy to moderate. All climbs in Country Park are short. Most of the trail is an easy cruise, though the constant roots in places can keep you working.
Technical difficulty: Tech 2. Lots of buff cruising track; some tech 3 logs; lots of roots and small drops.
Highlights: Logs; roots and rocks; tight singletrack cruising; the typical stuff.
Land status: Guilford county park.
Maps: USGS Greensboro; Greensboro Area Bike and Trail Map, available from Greensboro Parks and Recreation and area bike shops.
Access: From Interstate 40 in Greensboro, take Exit 128 and turn north onto East Lee Street. Follow signs for U.S. Highway 220 as this road changes names to Muro Boulevard, then Fisher Street, then finally Battleground Avenue. After a few miles, turn right onto Pisgah Church Road, then hang an immediate left at the entrance sign for Jaycee/Country Park. Turn left onto Forest Lawn Drive, then right into the parking lot for the Lewis Center (large brick building). A ballfield is at one end of the parking lot, and Safetyland (a surreal play/driving town setup for kids) is on one side. Trailhead is at the corner between the two.

Notes on the trail

This is a good beginner and intermediate cruising trail. You can get a warm-up on the paved greenway that circles the lake, or you can send your less-than-adventurous honey out to the greenway, while you get a little singletrack into your system. A well-maintained set of trails (if awfully confusing), Country Park offers lots of small, tech 2 roots and other challenges, along with a few big logs and lots of high-speed, twisting-through-the-trees cruising.

This place is a literal maze of trails. There are tons of intersections and cross-trails, and I'd be lying if I said you'll be able to follow my directions with no problems. In general though, the route given here runs a counter-clockwise loop between the lake and the cemetery. Try to follow the main track when in doubt; bearing to the right will generally keep you on the outside of the loop. You can't really get too lost, unless you get into the military park, so if you start to see lots of confederate statues, turn around.

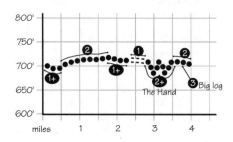

The Ride

0.0 Trail begins at the back of the parking area between the fence to Safetyland and the ballfield. Cross a small ditch and hang an immediate right at the first T you hit. Trail starts off with clean, hardpacked tech 1+ singletrack.

0.3 Turn left at the T. Small bridge and clearing off to right.

0.4 Pass a green, wooden swing and white arrows on the trees, then bear right at the Y into a small meadow. Shortly after, you'll cross a small playground area, and the trail bears uphill.

0.5 Bear right at this Y and follow the white arrows for a good, tech 2 climb.

0.6 Trail crosses the paved lake greenway. Cross the greenway, ride over a sizable wooden bridge, then immediately turn right onto more singletrack.

0.8 Nice 12-inch drop, then bear left uphill at the Y, heading away from the lake.

0.9 Ride up a long set of landscape-timber steps. Cross the paved greenway again, ride through a gap in the wooden fence, and cut straight across another playground area to pick up singletrack on the other side.

1.1 Turn left at this T (right takes you to the military park).

1.5 12-inch log-drop leads you into a five-way intersection. Turn sharp right, and you'll start to see the cemetery off to your right. Track is very twisty, mostly tech 1+, with some large tech 3 logs along the way.

2.1 Cross one small wooden bridge, then a second bridge constructed of an old Ping-Pong table. Head uphill, still by the cemetery.

2.2 Trail enters a clearing and turns into dirt doubletrack behind an old brick building. Track leads past several old trolley cars, and crosses a gravel path that leads to the cemetery.

2.6 Drop back into the woods; trail returns to singletrack.

2.7 Trail leads to "The Hand," an intersection with five or six possibilities. Turn sharply right for a steep, fast, tech 2+ drop, then a quick U-turn and a return to the Hand. Turn right again and repeat the drop/U-turn process. Return to the Hand once more and turn right again onto the next track.

Country Park

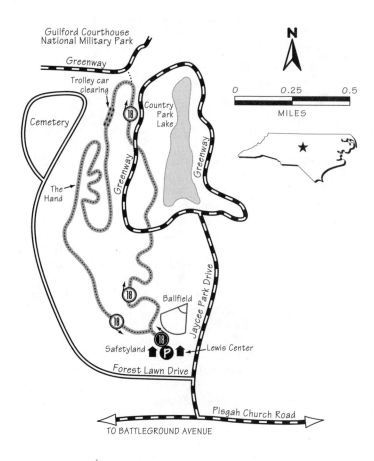

3.1 Trail loops out once more, running back along the edge of the cemetery fence, then returns to the Hand.

3.2 Turn right at the Hand one last time, following the sign for Long Trail of Peace. Bear right at the immediate Y that follows, following the red ribbons. Cross a little humpty bridge, then start cranking though some fast, twisty, tech 2 cruising track.

3.6 Nice, 24-inch log to practice your moves on—a tech 3 to clean it.

4.0 Trail comes back up along the Safetyland fence. Bear right at the Y, and pop back out into the parking area.

Hobby Park

Location: Winston-Salem, just south of Interstate 40.

Distance: 6.6-mile loop.

Time: 45 minutes to 1.5 hours.

Tread: All singletrack (except for final run up the paved derby track); mostly hardpack with some sand and loose surface.

Aerobic level: Moderate to strenuous. Almost constant up and down with little chance for a rest. Climbs can be tough (particularly the Hill). High adrenaline factor pushes things up a notch or two as well.

Technical difficulty: Tech 3+. Hobby Park tosses out one tough technical move after another. Jumps abound for some good air-time potential. Descent through the Rock Garden is a tech 4 number, particularly since it's tough *not* to carry a bunch of speed into it.

Highlights: Lots of jumps; cool log pyramids; fast, crazy downhills; multiple brakes-free zones; heart-breaking climb.

Land status: City park.

Maps: Sketch available on the North Carolina Mountain Bike Authority website, at http://members.aol.com/NCMBA/ home.html and also at www.mbinfo.com.

Access: From I-40 (*not* Business 40) in Winston-Salem, take Exit 189, Stratford Road West (U.S. Highway 158). Go about 3 miles and turn left onto Clemmonsville Road, then take an immediate left into the well-marked park entrance.

Notes on the trail

This trail has got it all: huge berms, rock gardens, streams, big logs, pyramids, a serious drop through a rock and log-infested erosion gully, and a climb that gives you the option of lung-busting or heart-breaking fun. It's Disneyland for the two-wheeled set—not a trail for first-timers or for anyone who really hates falling. This trail will test your technical skills (and courage) from all angles. Beginners will be scared—often. Intermediates will probably crash—often. Advanced folks can pound through it for an experience like riding a jackhammer.

The trail changes occasionally and often isn't well-marked. When in doubt, follow a general clockwise direction or head uphill to return to the airfields and parking area.

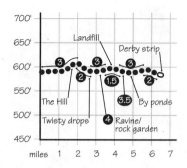

The Ride

0.0 Start from parking lot. Enter in past park sign and over a 3-foot red-clay hump. Trail starts with multiple bunny hops over sandy track littered with big rocks.

0.1 Quick left, right, left, at three Y's in row. If in doubt, follow clearest track and end up back near the parking lot. First of many extremely sweet brakes-free sections.

0.4 Ignore trail that peels in from right.

0.7 Turn right at four-way intersection. Lots of dips to dance over.

0.9 Sharp turn back left by orange fencing. Straight is a shortcut that avoids climbing Poop Plant Hill, but also misses some excellent zipping through the trees. Your choice, but I think it's worth it; besides, you ought to pay to play.

1.4 Several more grin-inducing brakes-free zones. Last one drops you onto a long wooden walkway. Start calling up your reserves now, 'cause the biggest climb in the ride is just around the corner.

1.7 Poop Plant Hill. A choice of tracks is now offered up this painful climb: snaking back and forth for prolonged agony or straight up the throat for a quick victory or demise. Call it a tech 3 but a mean one. Follow main track straight. Shortcut reenters from right by orange fence.

1.9 Sharp left turn. Straight leads to back of derby grandstands.

2.4 Track enters clearing behind derby track, follows left along the edge, then drops back into the woods. Tasty brakes-free zone, several short wooden bridges, and lots of twisty root-drops lead you back down by the poop plant.

3.2 Turn left at T, shortly after running into and back out of the field again. Stop, cinch your shorts, and prepare for the Rock Garden. This tech 4 descent tosses you a respectable rock ledge, then a large log, then drops you into a high-walled erosion gully that can be ridden high on the side. Ugly, but sweet: sort of like my bulldog.

3.5 Bear left as you enter the landfill. In summer this place is a sticker-filled wasteland and is best bypassed by going right. Decent chance to stretch your legs a bit otherwise. Follow track as it cuts across landfill then doubles back. Bypass peels in from right.

4.6 Sharp right turn drops you down toward lower pond.

4.7 Turn left at edge of lower pond to cross dam. Turn right at far end of dam, for a 5-foot weightless drop.

5.0 Turn right at T. Look for boards nailed across a huge root ball for some optional serious technical action.

Grinding up Poop Plant Hill at Hobby Park.

Hobby Park

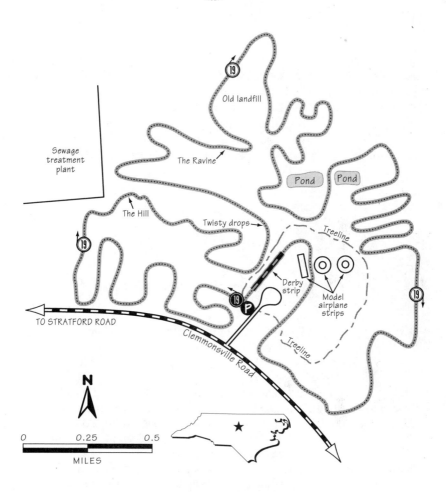

5.1 Cross bridge and follow dam between upper and lower pond.

5.5 Follow track across short section of field near airplane circle. Track reenters woods, then skirts along edge of field through a sandy hemlock grove.

5.8 Bear left at Y to drop down near Clemmonsville Road.

5.9 Follow track straight for one last chance at some speed (opening to left leads back to parking lot if you've had enough already). Track leads out into field for some smooth, fast cruising. Circle around airplane strip to enter bottom of derby track.

6.6 Zip down the derby track, then groan up the other side for a last bit of sweat before you return to the parking lot.

Charlotte, Statesville, and Morganton

The Queen City hosts a bevy of singletrack beauties. We included only four due to legal reasons, but there are several other open trails in the area. Catawba River Front, Cane Creek, and Renaissance Park are all located on public property, whereas Beech Springs is a private venture. South Mountain outside Morganton is as brutal a trail as you'll find anywhere. Signal Hill is Statesville's only legal ride (that we could find, at least).

Catawba River Front

Location: On the banks of the Catawba River, about 15 minutes west of Charlotte.

Distance: 8.5-mile loop.

Time: 1.5 to 2.5 hours.

Tread: 7.3 miles of singletrack; 1.2 miles of dirt doubletrack.

Aerobic level: Moderate. The warm-up climbs along the power line hit you hard, and then you get a dozen trips down to the river and back up. Plus, all the roots can just sap your strength. These 8 miles can feel like 18.

Technical difficulty: Tech 3 overall. Roots everywhere for a near constant pounding except along the power line, and then you get rocks and gullies. Lots of knee-high jumps, and at least one double, and a monster launch pad down by the river.

Highlights: Switchy downhills; jumps; bermed turns; slalom course; mudholes.

Land status: County park.

Maps: USGS Mount Holly.

Access: From Charlotte, follow Interstate 85 South to Exit 29, Sam Wilson Road. Turn right at the top of the ramp, then hang an immediate (and I mean immediate) left onto Performance Road. Turn left again onto Mores Chapel Road, then right onto Heavy Equipment School Road. Follow this 'til the road ends at a metal gate and the trailhead.

Notes on the trail

This is a top-notch ride, only 15 minutes from Charlotte. Catawba is the kind of trail that's doable for a determined beginner yet still challenging for an advanced rider. For the uninitiated, the climbs will require some pushing, and the rooty drops will keep you on your toes or your face, depending on your concentration and ability. You'll get lots of fast downhill action that slips back and forth through the trees. Speed comes quickly in many spots, but be warned that most of the downhills end with a sudden turn at the river's edge. Opportunities for air abound with dozens of dips and humps to fly from, including the River Monster—a 5-footer that'll show you its ugly side if you don't show proper respect.

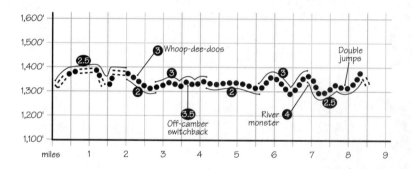

The Ride

0.0 From the parking area, ride straight past the gate onto a wide, dirt doubletrack. Follow this track as it curves under the power lines and up the hill.

0.4 Turn right, back under the power lines, as you reach the top of the hill. Track takes you to the edge of the woods, where some tasty singletrack picks up (tech 2+, small rocks and roots).

0.8 Pop out of the woods and run under the power lines. Watch for immediate singletrack on the right darting back into the woods. Ride the woods for about 200 yards, jump out onto the power lines track again for a steep downhill, then back in for more sweet singletrack.

1.5 Back out on the power line doubletrack again. Turn left just before two big power line towers and cross over to the singletrack on the other side.

1.8 Sweet, twisty track leads you into a cool gully for some roller-coaster action, then over some big ol' whoop-dee-doos. Bear right if you're given the option. (Several faint, older tracks peel off; just follow the clearest trail.)

2.2 Fast downhilling through the trees, heading toward the river.

2.4 Turn left as you bottom out at the river (or just go straight if you want to swim awhile). Trail works back and forth with good use of terrain, some big dips, tree tunnels, and several surprise mudholes—a little bit of everything.

3.1 Climb, turn right at the T, and head back to the river.

The Excitable Boy has good reason to be.

Catawba River Front

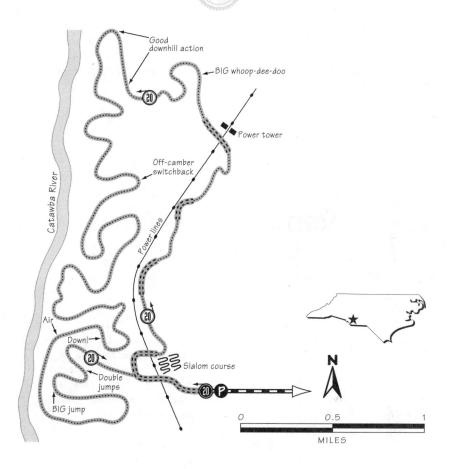

3.3 Climb some more, turn right at this T too, and head back to the river.

3.6 Turn right once more for another trip back down the hill. Challenging, off-camber switchback to maneuver (tech 3+).

3.8 Big dip with a bridge in the middle, then a steep climb, and another trip back to the river.

4.1 Turn left, up away from the river. You'll cross several old roads and doubletrack trails; just keep following the clear track and you'll eventually end up back by the river once again.

5.7 Bear right at this Y, dropping down across some old drainage pipes then into a tough, granny-gear climb.

6.0 Bear right as you pop out of the woods back up near the power lines. Look for an immediate right back into the trees. Get ready for the best downhill yet, a fast descent that swoops through the trees, with several surprise switchbacks.

6.2 Turn left as you reach the river again.

6.9 Slip along the river for a while, climb up, then roar back down to challenge the River Monster, a 5-foot behemoth of a jump that deserves respect and some good suspension.

7.7 Cool set of double jumps, each with a tight, bermed turn afterward.

8.1 Return once more to the power lines. Head downhill on the doubletrack to return to the parking area, or take the challenge of the slalom course hidden out in the middle of the field among the high weeds (beware the steep jumps).

8.5 Return to the parking area.

Renaissance Park

Location: Next door to the Charlotte Coliseum, in downtown Charlotte.

Distance: 4.7-mile loop.

Time: 45 minutes to 1.5 hours.

Tread: 4.4 miles of singletrack; 0.3 mile of gravel doubletrack.

Aerobic level: Easy to moderate. There's not much elevation change in these woods, but the singletrack makes the most of it, climbing, turning, and dropping almost constantly. And while none of the climbs are very long, many are rock strewn and turn into tortuous, slow-motion grinders.

Technical difficulty: Tech 2.5 overall. This track is very temperamental and can change from a tech 1 cruiser to a tech 3 root/rock/log playground with no warning. Many of the rooty sections will be overwhelming for beginners.

Highlights: Big pyramids; lots of humps and root drops; treacherous roots; view of coliseum; located almost in downtown Charlotte!

Land status: City park.

Maps: Sketches available on the North Carolina Mountain Bike Authority website, at http://members.aol.com/NCMBA/home.html and at www.mbinfo.com.

Access: From Interstate 77 in Charlotte, take Exit 5 onto West Tyvola Road. Go about 3 miles; pass the Charlotte Coliseum on your left. Go another mile or so, then turn left into the first Rennaissance Park entrance.

Notes on the trail

This little secret singletrack gem lies hidden only a long wheelie's ride from the Charlotte Coliseum. Don't be fooled as we were into expecting a smooth, cruising trail set up for Buffy on her Huffy, though. What begins with a friendly dirt path quickly turns into rock-and-root-strewn singletrack of surprising meanness. Pyramids and log crossings abound. Ugly, tech 3+ descent halfway in requires concentration, courage, or the sense to walk it.

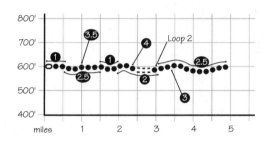

The Ride

0.0 Start from end of parking lot, near dumpster and dirt piles. To start with Loop 1, hop on track along the edge of the parking lot, and head toward the park entrance. As parking lot ends, look for obvious singletrack cutting straight through grassy field.

0.6 As it nears Tyvola Road, this singletrack suddenly changes from smooth, tech 1 hardpack to a rooty, eroded track full of drops and washouts. Beginners should keep their eyes open for the transition.

0.8 Cross short wooden bridge. **Caution:** Bridge is often slick with mud, and will slap you down faster than you can blink.

1.0 Trail wanders by second park entrance and edge of tennis courts, then reenters woods just past courts, offering up a nice 3-foot drop with a fat tech 3+ rock perched right at the lip for a world-class launching pad.

1.4 Trail varies from sweeping tech 1 track, to a series of large log pyramids, short drops, and tough, rooty climbs. Temperament seems to change almost constantly.

2.3 Nastiest drop on the trail; sometimes marked with a Danger sign or note. This is a 6-foot-high drop, with large roots snaking across its surface and even larger gaps in between the roots; call it a tech 4, mainly for the biff potential. Cut the roots as straight as possible, avoid the gully in the middle, use a little speed, resist the impulse to brake, and you should sail over it. Otherwise, walk it and hone your skills on the smaller versions along the trail.

2.5 Cross another bridge and immediately turn left by a large, unmarked wooden post. Trail winds through a bit more singletrack, then drops you onto a gravel road. Follow road straight.

2.8 Gravel road ends at edge of parking lot. Turn right to head back toward the truck and Loop 2 trailhead.

Renaissance Park

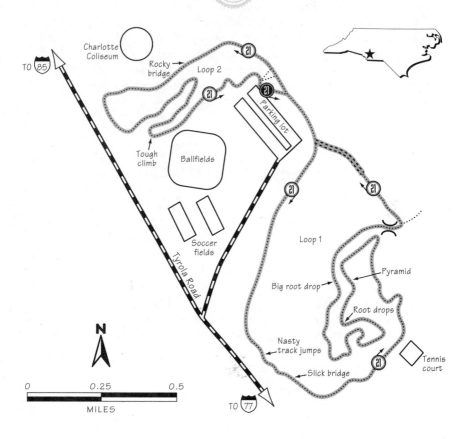

3.0 Shortcut to Loop 2 bears right from edge of parking lot onto singletrack back into woods. Watch closely for small arrow pointing to trailhead. Once you're in the woods, ignore several small trails peeling in from left. If you miss this entrance, go in by arrows near the dumpster and bear right (see map).

3.3 Tech 3 move over makeshift rocky bridge.

3.5 Opening to right reveals Charlotte Coliseum through the trees. Track from here dishes out some sweet drops, humps, and logs, served from a bed of smooth, fairly fast singletrack.

3.9 Trail turns sharply right across a short bridge, just after a series of major bunny hops. Watch that you're not still airborne when the turn shows up.

4.2 Tortuous, loose, rocky climb. Here's where you pay for all that fun you've just enjoyed.

4.6 End of Loop 2. Turn right to head back to the parking lot.

4.7 Return to parking area.

Beech Springs

Location: 20 minutes north of Charlotte.

Distance: 4.7-mile loop.

Time: 40 minutes to 1.5 hours.

Tread: Pure singletrack in all its incarnations: sandy, boggy, hardpack, loose, rocky, and eroded. Just what you wanted and more.

Aerobic level: Easy to moderate. None of the climbs are very long, but they're often steep and rooty enough to set your legs on fire. Those who want a more casual ride can just toodle along and push the tough stuff.

Technical difficulty: Tech 3 overall, though it ranges widely. Ribbons of lazy tech 1 singletrack wind gracefully through the trees in places. Elsewhere along the trail, Devil's Drop, Gravity Cavity, and the Rock Dam all push tech 4 with more logs, humps, and pyramids scattered about.

Highlights: BMX playground at trailhead with tons of jumps; big ravine drops; several tricky rock moves; one big-ass rooty descent.

Land status: Private land set up solely for mountain bikers. Fee: $2 per rider per day, a bargain wherever you come from. Contact Mike Andrews at 704-782-6134 for information or just to say thanks.

Maps: Trail map available at trailhead information shed.

Access: From Charlotte take Interstate 85 North and exit on Poplar Tent Road (Exit 52) heading west. Turn right at the top of the ramp. Go roughly 100 yards and turn right onto Goodman Road. Beech Springs Mountain Bike Park is clearly marked on the left about 1 mile down the road.

Notes on the trail

This is an excellent trail. It's a blast to ride with enough roots, rocks, jumps, and drops to satisfy the thrasher quotient in just about anyone. Devil's Drop gives you a choice of three insane descents with other treacherous drops at the Rock Dam and Gravity Cavity. And although novices will, or should, choose to dismount at a few spots, they should take heart knowing that most of the tough moves have bypasses cut.

Beech Springs is a shining example of a professionally designed and maintained mountain bike park. Besides the incredible riding, additional features include picnic benches for reviving and reliving the ride, and an information center filled with ads, maps, lost keys, notes for riding partners, waivers, and info sheets. Hats off to Mike Andrews, for having the foresight and the simple good grace to provide us with such a wonderful green playground.

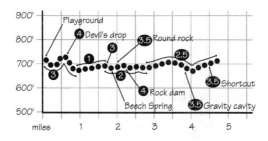

The Ride

0.0 Start from the info shack. Drop through the BMX humps, and start following the red arrows around to the right. Note: Be sure to sign a waiver and drop off your $2 in the shack first, so someone will know if you don't make it back, and so you won't look like a cheapskate if you stack at the dam and never make it back.

0.1 Cross small wooden bridge, then follow arrows straight. Sign: "No Horseback Riding."

0.2 Turn left for "Tough Trail Option," or stay straight for the main trail. Option trail is full of logs, roots, and twisty drops (solid tech 3), and main trail gives up some fast hardpack cut by narrow gullies. I enjoyed them both, so it's up to your own tastes. Same mileage either direction.

0.4 Follow red arrows straight on main trail. Option trail to right isn't really worth it, and you'll miss some really excellent water bars in the process.

0.5 "Option: Devil's Drop" turn left. I recommend this option highly, though only if you enjoy screaming 80 feet down a steep, root-encrusted hillside. Otherwise, continue straight and wait for your more foolhardy companions to join you by the stream at the bottom. Note that trying to bail out or even brake hard in the middle of any of these descents will result in serious penalties. Do not look at the padded tree in the middle of the first descent, lest it suck you into its woody embrace. Cross stream at bottom (via stream bottom or bridge) and follow arrows left. Ignore all other trail options as you start to climb.

1.4 Track flattens to tech 1, runs into old farm road, and turns sharply left by the yellow flagging. Following descent runs fast over some off-camber washouts (tech 3), then into three or four big, fun, sweeping turns.

1.7 Pass Beech Tree Spring. Clear, cool spring bubbles from the ground by the foot of a massive, silver-skinned giant. Picnic table makes for a nice break spot, if you need one already. Follow red arrows straight along edge of field.

Beech Springs

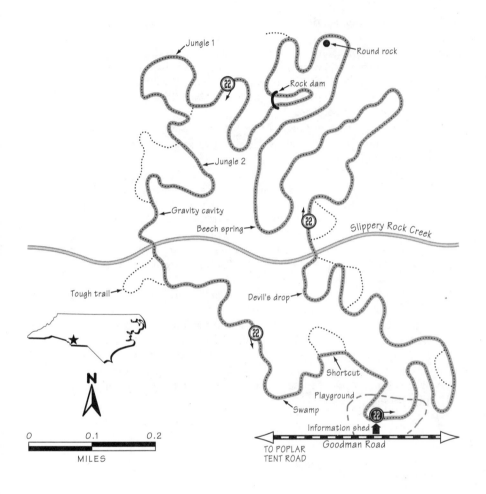

Jungle 1

Round rock

Rock dam

Jungle 2

Gravity cavity

Beech spring

Slippery Rock Creek

Tough trail

Devil's drop

N

Shortcut

Playground

Swamp

Information shed

0   0.1   0.2

MILES

TO POPLAR
TENT ROAD

Goodman Road

1.8 Multiple paths and bridges across muddy area. Hug the right side and follow red arrows uphill.

2.0 Trail turns left at edge of field, then drops back in past Round Rock. Tech 3 + move to ride up and over Round Rock (wheelie drop is probably your best choice).

2.1 Follow main trail to left. "Log Option" trail to right adds a little length, but not much else.

2.2 "Rock Dam Bypass" to left. The Rock Dam to right is a nasty, tech 4 drop down through some hungry-looking rocks. This is a very worthwhile move but pay heed to the Caution sign. Trip mileage includes the bypass trail to the left.

2.8 Turn right for "Jungle 1 Option" trail. Additional dosage of rooty, twisty track dotted with 12-inch drops.

3.0 Turn right again when Jungle 1 tees back into main trail.

3.2 Turn left for "Jungle 2 Option." Trail holds an excellent pair of 2-foot rock drops to leap from.

3.7 Turn left as Jungle 2 T's back into main trail. This brings you to the top of Gravity Cavity, a 15-foot deep network of gullies that offers sick drops, wall riding, and some serious, tech 3 and 4 roller-coaster action. Bypass trail along right side of gully provides an easy return for the multiple passes you'll have to take here. Turn left again at bottom of Gravity Cavity.

3.8 Cross Slippery Rock Creek, then turn left. "Tough Trail 2 Option" to right is fairly rough track with a tough and ugly climb woven in. I'd opt to stay on the main track.

4.2 Tough uphill rock move, as you enter a small clearing with fence on your right. Sign for Swamp, though I never saw one.

4.4 Sign: "Shortcut If You Can." Who could resist a dare like that? Turn right and prepare for an ugly tech 3 + descent, followed by some gully drops and short, tough climbs. Be careful crossing the slick wooden bridge at the bottom.

4.7 Return to parking area. Excellent hump/big drop/hump combo just before exiting woods—sort of like Mother Nature handing you a cookie as you leave her playground.

Cane Creek

Location: Waxhaw, 20 minutes south of Charlotte.

Distance: 11.9-mile loop.

Time: 1.5 to 3 hours.

Tread: 11.3 miles of singletrack; 0.5 mile of grassy doubletrack; 0.1 mile of gravel doubletrack.

Aerobic level: Easy. No significant elevation changes.

Technical difficulty: Tech 1+ overall. Occasional short tech 2 rock/root sections on beginner loop. Several tech 3 and 3.5 rock gardens and stream crossings on intermediate loop.

Highlights: Easy cruising on beginner's loop; lake views; rock gardens; tricky stream crossings; serious mudholes.

Land status: County park.

Maps: USGS Waxhaw; map available at park office.

Access: From Charlotte, take Interstate 77 South to I-485. Exit onto North Carolina Highway 16 South, and go about 8 miles to Waxhaw. At the stoplight in Waxhaw (there's only one), turn left onto NC 75 (Waxhaw Highway). Go about 0.5 mile and bear right onto Old Providence Road by the brown sign for Cane Creek Park. Somewhere along the way this turns into Old Waxhaw– Monroe Road. After 2 miles or so, turn right onto Providence Road. Cross NC 200, go another 2 miles, then turn right onto Harkey Road. Cane Creek Park is 1 mile on the right.

Notes on the trail

A number of trails lace the land around the lake. The directions given here lay out two loops: The first is a beginner's loop with a minimum of technical challenges, though it does contain some huge, skanky, horse-induced mudholes. The second loop offers a number of tricky rock gardens and stream crossings that can slap you down in a big way if you don't play them right. An excellent pair of jumps bookend the grassy area just before the dam. For an interesting—if somewhat unsavory—wildlife experience, keep an eye out for the buzzard tower.

The park offers several other really nice features. There are picnic facilities all over the place and a snack bar down by the beach. The bathhouses contain free showers and flush toilets. If you ask nicely at the office, they'll

Cane Creek

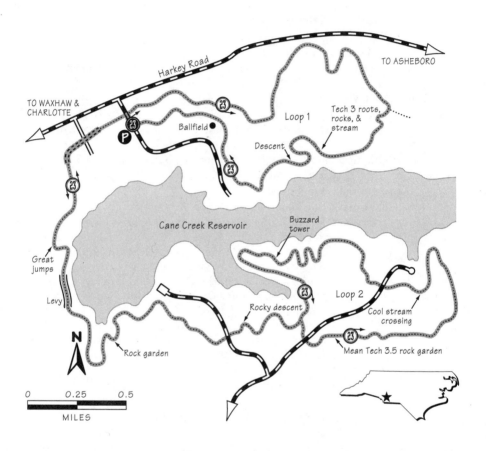

Harkey Road

TO ASHEBORO

TO WAXHAW &
CHARLOTTE

23

23

P

Ballfield

Loop 1

Tech 3 roots,
rocks, &
stream

Descent

23

23

Cane Creek Reservoir

Buzzard
tower

Great
jumps

Levy

Loop 2

23

Rocky descent

Cool stream
crossing

N

Rock garden

23

Mean Tech 3.5 rock garden

0   0.25   0.5

MILES

let you use a hose to wash your bikes off. And for a measly $2, you can go swim in the lake and wash the dust from your weary bones.

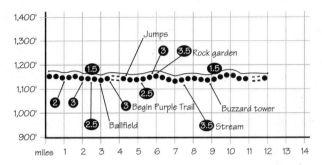

The Ride

0.0 From the parking area, ride back up past the park office. Turn right onto the second red trail entrance, the one closest to Harkey Road. You'll follow the red blazes for this entire loop. Mileage starts at this point.

0.3 Bear left at this Y, following the red blazes. Track is tech 1+ hardpack, with a few tech 2 roots. You'll find some small bunny hop opportunities along the way, but other than that it's a cruiser.

0.7 First of several mondo mudholes, like equine-induced bomb craters. These things can swallow you.

1.0 Trail runs near Harkey Road, then you get a short but fun twisty descent into several small tech 2 rock gardens.

1.4 Pass through a power line opening.

1.5 Turn right to follow blazes. Straight leads to private property.

1.8 Red trail turns right onto a short section of pea-gravel doubletrack, runs down near the lake, then back under the power lines again.

2.0 First real technical offering of the day: a tasty, tech 3 trail-salad of roots and rocks, surrounding a shallow stream and a fat, skanky mudhole. Yum!

2.2 Red trail turns left at this T.

2.5 A short, fun descent into a small ravine and over some tech 2+ roots, leads you to a four-way intersection. Go straight to follow the red blazes; left and right are *orange*, which all look the same if you're wearing glasses.

2.6 Turn right to follow red blazes.

2.7 Turn right again to follow red blazes. A noticeable tech 2 climb leads you up past a picnic table.

2.8 Go straight to follow red blazes.

2.9 Turn right in quick succession leads you out into a grassy field. Hug the right side of the field as you go around the baseball diamond. There's no real trail across the field, but you will still see some red blazes. Trail clearly picks up and enters the woods past the ballfield.

3.5 Trail drops you back out onto the park entrance road. Turn right on the hardtop, heading toward Harkey Road. Go 30 feet, then turn left onto the start of the second (purple) loop. The welcoming mat of tech 3 roots and rocks will let you know that you're no longer on the beginner's loop.

3.7 Trail crosses a wide, grassy field and a gravel road, then heads back into the woods for more fun.

4.0 Turn right at the T to follow the purple blazes.

4.2 Bear left at the Y toward the lake. You'll enter another small grassy field that's bracketed by two excellent 3-foot jumps. The play-out for both jumps is perfect, and you'll surely want to spend some time here polishing your soaring techniques.

4.3 When you finish jumping around, bear left along the top of the lake's dam, then left again at the far end, following the purple blazes. Lots of smooth, twisty-turny track follows, with some occasional mudholes.

5.1 Long technical section: a tech 2+ rock garden, then a rocky descent, a rocky climb, and a zippy downhill. Expect some serious grin inducement and possibly the first big bust of the day.

5.6 Turn right just before the edge of a parking lot. Shortly after, bear right again, around the end of a chain-link fence and past an RV camping area.

6.0 Hit a paved service road. Trail picks up across the road, maybe 15 feet up to the left, and starts with a banging tech 3 descent/mudhole/climb combo.

6.2 Turn right at the T, then pass under the power lines. Not long after, you'll dive into a choice tech 3+ root/rock garden that runs along the edge of a stream. You'll eventually return from across the stream here on the blue trail.

6.5 Hit another paved service road. Jag left, then right back into the woods.

6.6 Continue straight at this intersection. Purple trail ends and red blazes begin. Watch for a mean, tech 3 rock garden.

7.5 Excellent stream crossing, with many options, from a smooth, tech 2+ nose-in to a tech 3+ leap off a root lip. Shortly after, cross a second stream over a short log bridge; bridge is ridable, the gaps between the logs are treacherous.

7.6 Continue straight past branch to the right (both ways are blazed red).

7.7 Turn right as you hit a gravel road. Ride down past a wooden cabin, cross the hardtop road, and pick up the green trail on the other side.

7.8 Bear right at the Y and run along the edge of a field for a 100 yards or so, then dart back in among the trees.

8.7 Go under the power lines. Be sure to check out the tower on a sunny day, as it's often a roosting spot for a dozen black buzzards. Not especially attractive fellows, but an important part of the food chain all the same.

8.9 Sharp right turn onto the blue trail.

9.2 Tech 3+ rocky stream crossing, then turn right to put you back onto the purple trail and into the rock garden from mile mark 6.2.

9.5 Cross the hardtop service road again. Trail picks up just to the left across the road.

9.9 Bear left as you return to the RV campground, going around the fence and back into the woods.

10.8 Bear right and ride back across the dam. Get ready for those wonderful jumps that wait for you again on the far side.

11.9 Cross the wide, grassy field, grind your way up one last tech 3 rocky climb, and return to the park entrance road. Parking area is down to your right.

South Mountain

Location: South Mountain State Park; 32 miles southwest of Morganton.

Distance: 17.7-mile loop.

Time: 4 to 6 hours.

Tread: 15.7 miles of old Forest Service road/doubletrack; 2 miles of pavement.

Aerobic level: Strenuous. These climbs will kill you, no matter where you ride. They're mean, and there's a lot of them. Ride it once, and you'll believe.

Technical difficulty: Tech 3 overall. The saddles are flat and smooth, easy tech 1 rides. But most of the downhills are steep, covered with loose rocks, and littered with water bars of various construction. At least one tech 4 rocky section.

Highlights: Formidable climbs; outrageous, rocky descents full of water bars; long-range views; wildlife; waterfall.

Land status: North Carolina state park. The only one to offer any real mountain biking. Thank you, South Mountain, for your foresight and consideration. We love these mountains too. Note: The park closes between 6 P.M. and 9 P.M., depending on the season. Check at the office for closing time, because you'll be sleeping in the car if you don't get out before the gates are locked.

Maps: USGS Morganton South, Benn Knob; North Carolina State Parks Map Guide by Graphics, 2000; park map available at ranger station.

Access: Traveling on Interstate 40 West, south of Morganton, watch for the South Mountain State Park sign. Take Exit 105 and turn onto North Carolina Highway 18 South. Follow this for about 10 miles, then turn sharply back right onto Sugar Loaf Road. Go another 5 miles, then turn left at the Citgo station onto South Mountain Park Road. After another 2 miles, turn right onto a gravel road at the sign for South Mountain State Park. Follow the gravel road to the park entrance. The HQ Trail starts just at the edge on the parking lot.

Notes on the trail

The South Mountain Trail climbs up to series of ridges that encircle a large cove. Ridgeline running isn't usually that tough, but this is a severe trail.

Imagine the longest, rockiest, most painful single climb you've made in recent years. Now imagine it a dozen or more times in the space of 18 miles; not a pretty picture. But the descents are worth it: crazy-fast over loose rocks with dozens of water bars. Even the paved section runs a ridgeline, and we hit 40 miles per hour coasting it at one point. If you think you can hammer *anything* for 16 miles, then come to South Mountain, but consider yourself warned about spending the night on the mountain.

"This section is 'strainuous.' And this other section is 'strainuous' too." — Lady at the park desk. We scoffed. Now we believe.

"The mountain must stop; but we can continue." —David T, the Mango Medic

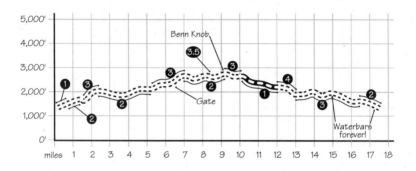

The Ride

0.0 Start from the parking lot. Turn left onto the Headquarters Trail, up past the gate and the white house with the barking dogs. Flat, tech 1 gravel doubletrack. Be sure to sign in at the gate so the rangers will know how much we love their trail, and so they'll know if you don't make it back out.

0.2 Amphitheater down to left.

0.3 Continue straight. Chestnut Knob Trail breaks off to the right.

0.4 Small downhill with your first taste of water bars. Trail leads across a small wooden bridge.

0.5 Turn right uphill at this Y. Sign says "To Sites 5–8." Ride up steep, hardpacked gravel doubletrack with heavy erosion cuts and quick elevation gain.

0.7 Pretty cascade and swimming hole in stream down to left.

0.9 Wooden bridge.

1.3 Short descent, then cross another bridge. And now, my friends, the pain begins. Don't even look up; just start climbing. Tread is hardpacked dirt doubletrack sprinkled with loose chicken heads. This is one long, mean, tech 3 climb.

2.5 Turn right at this major intersection. Signs point right for Headquarters Trail, Shinny Trail, and Lower CCC Trail, and left for Upper Falls Trail, sites 1 through 4, and High Shoals Falls. Rest at this intersection until you're sure your heart won't explode. Then follow the trail right. Short climb, then the first of many scary descents with some wicked water bars and some serious speed.

3.0 Continue straight. Jacobs Trail (walking only) breaks off to the left. Along the ridgetops, the trail is a wide-open dirt doubletrack. On the slopes, it's loose, rocky, and either deadly fast or heartbreakingly steep.

South Mountain

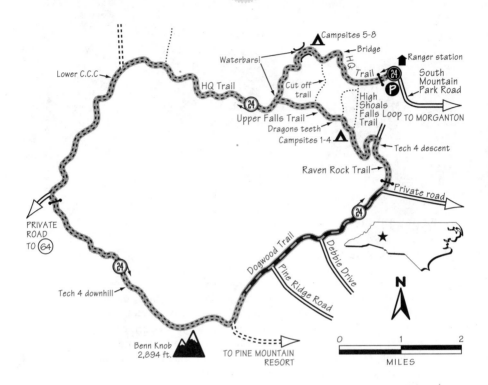

3.6 Continue straight. Shinny Trail breaks to right.

4.4 Continue straight. Old road (Horseridge Trail) breaks off to the right. By now you'll have noticed that you're surrounded by an emerald paradise. Relax and enjoy it—when you're not holding on for dear life.

4.9 Continue straight. Fox Trail breaks to left. Very difficult, tech 3+ climb; cluttered enough to keep you always searching for a cleaner line.

5.2 Top a ridge, then the bottom just falls out. Here's your first set of really big water bars with an excellent waist-high berm set in the middle: 8.5 on the fun meter.

5.7 Enormous steep, rocky climb (what else). Get in granny early or plan on standing the whole way. Remember that you can ride every one of these climbs; it's just a matter of how much pain you can stand.

6.6 Turn left at the big yellow gate. Track straight is signed "No Bikes"; I think it leads to a private road.

The ride gets rocky at South Mountain.

7.1 Sign for park boundary; double orange blazes. Flat, wide-open cruising terrain for a nice long while. Then back to falling down the mountain.

7.8 White sign: "Park Boundary. No Guns." What a reassuring thought. Following downhill is a serious gravity run. It's steep, way fast, and sketchy as can be with lots of loose rocks that shift as you hit them. It was a squirrelly tech 4 descent, and we were all glad to survive it.

8.9 Unbearably long, hemorrhaging climb. Then a long saddle, then some more climbing. Then another flat, then some more climbing. This hill is all about pain and determination.

9.2 Continue straight. Singletrack to right signed "No Bikes" probably leads to Benn Knob.

9.7 Turn sharp back left at this intersection, following sign for "Bikes." Descent is fast and furious (like you expected something else). Then you get another serious granny-gear climb.

10.1 Trail dumps you onto Dogwood Trail, a paved road, that continues to run up and down the same ridgeline you've been on. You can *cook* on this puppy; I hit 40 miles per hour coasting!

10.7 Continue straight. Pine Ridge Road to right.

11.2 Continue straight. Debbie Drive to right, then Fern Lane. Incredible view that probably reaches out 100 miles on a clear day.

12.0 Continue straight past gate onto Raven Rock Trail. Paved road turns right. Now that you've had a taste of something more civilized, it's back to a steady diet of loose, sketchy downhills covered with chicken heads. Continual tech 3+ assault.

12.4 Trail cuts back sharply left. Now you get an even nastier downhill than the last one: a tech 4 field of loose boulders and mean water bars, tilted to a severe angle. Some of these water bars are 4 feet tall with some really ugly landing zones behind them. This is not a place for front brakes or for the faint of heart.

12.9 Trail turns back left again, this time onto Upper Falls Trail. Raven Rock continues straight with a "No Bikes" sign. Continued descent snakes through a deep, dark, rhododendron forest with the ever-present water bars here and there.

13.4 Cross stream (Jacob's Fork) and ride past campsites 1 through 4. Portable toilet conveniently located here.

13.5 Turn left at this T. Right branch is one side of Falls Loop Trail (hiking only).

13.8 Tech 4 descent with dragons teeth outlining the water bars. Hit the gaps in the teeth or jump them. Straight on is a bad idea.

14.1 Turn left again. The last real climb of the ride; and it's the ugly runt of the litter. If none of the other climbs broke you, this one just might do it. Trail straight ahead was the other side of Falls Loop Trail (hiking only).

14.5 Continue straight past the Cut-Off Trail (hiking only) to the right.

15.1 Enter at the large, signed intersection where you started the loop and hang the sharp right turn back onto Headquarters Trail. Swallow hard and hang on, 'cause you've probably never dropped a run like this before. Nearly 30 water bars on the way down, coming at you at warp speed. Just hang on, keep your butt back and your front wheel pointed downhill, and you'll probably be okay.

16.3 Cross bridge at bottom, near campsites 5 through 8. Only one last climb to make, and this one's a baby compared with the monsters you've already survived.

16.8 And one last serious descent. A number of big water bars, then a sizable boulder to launch from, backed up by a huge water bar that will probably send you for the record jump of the ride.

17.2 Bear left as trail drops you down to the lower intersection. Easy, flat run from here on out.

17.7 Return to parking lot. If you don't have a cooler full of cold drinks, you should probably go lie in the stream for a while.

Signal Hill

Location: Statesville.
Distance: 4.8-mile loop.
Time: 30 to 45 minutes.
Tread: Singletrack, nothing but singletrack.
Aerobic level: Easy to moderate. No major elevation changes, though one or two hills will leave you gasping.
Technical difficulty: Tech 2 overall. Some tech 2+ roots and a tech 3 off-camber climb. But although the trail is relatively smooth, there are lots of dips, humps, and jumps that could spell disaster for beginners or anyone else liable to grab a handful of brakes at an inappropriate time.
Highlights: Humps; jumps; dips; roots; typical singletrack fare.
Land status: County park.
Maps: USGS Statesville East; map posted at trailhead.
Access: From Interstate 77 in Statesville, take Exit 50 for Broad Street. Head east on Broad Street, passing a bunch of retail sprawl. Turn left at the third light onto Signal Hill Road. The park is less than a half mile on the right. The trailhead starts at the edge of the parking lot, just behind the information sign.

Notes on the trail

This is an excellent singletrack playground, particularly considering that it's 1 minute off the interstate. The builders have made excellent use of a limited space with a trail that twists and swoops over humps and bumps without seeming congested or slow. Lots of tight turns, multiple dips, and a half-dozen excellent jumps along the back stretch keep it interesting. The trail is clearly marked and fairly easy to follow. Any time you're running past Statesville, take your bike and check it out; it's probably the best half hour you'll spend all day.

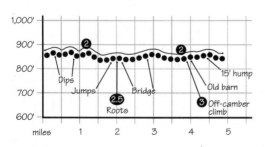

Signal Hill

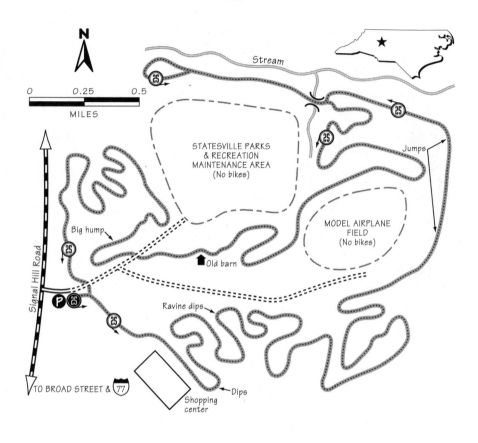

N

0   0.25   0.5

MILES

Stream

STATESVILLE PARKS
& RECREATION
MAINTENANCE AREA
(No bikes)

Jumps

MODEL AIRPLANE
FIELD
(No bikes)

Big hump

Signal Hill Road

Old barn

P

Ravine dips

TO BROAD STREET & 77

Dips

Shopping
center

The Ride

0.0 Trail begins just behind the information sign. Be sure to sign in on the sheet provided. Follow the hardpack track to the right, up behind the shopping center, then dive into the woods and start playing.

0.4 Lots of dips, one after another. Trail snakes down a little ravine and twists back and forth over some small roots for a constant tech 2 ride.

1.0 Trail runs the edge of the woods behind a red brick building. By now you've been grinning constantly for a mile, and there's more to come.

1.6 Bear right as the trail runs along the edge of the model airplane field. This leads you to five or six cool jumps along the back stretch. Good play-out after each jump; just stay out of the rough grass on either side.

2.2 Turn right across a fairly wide wooden bridge, then bear left along the edge of a field. Maintenance buildings up to your left, stream down to the right. Close trees make for some fun, tight gates to thread.

2.5 Trail loops for a short climb, then takes you back across the field on the same track you took in.

2.8 Recross the bridge and hang a right onto some freshly cut track.

3.2 Come out near the airplane field again. Cool, bermed sweeper turn shortly after.

3.4 Bear left at the Y, just at the far edge of the airfield.

3.9 Mean, off-camber, tech 3 climb. Pass an old tin-sided barn, and ride over a funky little bridge/pyramid, then cross a gravel service road; trail clearly picks up on other side of the road.

4.2 Get cranking to zip up a sudden 15-foot-tall hump, then drop off the back side and hit another 6-footer.

4.3 Trail closely parallels Signal Hill Road, heading toward a small power station and back toward the parking lot.

4.8 Return to parking lot, and probably set off on another loop because you haven't had your fill of fun yet.

Uhwarrie National Forest

Uhwarrie National Forest sits alone in the middle of the Piedmont, its 1,000-foot peaks perching over the rest of the rolling hills. Through the diligent efforts of the Uhwarrie Mountain Biking Association (UMBA), two loops of dedicated mountain bike trail are now open with as many as four more slated for construction. Off-road vehicle trails are open in the upper section of the forest, though they are legendary in their brutality.

Uwharrie-Supertree

Location: Uwharrie National Forest; 40 miles southeast of Asheboro, or 30 miles east of Charlotte.

Distance: 7.7-mile lariat.

Time: 45 minutes to 1.5 hours.

Tread: 1.5 miles of singletrack; 2.2 miles of dirt and gravel doubletrack; 4 miles of gravel road.

Aerobic level: Easy to moderate. Wood Run Road is an easy cruise, but it feels a lot longer than it is. The drop down Supertree is fast and easy, and the return climb back up to Wood Run really isn't too bad.

Technical difficulty: Tech 2. Supertree is fairly smooth for most of its length. However, multiple, knee-high water bars on the descent can up the ante a bit—particularly if you're cooking—and a few of the landing zones are a bit dicey. Wood Run Road is a tech 1 run, just long enough to give your legs a good warm-up and cool-down.

Highlights: Fast swoopy descent with big water bars; easy climb and return.

Land status: Uwharrie National Forest.

Maps: USGS Morrow Mountain; *Uwharrie Lakes Region Trail Guide,* by Don Childrey (excellent reference for all biking, hiking, and off-road vehicle trails in the area). Maps are posted at trailhead.

Riding out of control often leads to biffing, but it can be fun.

Access: From Asheboro, take U.S. Highway 220 South. Exit onto North Carolina Highway 24/27 toward Troy. After you pass through Troy, go another 10 miles on NC 24/27 and watch for the Uhwarrie National Forest–Wood Run Trails sign on the right. If you cross the Pee Dee River, you went too far. From Charlotte, take US 74 East. Exit at Albemarle Road, which is NC 24/27. Follow NC 24/27 through Albemarle and over the Pee Dee River. Park entrance is on the left.

Notes on the trail

If you just want to enjoy the downhill and don't want to bother with long climbs or gnarly track, then you need to make several loops around Supertree. Once you start descending, it gets fast as hell with wide bermed turns swooping through the trees and a dozen or more magnificent water bars for some supreme air. An easy return back up Wood Run Road sets you up for multiple trips around, sort of like a free pass to your favorite ride at the carnival.

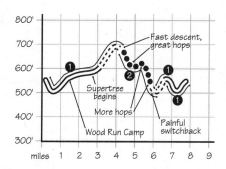

The Ride

0.0 From the parking area, ride in past the gate onto Wood Run Road (gravel). Easy, wide-open cruising for the next several miles.

1.4 Continue straight past the Wood Run campsite.

2.6 Turn right at this signed intersection onto the entrance to Supertree Loop. Tread starts off as gravel doubletrack, but don't despair, 'cause there's plenty of fun stuff farther on.

3.2 Bear left at this split, following the UMBA sign. Tread is still gravel doubletrack.

4.1 Doubletrack ends and true singletrack begins. Pass under the power lines and cross Dutchman's Trail (hiking only).

4.3 And now Supertree delivers. You get one teaser downhill with a few hops, a short climb, and then a long, raging descent. Numerous smooth-topped water bars along the drop with excellent launching potential. Beginning riders really need to keep their speed down, unless they want some impromptu flying lessons.

Uwharrie–Supertree

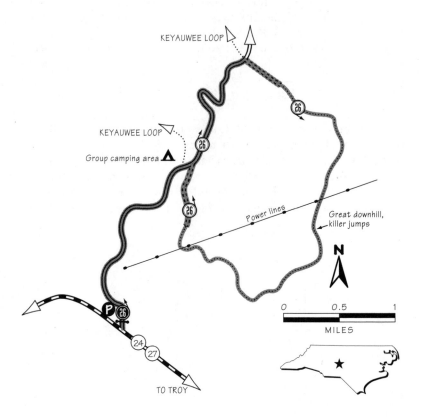

KEYAUWEE LOOP

KEYAUWEE LOOP

Group camping area

Power lines

Great downhill,
killer jumps

N

0   0.5   1

MILES

TO TROY

5.6 Trail turns sharply right as it hits the bottom and changes to dirt doubletrack. Some loose, fast running with a few small hops and some sharp corners. Good place to race your buddy until one of you stacks.

5.8 Trail pops out to run along under the power lines for a bit. Cross a small stream then hit a respectable switchback and climb to get back out of the bottom. Tread changes from dirt to gravel doubletrack.

6.3 Turn left as you pop back out onto Wood Run Road, just across from the campsite.

7.7 Return to the trailhead and parking area.

Uwharrie–Keyauwee

Location: Uwharrie National Forest; 40 miles southeast of Asheboro, or 30 miles west of Charlotte.

Distance: 8.9-mile lariat.

Time: 1 to 2 hours.

Tread: 3.9 miles of singletrack; 0.7 mile of doubletrack; 4.3 miles of gravel road.

Aerobic level: Moderate. Wood Run Road is an easy cruise. However, the climbs along Keyauwee are rocky and long enough to have your legs protesting at the abuse.

Technical difficulty: Tech 2 +. Keyauwee is a solid tech 2 singletrack for most of its length with a handful of tech 3 rocks and roots sprinkled along both the climbs and descents. Wood Run Road is a tech 1 run, just long enough to give your legs a good warm-up.

Highlights: Sweet rocky downhills; water bars; long-range views.

Land status: Uwharrie National Forest.

Maps: USGS Morrow Mountain; *Uwharrie Lakes Region Trail Guide,* by Don Childrey (excellent reference for all biking, hiking, and off-road vehicle trails in the area).

Access: From Asheboro, take U.S. Highway 220 South. Exit onto North Carolina Highway 24/27 and head toward Troy. After you pass through Troy, go another 10 miles on NC 24/27 and watch for the Uhwarrie National Forest–Wood Run Trails sign on the right. If you cross the Pee Dee River, you went too far.

From Charlotte, take US 74 East. Exit at Albemarle Road, which is NC 24/27. Follow NC 24/27 through Albemarle, and over the Pee Dee River. Park entrance is shortly on the left.

Notes on the trail

Keyauwee offers up a little bit of everything: fast, snaky singletrack; sketchy downhills; mean, rocky climbs; big whoop-dee-doos. It's the kind of trail that makes you work for your fun, but still feels like a bargain. The good folks at UMBA did a great job with this one. At the end of Keyauwee, you can run right into Supertree Loop for some more serious downhilling, extending the ride by another 3 miles.

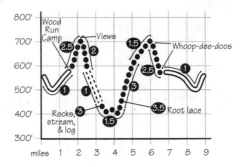

The Ride

0.0 From the parking area, ride in past the gate onto Wood Run Road (gravel). Easy, wide-open cruising for the next mile or so.

1.4 Turn left as you hit the opening for Wood Run campsite. Turn just before the portable toilet, hug the side of the clearing, and run right up to the entrance sign for Keyauwee Loop. Trail starts off with a tough, tech 2+ rooty section, sort of an entrance toll.

1.6 Bear left at the Y. Track straight is blocked off; may be an old hiking trail.

1.8 Hit a long, painful, rocky climb. This one will have you howling *No más!* by the time you reach the top.

2.0 Climb finally ends, and you get an adrenaline-boosting descent along the edge of an old clearcut. Fast run with lots of loose chicken heads and a few small bunny hops, through some tight undergrowth. Nice view from the top.

2.3 Trail flattens and feeds into an old gravel doubletrack.

2.7 Another pretty long-range view to left.

3.0 Trail gets a bit fast and loose as it changes from doubletrack to gravel road.

3.3 Turn right onto clear singletrack that peels off and drops down into the trees. UMBA sign is hidden in bushes, but trail entrance is very clear. Immediate, tech 3 descent over some big rocks, ending in a tech 3 stream crossing with a respectable log to back it up.

3.6 Keyauwee mellows and offers some gentle tech 1+ up-and-down for a while. Red blazes mark the trail.

3.9 Triple set of shallow dips set into an otherwise smooth section of trail, just to remind you not to take things for granted. These hungry little suckers are just deep enough to grab your front wheel and either toss you on your face or bring delicate parts of your anatomy into painful contact with your bike stem.

4.4 Tech 3 stream crossing leads you into a long, ugly, and off-camber climb.

4.7 Straight at this crossroads, continuing on Keyauwee. Cross the Uhwarrie Trail (hiking only). Long, tech 3+ root lace just after the intersection, then some more off-camber climbing dotted with tech 3 rocks.

5.8 A little flat, tech 1+ cruising leads you to the start for a rip-roaring downhill. Descent is fast and more than a little loose in spots with some great whoop-dee-doos and a few small logs as incentive to improve your hopping skills. Excellent run!

Uwharrie-Keyauwee

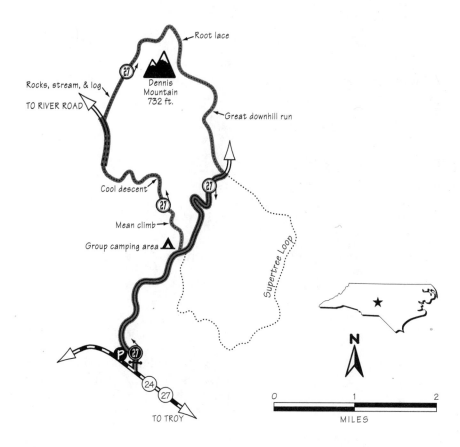

Root lace

Rocks, stream, & log

TO RIVER ROAD

Dennis
Mountain
732 ft.

Great downhill run

Cool descent

Mean climb

Group camping area

Supertree Loop

N

0   1   2

MILES

TO TROY

6.3 Turn right as Keyauwee drops back onto Wood Run Road. If you've had enough, follow Wood Run (and the following trail notes) back to the trailhead. The gravel can get really loose in the corners, so take it easy or be ready to drift. If you still want more, hang an immediate left and dive into Supertree.

7.5 Pass the Wood Run camp on your right. Continue straight for the trailhead.

8.9 Return to the trailhead and parking area.

Boone

Boone sports several cool rides right within town limits. But the real riding is in the Wilson Creek area, about 20 minutes southeast of town, in the heart of Pisgah's Grandfather Mountain district. The entire Yancey's Ridge, Schoolhouse Ridge, and Wilson Creek system probably contains more than 35 miles of phenomenal track.

Woodruff Ridge

Location: Globe, about 15 miles south of Blowing Rock.

Distance: 7.5-mile loop.

Time: 45 minutes to 1.5 hours.

Tread: 1.8 miles of singletrack; 0.5 mile of gated Forest Service road; 5.2 miles of gravel road.

Aerobic level: Moderate. The climb up is long but not too steep. Initial singletrack is fairly flat. Descent back down to the start is so furious it barely gives you time to breathe.

Technical difficulty: Climb up the roads is a long, tech 1 grinder. Singletrack starts off as tech 2, then jumps to tech 3+ on the downhill with several tech 4 stream crossings and a pair of tech 4+ boulder drops.

Highlights: Hardcore descent; technical creek crossings; steep narrow track; big rocks; beautiful lush undergrowth and big trees.

Land status: Pisgah National Forest.

Maps: USGS Globe; USDA Forest Service Wilson Creek Area Trail Map.

Access: From Blowing Rock, turn off Main Street (U.S. Highway 321 Business) onto Globe Road. Follow this twisting gravel road south for about 6 miles until you hit the tiny town of Globe. Turn right onto Anthony Creek Road (North Carolina Highway 1362). Go about 2 miles and watch for a parking spot on the right on an inside curve. Very nice campsite and excellent waterfall on Anthony Creek to the right. Trailhead is just across the road on the left.

Notes on the trail

This is one crazy—if short—downhill. If you like it fast and ugly, this is your place. Beginners should avoid this place; everyone else should use (or abandon) caution. Extremely tough stream crossings, narrow and unpredictable lines, and a pair of boulder drops make for some serious launch (and damage) potential. The waterfall below the parking area provides the perfect place to soak your wounded pride and body after the ride.

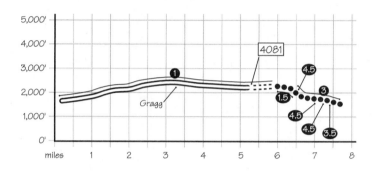

The Ride

0.0 From the parking area, turn right, continuing up Anthony Creek Road (NC 1362). Follow this gravel road up to the hamlet of Gragg.

3.2 At Gragg, turn left onto Edgemount Road (Forest Road 45).

5.2 Turn left onto Forest Road 4081 (gated Forest Service road).

5.7 Turn left onto dirt singletrack. Starts off with some slight downhill, fairly level, tech 1+ track. Don't be fooled though; this is like the first sip of grain alcohol punch: deceiving and deadly.

5.9 Cross old logging road. Begin some narrow contour running.

6.2 Drop down a narrow ledge back onto FR 4081 and turn right just for a bit. Watch for immediate sharp left back onto the singletrack. Here starts the downhill assault with an initial salvo of tech 4 roots. Then you get an extremely dicey tech 4+ rock field, followed by a pair of tech 3 stream crossings.

6.8 3-foot-high boulder planted in the middle of the trail for a *big* rock move (tech 4+). This puppy can launch you 12 or 15 feet down the trail with a narrow, sketchy landing zone. While you're celebrating your successful landing, don't bust in the pair of bad, tech 3 stream crossings that follow.

7.1 Trail bears right; old, unused track crosses stream to left. Just after, watch for some slippery and downright dangerous rock slabs, tech 4+, that carry some serious bust potential. Then more crazy speed, roots, and rocks.

7.3 Second rock launching pad, though this one is only a tech 3+ and good for only 8 to 10 feet of air time.

7.5 Drop down onto the road, and return to parking area.

Woodruff Ridge

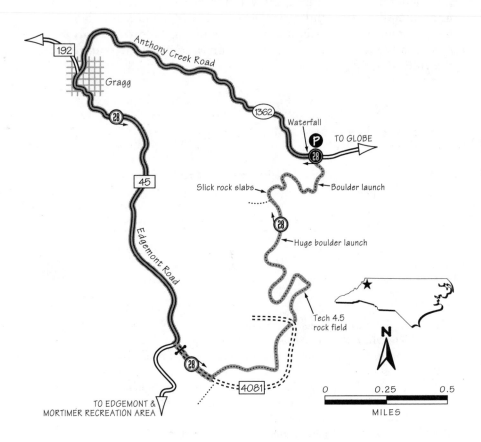

192

Anthony Creek Road

Gragg

1362

Waterfall

28

P

28

TO GLOBE

45

Slick rock slabs

Boulder launch

28

Huge boulder launch

Edgemont Road

Tech 4.5
rock field

28

4081

TO EDGEMONT &
MORTIMER RECREATION AREA

N

0   0.25   0.5

MILES

Long Yancey

Location: Roseborough; about 25 minutes south of Blowing Rock.
Distance: 17-mile loop.
Time: 3 to 5 hours.
Tread: 3.1 miles of singletrack; 4.6 miles of old Forest Service road; 9.3 miles of gravel road.
Aerobic level: Strenuous. Initial climb up Forest Road 192 is long and brutal in parts. Old doubletrack climb up to FR 45 is not as long but much more painful. Return climb up Roseborough Road seems to last forever.
Technical difficulty: Tech 3 overall. Several tech 4 descents of various flavors and textures will have you shaking in your shoes. Several tough technical climbs and creek crossings. It would not be kind to take novices on this trail.
Highlights: Rocky climbs; crazy rocky descents; whoop-dee-doos; rhododendron tunnel running; creek crossings; huge erosion gully; high-speed gravel road run; excellent swimming hole; Coffey's General Store.
Land status: Pisgah National Forest.
Maps: USGS Globe; USDA Forest Service Wilson Creek Area Trail Map.
Access: From Blowing Rock or Boone, take the Blue Ridge Parkway south. Turn left onto North Carolina Highway 1511 (Roseborough Road), near Grandmother Mountain and the town of Linville. Follow NC 1511 for 7 miles or so past the tiny town of Roseborough. Watch for a wide parking area on the right, just before a short concrete bridge over Webb Creek. FR 192 heads uphill across the road.

Notes on the trail

This trail offers you everything you can handle and more. It starts with Short Yancey's long, brutal climb, then throws in some even nastier ones later for good measure. Along the way, it hands out insane switchbacks that go on for days; boulder fields; incredibly tight tunnel running; whoop-dee-doos; and a hair-raising gravel road run. The swimming hole along FR 45 is a required stop, along with Coffey's General Store.

Smart riders will leave a shuttle vehicle at Coffey's and avoid the 4-mile gravel road climb back to the start. You won't be missing out on much other than a whole lot of pain.

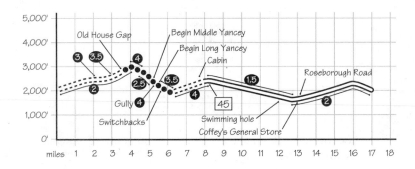

5,000'
4,000'
3,000'
2,000'
1,000'
0'

Old House Gap Begin Middle Yancey
Begin Long Yancey
Cabin
Roseborough Road
③ ③.5 ④
④
②.5 ③.5 1.5
② ④
Gully ④ ④ 45 ②
Switchbacks Swimming hole
Coffey's General Store

miles 1 2 3 4 5 6 7 8 9 10 11 12 13 14 15 16 17 18

The Ride

0.0 Like all the Yancey Ridge trails, this one leaves the parking area, crosses Roseborough Road and starts up FR 192. This time, it's the first of many long, painful climbs, though this one is probably the worst. Ignore all the various side trails and turn-offs until you reach Old House Gap. Just find a good gear and keep chugging.

2.0 Tech 3 rock garden. Only one good line, and that switches back and forth all over. Red -blazed trail down left toward the stream.

2.6 Shallow cave to the right. Gorgeous cascade and swimming hole down left at the stream.

2.7 Steep and painful tech 3+ rocky climb. Believe it or not, we once met a small Ford station wagon coming down the trail at this spot! What were those guys drinking?

2.8 Continue straight past gated road on the left. Sign: "Road Closed. Foot Traffic Welcome." I believe this leads to the old Gragg Cemetery.

3.2 Enter intersection at Old House Gap. Turn right up short incline onto singletrack; stub of brown USDA Forest Service sign can be found if you look hard. Gated road to the left leads up to the Blue Ridge Parkway. Gravel road straight is continuation of FR 192, which leads to Gragg.

3.4 Bear left uphill at this Y. Trail tops along a ridgeline, then drops with several sweet whoop-dee-doos.

4.6 Go straight onto Middle Yancey. Get set for a mean, rocky climb that's no fun at all. Turn back right leads to Short Yancey.

5.0 Major erosion gully with steep sides and big drops. Lines wander and often just disappear, so be prepared to hop a lot. Call it a tech 4 move to clean the whole thing.

5.4 Fast contour running leads you to a couple of awfully skanky mudholes. Then some faster, rooty descending.

5.6 Turn sharp back left onto Long Yancey (straight is continuation of Middle Yancey). You'll run through a long, tight rhododendron tunnel filled deep with leaves, then hit a crazy section of steep, tech 3+, 180-degree switchbacks.

5.9 Follow Long Yancey as it bears left, down over some whoop-dee-doos, out on a finger, then down some more. Turn right at the T that follows. More insane switchbacks, these filled with rocks and roots.

Long Yancey

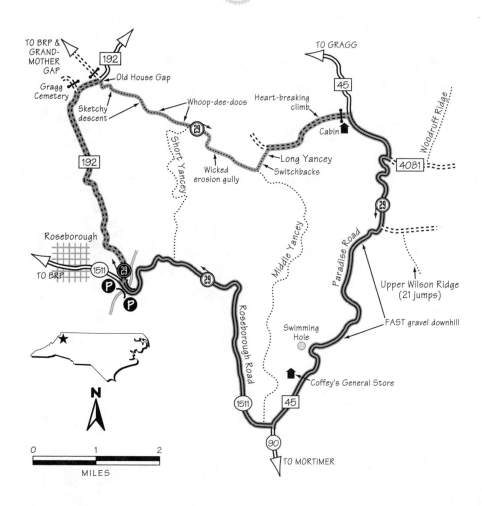

TO BRP & GRAND-MOTHER GAP

192

Old House Gap

Gragg Cemetery

Sketchy descent

Whoop-dee-doos

Heart-breaking climb

TO GRAGG

45

Cabin

Woodruff Ridge

192

Short Yancey

29

Wicked erosion gully

Long Yancey Switchbacks

4081

Roseborough

TO BRP

1511

29

P
P

Middle Yancey

29

Paradise Road

Upper Wilson Ridge (21 jumps)

FAST gravel downhill

Roseborough Road

Swimming Hole

Coffey's General Store

N

1511

45

90

TO MORTIMER

0   1   2
MILES

There are many creeks in the Wilson Ridge area.

6.1 Straight across Wilson Creek. This wide stream crossing is doable, but tough, with a mean little boulder field on the far side: call it a tech 4.

6.2 Second stream crossing is more ridable but shouldered by a tech 4+ climb. After pushing your way up this, you get dropped onto an old doubletrack beside an old cabin. Then the series repeats itself for a while: rock, stream, more rocks, bigger stream, fall down, get up, more rocks.

7.0 Begin the worst climb of the ride: just a steep, eroded, long dirt road. Don't look up, just keep grinding.

7.6 Pass a white gate and pop out onto FR 45, Paradise Road (gravel). Another cabin sits just to the right. And now's a good time for a break, before the long drop back. Gravel road descent that follows is fast and crazy with loose, deep gravel and erosion bumps filling the inside corners, 180-degree switchbacks, and occasional drainage ditches. Watch for auto traffic.

8.5 Continue straight down FR 45. Gated road to left leads to Woodruff Ridge Trail

9.4 Continue straight down FR 45. Gated road to left leads to Upper Wilson Ridge Trail (21 Jumps).

12.0 Cross concrete bridge. Wilson Creek provides a gorgeous, deep, cool swimming hole. This is a required stop if you've been cranking all day in the heat. At some unknown point, FR 45 has changed into NC 90.

13.0 Stop at Coffey's General Store. Go through the doors here and you take a step back in time. They even sell those tiny, ice-cold bottles of Coca-Cola. The folks here are real friendly and have great stories to tell. Ask politely, and they'll let you park your shuttle vehicle across the road and save yourself the next 4 miles of climbing, an option I highly recommend.

13.2 Turn right at the Edgemont Baptist Church onto Roseborough Road.

17.0 Return to the parking area near Roseborough.

Short Yancey

Location: Roseborough; about 25 minutes south of Blowing Rock.

Distance: 9-mile loop.

Time: 2 to 3 hours.

Tread: 4.8 miles of singletrack; 3.2 miles of old Forest Service road; 1 mile of gravel road.

Aerobic level: Moderate to strenuous. Initial climb up Forest Road 192 is long and brutal in parts. Other climbs are short but steep. And even the downhills keep your heart pumping.

Technical difficulty: Tech 2 overall. Several tech 3 rock sections on both climb and descent. The first drop after Old House Gap is a long, nasty tech 4 that will chew you up and spit you out if you're not careful.

Highlights: Whoop-dee-doos; screaming descents of various flavors; big berms; hemlock coves.

Land status: Pisgah National Forest.

Maps: USGS Globe; USDA Forest Service Wilson Creek Area Trail Map.

Access: From Blowing Rock or Boone, take the Blue Ridge Parkway south. Turn left onto North Carolina Highway 1511 (Roseborough Road), near Grandmother Mountain and the town of Linville. Follow NC 1511 for 7 miles or so past the tiny town of Roseborough. Watch for a wide parking area on the right, just before a short concrete bridge over Webb Creek. FR 192 heads uphill across the road.

Notes on the trail

You pay your money up front for this ride; that means starting out with an unrelenting 3.2-mile climb. But such pain buys you a buffet of downhills to enjoy on the way back: smooth, fast, dirt cruisers; eroded and fickle hardpack; sick, tilted boulder fields; and slippery gravel screamers. Although novices might walk a section or three, anyone with the grit to make the opening climb will enjoy this trail thoroughly.

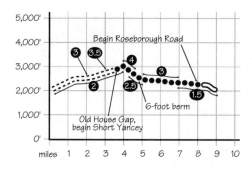

5,000'
4,000' — Begin Roseborough Road
3,000'
2,000'
1,000' — Old House Gap, begin Short Yancey

6-foot berm

0'
miles 1 2 3 4 5 6 7 8 9 10

The Ride

0.0 From the parking area, cross Roseborough Road an start up FR 192, an old, rocky, tech 1+ doubletrack. And thus begins one long, painful climb. Ignore all the various side trails and turnoffs 'til you reach Old House Gap. Just find a good gear and keep chugging.

2.0 Tech 3 rock garden. Only one good line, and that switches back and forth all over. Red-blazed trail down left toward the stream.

2.6 Shallow cave to the right. Gorgeous cascade and swimming hole down left at the stream.

2.7 Steep and painful tech 3+ rocky climb.

2.8 Continue straight past gated road on the left. Sign: "Road Closed. Foot Traffic Welcome." I believe this leads to the old Gragg Cemetery.

3.2 Enter intersection at Old House Gap. Turn right up short incline onto singletrack; stub of brown Forest Service sign can be found if you look hard. Gated road to the left leads up to the Blue Ridge Parkway. Gravel road straight is continuation of FR 192, which leads to Gragg.

3.4 Bear left uphill at this Y. Trail tops along a ridgeline, then drops with several sweet whoop-dee-doos.

3.8 Turn sharp right, downhill. Sign straight says "No Bikes. No Horses." The following downhill is certainly scary and probably dangerous. It's loose, fast, and filled with some nasty, hungry-looking rocks. It's a tech 4 descent for certain. After it flattens and clears up, you get a long, fast tech 2 tunnel run that's smooth and sweet and some great whoop-dee-doos.

4.4 Turn sharply back right at this T. More fast descending with a long series of sweeping inside turns.

4.9 Berms keep getting bigger and bigger until you hit one monster that stands 6 or 7 feet tall. More whoop-dee-doos to follow, then a sketchy, eroded, tech 3+ descent with lines that wander and disappear unexpectedly.

5.8 Super mudhole maze with holes that are hub-deep. Thread your way through or guess which is the shallow one.

6.5 Climbing through a thick rhododendron tunnel. Pass an old road to the right, then bomb another rocky, tech 3 downhill. Big, tight switchback into a mean-spirited climb.

Climbing up Short Yancey. DAVID TOLLERTON PHOTO

Short Yancey

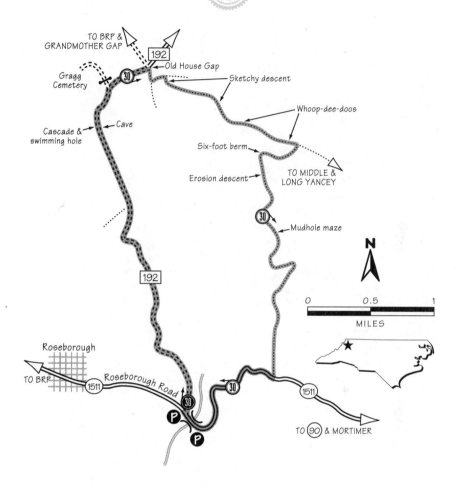

TO BRP &
GRANDMOTHER GAP

192

Old House Gap

Gragg
Cemetery

30

Sketchy descent

Whoop-dee-doos

Cascade &
swimming hole

Cave

Six-foot berm

Erosion descent

TO MIDDLE &
LONG YANCEY

30

Mudhole maze

N

0   0.5   1

MILES

192

Roseborough

TO BRP

1511

Roseborough Road

30

P

30

P

1511

TO 90 & MORTIMER

7.3 Flat, tech 1+ contour running through a majestic hemlock grove.

7.9 Turn right when you drop back out onto Roseborough Road. Now, for one last shot of adrenaline: a long, fast gravel downhill with a huge switchback in the middle. Watch for car traffic.

9.0 Return to the parking area. Nearby Webb Creek is the perfect spot for cooling your feet, head, or entire body.

Wilson Ridge–Schoolhouse Ridge Loop

Location: Mortimer; about 35 minutes south of Blowing Rock, or 30 minutes north of Morganton.

Distance: 13.6-mile loop.

Time: 2 to 3.5 hours.

Tread: 8.3 miles of singletrack; 5.3 miles of gravel road.

Aerobic level: Moderate to strenuous. Even if you shuttle and avoid the climb, the drop down Schoolhouse will take its toll on you. The ride up North Carolina Highway 90 is a hateful, pain-filled grinder, simple as that.

Technical difficulty: Tech 3 to 4.5. Wilson Ridge has only one tough rooty section, but lots of smooth-topped launching pads masquerading as water bars. Schoolhouse Ridge on the other hand is a war zone, filled with expert-level root drops and erosion gullies.

Highlights: 21 (or more) gorgeous jumps; ridge running; horrific root drops and ravines.

Land status: Pisgah National Forest.

Maps: USGS Globe; USDA Forest Service Wilson Creek Area Trail Map.

Access: From Morganton, take NC 181 north for 15 to 20 miles. Turn right onto Brown Mountain Beach Road (which is North Carolina Bike Route 2). Go about 4 miles, and turn left onto Ralph Winchester Road (Forest Road 1328); there's also a brown sign for Brown Mountain Beach), immediately after a good-sized concrete bridge over Wilson Creek. Follow FR 1328 about 6 miles to its end and a T with NC 90. Mortimer Recreation Area and parking for a second shuttle vehicle (if you're so fortunate) are straight ahead at this intersection. Turn left and follow NC 90 for 5.5 miles up the mountain, past Edgemont, Coffey's General Store, then past FR 4068. After a particularly steep section in the road, watch for a short, unmarked dirt road to the right, which immediately dead-ends at a metal gate (if you pass FR 4081, you went too far). Park here, ride in past the gate into a small meadow. The entrance to Wilson Ridge is immediately to your right; look closely, as it's sometime overgrown.

Notes on the trail

This is a true Jekyll and Hyde ride. Wilson Ridge is a cultured sort of trail, a smooth, dirt-faced roller coaster for most of its length, with whoops and jumps to delight even the most jaded bike pilot; the locals lovingly refer to this section of trail as 21 Jumps. Schoolhouse Ridge, however, is its homicidal, crackhead cousin. Blind turns through the mountain laurel suddenly drop you into 4-foot erosion gullies, ravines, and packs of sick root drops that would like nothing more than to break your bones. It's a sadistic piece of riding. Put the two together, and you've got something to alternately delight and terrify just about anyone.

If you'd like to leave out the blood-letting, then just ride Wilson Ridge, skip Schoolhouse entirely, and loop back on FR 4068. However, if you just can't get enough of sick, pounding riding, then not only ride Wilson and Schoolhouse, but start off with a trip around Long Yancey, which will eventually bring you right to the Wilson Ridge trailhead.

"Doooode! That was hardcore, man!" —Excitable Boy

"Wilson Ridge is a dream. But Schoolhouse is just continual brutality." —Author

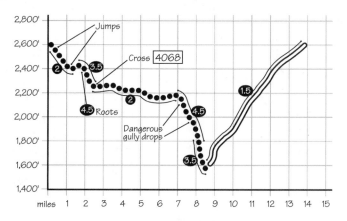

The Ride

0.0 From the entrance off NC 90, ride around the metal gate out into a small meadow. Hug the right side and immediately hit the (unsigned) entrance to Upper Wilson Ridge, better known as 21 Jumps. Buffed launching ramps start almost immediately with clear landings and plenty of fun. Easy, tech 2 track. Not an especially fast descent, just fun to the core. Watch for a couple of deep mudholes that span the trail.

0.8 Short but steep climb up, over some of those fine water bars.

1.0 Continue straight past an old road on the right. More descending and more water bars, but this time it's a bit dicey and loose—steeper too. Try your luck on the big log at the bottom, then get ready for a long, rooty climb.

Wilson Ridge–Schoolhouse Ridge Loop

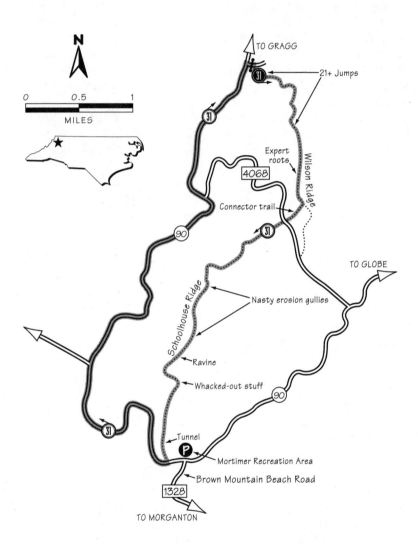

N

0   0.5   1
MILES

TO GRAGG

21+ Jumps

Wilson Ridge

Expert roots

4068

Connector trail

90

31

TO GLOBE

Nasty erosion gullies

Schoolhouse Ridge

Ravine

Whacked-out stuff

90

31

Tunnel

P

Mortimer Recreation Area

Brown Mountain Beach Road

1328

TO MORGANTON

1.5 An ego-crushing, tech 4+ move opens into a 30-foot-long puzzle of roots, hungry for front wheels and kneecaps. (Note: If this section proves too much of a technical challenge, you may want to consider opting out before Schoolhouse begins.)

1.9 Turn right at the T onto the connector trail for a quick trip down to FR 4068. The connector is steep and rocky, a sketchy tech 3+ run with lots of hops and drops. Left is the continuation of Wilson Ridge Trail and will also bring you down to FR 4068, just a little farther down.

2.3 Drop onto FR 4068 (gravel) and cut straight across for the entrance to Schoolhouse Ridge. Picks up with some fairly flat ridgeline running and lots of nice, gooey mudholes, perfect for decorating your buddies' jerseys with. (Here's the bailout point for anyone who just wants to play on 21 Jumps, without risking the wrath of Schoolhouse. Just turn right onto FR 4068, run it out 'til you hit NC 90 again, then turn right and ride a mile or two back up to your vehicle.)

3.8 Easy descent through a saddle, then a long, rambling climb.

6.6 Trail peaks along the top of the ridgeline; it's a good place for the application of both body armor and prayers of safety. The descent down Schoolhouse starts right off steep, rocky, and nasty with a long series of tech 4 root drops and deep erosion gullies. The worst of the drops approach tech 5 with some serious crash and burn possibilities.

7.2 Track runs down the throat of a steep-sided ravine. Your only hope to ride this is to just let it roll and hope for the best. It's a good tech 4+ move that'll put a lump in your throat.

7.9 The pounding finally slacks off as the trail runs out along a finger through some tight rhododendron tunnels. Fast tech 3 roots are almost unnoticeable after the insanity up top. Some steep, loose sections remind you not to relax too much.

8.3 Drop very suddenly out onto NC 90, just up from the Mortimer Recreation Area (watch for traffic). Turn right onto NC 90 if you were unfortunate enough not to have a shuttle vehicle. In this case, get ready for a long, long gravel road ride. Turn left if you parked a shuttle truck at Mortimer for the quick trip back. Celebrate your survival appropriately.

9.8 Continue straight on NC 90, past the Edgemont Baptist Church and the intersection with Roseborough Road.

10.0 Pass Coffey's General Store, the perfect spot to refuel yourself before the grind back to the top.

11.0 Cross over Wilson Creek on a wide, concrete bridge. On a hot summer day, nothing beats this swimming hole. And you'll need it to face the climbing yet to come.

12.1 Continue straight past FR 4068.

13.6 Turn right into the trailhead and parking area for Wilson Ridge.

The Biltmore Estate

Historic Biltmore Estate includes the Biltmore House, a 250-room mansion, and is located on more than 8,000 acres between two rivers in Asheville, North Carolina. In 1895 George Vanderbilt decided that there could be no finer setting for his planned estate than here in the Blue Ridge Mountains. After enlisting such notable help as Richard Morris Hunt, the renowned architect, and Frederick Law Olmstead, the designer of New York's Central Park, Vanderbilt set out to create what has become the largest private home in America and certainly the most beautiful.

Vanderbilt's descendents have dedicated themselves to preserving the Biltmore Estate in all its native beauty. That means restoring the magnificent house and gardens, creating award-winning wines, and opening the grounds to nature hikes, float trips, horseback riding, and, most recently, mountain biking.

Although at the time of this writing, biking is allowed only during prearranged tours, the staff at Biltmore eventually hopes to open up more trails, including some of the 4,000-acre track on the west side of the French Broad where the estate pastures and vineyard are located.

Treat yourself and your partner to a tour of this marvelous estate. The architecture, the innovative technological advances, the unbelievable gardens, the tapestries, paintings, and other fine furnishings are all treasures from an earlier, less complicated age.

Diana

Location: The Biltmore Estate, on the southern edge of Asheville.
Distance: 7.2-mile loop.
Time: 1 to 2 hours.
Tread: 2.7 miles of singletrack; 1.5 miles of doubletrack; 1.8 miles of gravel road; 1.2 miles of paved road.
Aerobic level: Easy to moderate. The climb up Overlook Road is an even 1 mile long but feels like 5. Short uphills in the woods can make you sweat a bit, but most of the trails are easy running.
Technical difficulty: Tech 1 +. No real technical challenges, except for a few mudholes here and there. The descent from the rear overlook is steep but wide open.
Highlights: Incredible views of the Biltmore Estate; statue of Diana; long cruising downhills; pleasant riverside riding.
Land status: Private estate. Mountain biking tours by appointment only. Contact Gina Elrod at 828-255-1785.
Maps: USGS Asheville.
Access: From Interstate 40 West in Asheville, take Exit 50B onto U.S. Highway 25 North, then follow signs to the Biltmore Estate.

Notes on the trail

This scenic ride takes in all the grandeur of the Biltmore Estate. It starts with an amazing view of the back of this modern castle, then drops steeply down to the lagoon and a long ride along the river. A mile-long climb drops you onto a dimly lit but lively little singletrack. This trail then empties into an emerald clearing, featuring a beautiful marble statue of the goddess Diana and an amazing view of the estate's front entrance. The trail finishes with a run through the leaves along an old forest doubletrack.

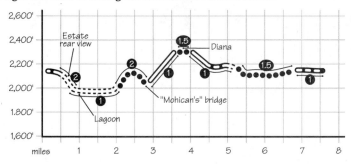

Diana

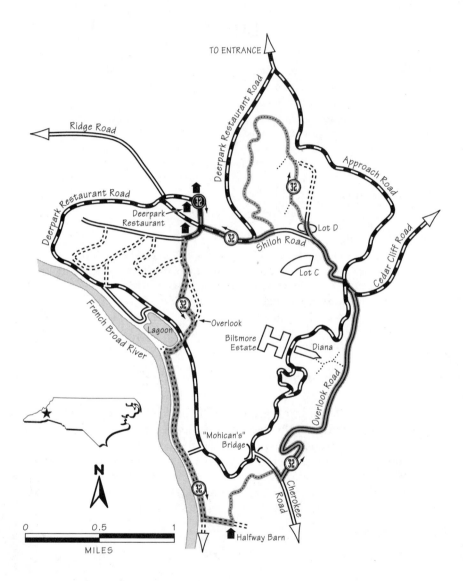

TO ENTRANCE

Ridge Road

Deerpark Restaurant Road

Deerpark Restaurant Road

Approach Road

Deerpark Restaurant

Lot D

Shiloh Road

Lot C

Cedar Cliff Road

Overlook

Lagoon

Biltmore Estate

Diana

French Broad River

Overlook Road

"Mohican's" Bridge

N

Cherokee Road

0   0.5   1

MILES

Halfway Barn

The Ride

0.0 Begin the at parking lot behind the Deerpark Restaurant. Ride out of the parking lot and head toward the hay barn. Cross the hardtop road and follow old road around barn.

0.2 After the barn, bear left at a choice of dirt doubletrack trails. Shortly after, bear left again at a choice of dirt doubletrack trails.

0.5 Track tops a little knoll and turns left. Fantastic view of the back of Biltmore Estate. Follow track straight down the hill, then bear right at the bottom and follow beside the stream toward the road.

0.8 Turn left on the hardtop road, then an immediate right onto a dirt doubletrack heading around the edge of the lagoon.

0.9 At the edge of the river, turn left onto another dirt doubletrack.

1.5 Turn right onto Bear Pen Road.

1.8 Turn left onto Sodfield Road. Keep a sharp eye out for this grassy doubletrack, as it heads back across the field toward Halfway Barn.

2.0 Turn left at Halfway Barn for some true singletrack. Cycling sign points the way.

2.6 Turn right onto Cherokee Road (gravel) by the sluice gate. The brick bridge upstream was used for footage in the film *Last of the Mohicans*. Take a quick left turn onto Overlook Road (gravel), marked by red arrows. Now begins a 1-mile climb.

3.6 Turn left onto singletrack at the intersection by old nursery and large wood chip piles. Trail splits; bear right. Trail splits again; bear left.

3.8 Diana's clearing. This emerald glade holds a statue of Diana and a magnificent view of the Biltmore Estate with all of Pisgah National Forest in the background. Once you finish taking pictures, turn around for the return trip back up to the road.

4.0 Return to the wood pile intersection. Turn left for a long, fast downhill run. Be careful of cars and loose gravel.

4.3 Track turns into Cedar Cliff Road past a funky little guardhouse. At the immediate intersection with Approach Road (paved), continue straight toward lot C. Beware of merging traffic.

4.6 Continue straight past lot C.

4.7 Turn right into lot D (dirt lot). Go to end of lot and look for dirt doubletrack heading down into the woods.

4.8 Turn left at the first available singletrack. A bit of speed, a bit of a swervy descent.

5.0 Trail hits a T. Turn right, following the red arrows.

5.3 Trail hits another T. Turn left, following the red arrows. Some cool contour running.

5.5 Trail hits another T. Turn right, following the red arrows.

6.2 Trail enters from right. Continue straight, following the red arrows.

6.4 Pass selective logging area.

6.5 Turn right onto Shiloh Road (gravel).

6.6 Continue straight through intersection onto Deerpark Road (hardtop).

7.2 Turn right by the barn and return to the Deerpark Restaurant parking area.

33

Patch Adams

Location: The Biltmore Estate, on the southern edge of Asheville.
Distance: 4.6-mile loop.
Time: 1 hour.
Tread: 0.1 mile of singletrack; 2.6 miles of doubletrack; 1.1 miles of gravel road; 0.8 mile of paved road.
Aerobic level: Easy to moderate. Nothing too tough or long, though some of the climbs in the woods below Patch Adams are steep and rocky enough to have you panting.
Technical difficulty: Tech 1+ overall. Mostly easy cruising, though you get a tech 2 descent down to Frog Pond Road, then a tough tech 2+ climb back up. The drop after the overlook is always good for a few wide eyes as well.
Highlights: *Patch Adams* movie site; reflected view of Biltmore Estate from the lagoon; long-range views of Pisgah National Forest; quick descents; technical climb.
Land status: Private estate. Mountain biking by appointment. Contact Gina Elrod at 828-255-1785.
Maps: USGS Asheville.
Access: From Interstate 40 West in Asheville, take Exit 50B onto U.S. Highway 25 North, then follow signs to the Biltmore Estate.

Notes on the trail

This ride takes you out to the cabin site used in the movie *Patch Adams*, where you get a gorgeous view of the Pisgah National Forest. A quick descent takes you down to the lagoon and a marvelous rear view of the estate. The climb back up through the woods requires some technical work, then easier doubletrack riding out to the overlook and back.

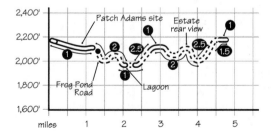

Patch Adams

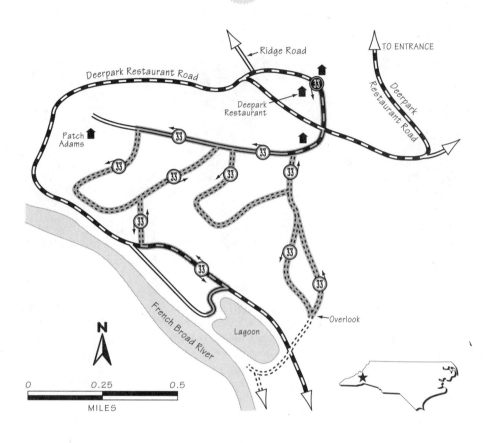

Deerpark Restaurant Road

Ridge Road

TO ENTRANCE

Deerpark
Restaurant
Road

Deerpark
Restaurant

Patch
Adams

Overlook

N

French Broad River

Lagoon

0   0.25   0.5

MILES

The Ride

0.0 Begin at the parking lot behind the Deerpark Restaurant. Ride out of the parking lot, heading toward the hay barn. Cross the hardtop road, and hop onto the old gravel road that skirts the barn. This road is generally known as Patch Adams Road.

0.6 Patch Adams Road bears right past a pasture gate. Continue following the road, but note the singletrack that peels off left just before you pass a metal gate; that's for later.

0.8 Pasture gate on left leads out onto the *Patch Adams* cabin site. Spectacular view of the Pisgah National Forest in the distance, which was all part of the Biltmore Estate grounds at one time. Thanks to Mr. Vanderbilt for such a tremendous gift to the public. Turn around here and head back along Patch Adams Road.

1.0 Turn right at the next pasture gate onto the singletrack that you noticed on the way up.

The Patch Adams Trail leads you past the lagoon on the Biltmore Estate.

1.1 Foundation and clearing for the old farm manager's homestead. Trail from here turns into a grassy doubletrack that descends quickly down toward the hardtop road and the lagoon. Nice mud bog along the way.

1.4 Turn left onto old doubletrack just before you hit the paved road. This section of track is known as Frog Pond Road, as it skirts a swampy area filled with amphibious peepers. Trail parallels the road, then turns back up into the woods.

1.6 Turn right at the T and head downhill toward the lagoon. You'll return to this intersection on the trip back.

1.8 Turn left onto the hardtop road.

2.0 Turn right onto a dirt doubletrack that runs along the edge of the lagoon. Follow this track to a nice viewing spot of the estate. Note that the lagoon was originally designed to be a reflecting pool, and on a clear day you can see a wonderful double-view of the estate. After shooting enough pictures, turn around and return the way you came.

2.2 Turn left back onto the hardtop road.

2.4 Bear right onto the grassy doubletrack that brought you down from Frog Pond Road. Watch closely, because it's hard to spot from this direction.

2.6 Return to the intersection with Frog Pond Road. This time, go straight and begin a steep tech 2+ climb.

2.8 Turn right at the T onto another doubletrack and climb back up to Patch Adams Road. Turn is marked with red arrows. After about 100 yards, turn right onto Patch Adams Road.

3.1 Turn right, drop off the road onto another dirt doubletrack. This one winds along through the bushes then descends at a fair clip.

3.5 Turn right at the T onto the dirt doubletrack that leads to the rear overlook.

3.8 Trail emerges at the rear overlook. This is a fantastic view of the estate, one that really displays Vanderbilt's appreciation of 16th-century French castles. From here, follow the track as it drops down the steep hill in front of you. Hang a sharp left at the bottom for a gradual return to the hay barn.

4.4 Continue straight past the hay barn and cross the paved road toward Deerpark.

4.6 Return to Deerpark Restaurant parking lot.

Power Line

Location: The Biltmore Estate, on the southern edge of Asheville.

Distance: 2.2-mile loop.

Time: 30 minutes.

Tread: 1.1 miles of singletrack; 0.7 mile of gravel road; 0.4 mile of paved road.

Aerobic level: Easy. This is a short ride, and all the climbing is fairly easy.

Technical difficulty: Tech 1+ overall. However, the descent under the power line is fast and steep with some nasty erosion gullies cutting across the face. Call it a tech 3+ move at speed.

Highlights: Fun, easy singletrack cruising; fast sketchy power line descent.

Land status: Private estate. Mountain biking by appointment only. Contact Gina Elrod at 828-255-1785.

Maps: USGS Asheville.

Access: From Interstate 40 West in Asheville, take Exit 50B onto U.S. Highway 25 North, and follow the signs to Biltmore Estate.

Notes on the trail

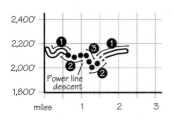

This trail adds a little shot of adrenaline, when tacked onto the end of either of the other rides. Singletrack dives into some deep woods for some fun cruising. The power line descent is fast and sketchy, though it ends all too quickly.

Power Line

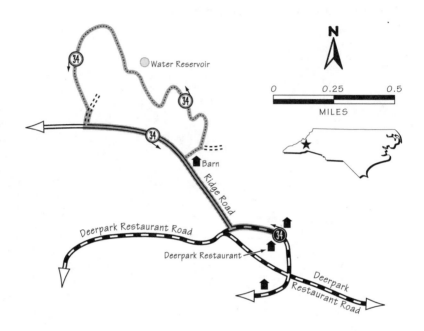

The Ride

0.0 From Deerpark Restaurant parking lot, turn right onto Deerpark Road (paved).

0.2 Continue straight past the stop sign toward a little brown cottage. Track changes to gravel road (Ridge Road).

0.4 Turn right at an old barn onto singletrack (red arrows). Bear left at each of the Y's that shortly follow (red arrows).

0.8 Turn right at the T. Sign says "30-B." No one seems to know what this means. Trail soon passes a large black tank.

1.0 Turn right under the power lines. Now get ready for a steep, eroded, tech 3 descent with a sharp left at the bottom. First-timers will want to walk this one.

1.1 Turn left at the T. Track to the right is gated.

1.2 Bear left at the Y (even though the red arrows point right).

1.3 Turn right at the T onto a dirt doubletrack.

1.4 Track dumps you back out onto Ridge Road. Turn left to return to Deerpark Restaurant.

2.2 Return to parking area.

Pisgah National Forest

Pisgah National Forest is the Queen Mother of eastern singletracking. If Tsali is the Autobahn of riding, then Pisgah is the Eco-Challenge. The trails here will thrash you, thrill you, scare the bejeebers out of you, and send you home with a grin that will make people worry about you. These woods contain some of the most beautiful trails, as well as some of the most hideous goat paths that you can find anywhere. Enjoy, but be aware that the Queen often demands a sacrifice—in blood.

Little Avery Loop

Location: Pisgah National Forest; Davidson River Campground area; 45 minutes south of Asheville.

Distance: 2.2-mile loop.

Time: 30 minutes to 1 hour.

Tread: 1.8 miles of singletrack; 0.4 mile of gravel road.

Aerobic level: Easy. Almost all the singletrack is downhill, with an easy return on the road.

Technical difficulty: Tech 2. Excellent introductory ride to give someone a small taste of what Pisgah has to offer. Some rocks, a tech 3+ root section, and a seriously mean tech 4+ stream crossing to keep newbies from getting too cocky.

Highlights: Fast cruising; rocks and roots; stream crossing.

Land status: Pisgah National Forest.

Maps: USGS Pisgah Forest; USDA Forest Service Pisgah District Trail Map; National Geographic Trails Illustrated Pisgah Ranger District.

Access: From Asheville, take Interstate 26 East (actually south) to North Carolina Highway 280 South. Follow NC 280 for about 15 miles to the town of Brevard. Turn right onto U.S. Highway 276, which leads up into the heart of the Pisgah National Forest. About 2 miles in, pass the Pisgah Ranger Station and turn right onto Forest Road 477 (gravel road), following the sign for the Pisgah Horse Stables. Go about another 2 miles, pass the gated road for the horse stables on your right, then watch for the second parking area on the right. Look close, and you'll see the sign for Buckhorn Gap Trail.

Notes on the trail

Don't know if you're up for Pisgah's charms? This short loop offers a chance for some easy speed, some respectable roots, and an advanced stream crossing before the quick return back to the start. If all that does is whet your appetite for further adventure, then check out the Buckhorn Gap Loop or parts of Big Avery Creek. This is a good trail to gauge an unknown rider's skills on before venturing on to the serious riding that awaits up above.

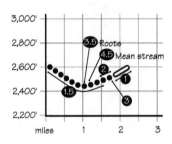

The Ride

0.0 Head in from the parking area, onto Buckhorn Gap Trail. A smooth, tech 1+ run, maybe the smoothest run you'll find in Pisgah. Small dips and root drops along the way.

0.9 Turn sharply back right onto the lower section of Avery Creek Trail. Watch for a particularly mean section of tech 3+ roots.

1.3 Extremely tricky tech 4+ stream crossing with a nasty, root-strewn lead in. Several log bridges both before and after.

1.5 Small waterfall on your right.

1.6 Continue straight past Clawhammer Cove Trail (hiking only) on your left.

1.7 Tough, tech 3 climb up some slippery water bars.

1.8 Turn right as you come out onto FR 477. Watch for cars.

2.2 Return to the parking area.

Little Avery Loop

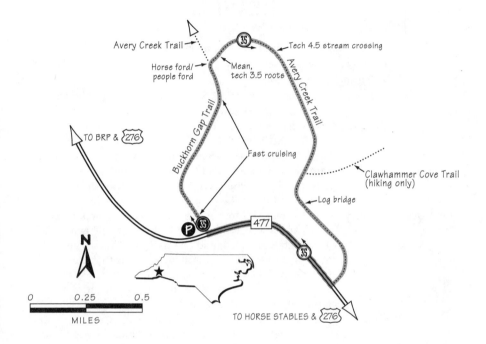

Avery Creek Trail

Horse ford/ people ford

Mean, tech 3.5 roots

Tech 4.5 stream crossing

Avery Creek Trail

Buckhorn Gap Trail

TO BRP & 276

Fast cruising

Clawhammer Cove Trail (hiking only)

Log bridge

P 35   477   35

N

0   0.25   0.5

MILES

TO HORSE STABLES & 276

Kitsuma

Location: Between Black Mountain and Old Fort.

Distance: 10.3-mile loop.

Time: 1.5 to 2.5 hours.

Tread: 5 miles of singletrack; 3.8 miles of abandoned highway; 1.5 miles of pavement.

Aerobic level: Moderate. The initial climb is a bit tough with 12 switchbacks in a row for some quick elevation gain. The downhills are furious enough to keep your hands and legs cramping from strain and your face cramping from grinning. Return climb on old U.S. Highway 70 is very gradual, but it's still a long time to be climbing.

Technical difficulty: Tech 2+ overall. Most of the singletrack is smooth, fast, and clear. However, a number of the downhill switchbacks rate a tech 3 to tech 4, and one nasty root/rock combo rates a tech 4+. The real difficulty here is that the trail is so fast and so bloody narrow, in places, it's barely wider than your tires. You could sleep on the return trip, if you could only keep pedaling.

Highlights: Knife-edge ridge running; fast contour runs; switchbacks a-plenty; tight mountain laurel thickets; incredible views.

Land status: Pisgah National Forest.

Maps: USGS Old Fort.

Access: From Interstate 40, take Exit 64 for Black Mountain. Follow this into Black Mountain, then turn right onto State Street, which is the main drag through town. After a block or two, you'll see a Food Lion grocery store; hop onto the service road (old US 70) that runs right in front of Food Lion. Follow this road for about a mile until you come to a stop sign. Go straight across onto King George Road, and follow it to the end. There you'll find a small parking area and a sign for Kitsuma Peak Trail and Old Fort Picnic Area.

Notes on the trail

Kitsuma is an awesome ride—period. Once you climb past the dozen or so initial switchbacks (which, strangely enough, are kind of fun in their own right), you're faced with a torpedo run down along knife-edge ridgelines that drop forever. You'll drop a ridge, switchback, then contour run until the next ridge peels off, over and over again. Most of the trail is smooth and buff, but screaming down an 8-inch-wide track along a 60-degree fall line brings its own form of adrenaline. The return trip is 5 miles of easy cruising on an abandoned and gated section of old US 70, with excellent views of the ridgeline you just descended. I can't do it justice; just ride this trail and it'll instantly be one of your top five favorites.

"That was some sick singletrack. I dug it." —David T

"Actually staying on the trail is imperative." —Author

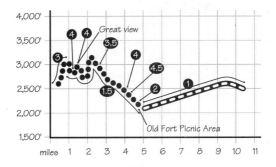

The Ride

0.0 Trail begins by sign for Kitsuma Trail and Old Fort Picnic Area. Tread starts as grassy doubletrack. The semis on I-40 will be rolling by only 20 feet away, but you'll soon leave them far behind and below.

0.3 Trail cuts sharply left uphill: true singletrack with a steep, tech 3 rocky and rooty climb. Yellow blazes lead you through the first two switchbacks.

0.5 Another eight switchbacks in a row. All of them are tight, with some sporting mean tech 3 roots and others wide open. Fairly flat, tech 1+ riding in between.

0.9 Switchback 11 brings you by a rocky ledge with views of Black Mountain and Montreat. In June the blooming mountain laurel walls the trail with pink-and-white blossoms.

1.0 Trail enters a small campsite clearing, and continues on the other side across some large rock slabs. The first descent of the ride starts here, and it's probably the toughest: a seriously steep, eroded, tech 4 drop that requires you to just let it go and hang on.

1.2 Round a corner and start dropping again. This time, you're running an 18-inch-wide trail across a 60-degree fall line, then through a tight switchback, with little room for error.

1.3 Gorgeous view over the entire valley. After you pocket the camera, get ready for a very sketchy, tech 4 switchback, followed by some narrow, slippery, off-camber contour running. Trail here is only a tech 1+, but then again it's only about as wide as your tires, and the drop off the side is pretty imposing.

1.7 Pair of switchbacks up, both very tight, for a last bit of elevation gain. Then the bottom drops out, and you're zooming down a saddle through extremely tight laurel thickets. Sometimes, all you can do is drop your head and follow your

Kitsuma

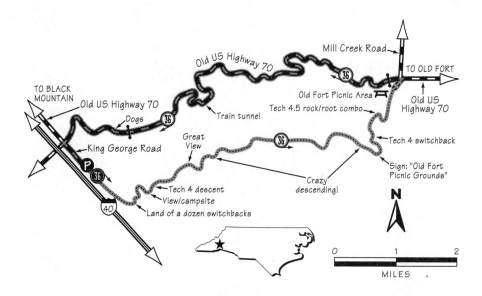

wheel. From here out, Kitsuma hits a really sweet rhythm: fast saddle, ridgeline run, tight switchback, scorching contouring, then into the next saddle. It's a 9 on the fun scale that just doesn't seem to end.

3.5 Tight, tech 3+ switchback. You're simply bombing it at this point, so keep an eye peeled for the sudden turns.

3.9 Trail turns left at sign: "Old Fort Picnic Grounds." Watch out for the off-camber contouring just after this, as my back wheel dropped over the edge three times within 50 feet.

4.0 Another extremely tight, tech 4 switchback. Contouring that follows holds a huge inside berm. Try really hard not to look over the side as you're running, 'cause the drop will make you woozy. Watch for a nasty washout along the way.

4.3 Really, really mean tech 4+ rock/root combo. Blowing this will probably send you off the side, so do it right or walk it. Shortly after, you'll fly over a crazy, tech 3+ rootball in the middle of the trail and try to land on a 10-inch-wide ledge on the other side. It's a screamer, whether you make it or not.

4.6 Trail flattens and starts running beside a small creek. Tech 2 trail gives you a few small roots to bunny hop.

4.9 Kitsuma finally ends, dumping you out into the Old Fort Picnic Area. You'll find bathrooms and water here, along with some wide-eyed picnickers who may either offer you some cake or grab their children and prepare to run. Follow the gravel access road straight out to the hardtop.

Take time to appreciate the view of Kitsuma Trail on the return trip.

5.0 Turn left at this four-way intersection, onto old US 70 (paved) with a Dead End sign posted.

5.3 Pass a white metal gate. Follow this abandoned section of US 70 up into the hills. In June and July, watch for thickets of ripe blackberries to sweeten the ride back.

6.7 Just past a landslide on the road, you get an excellent view of the Kitsuma ridgeline off to the left. You'll be astonished at how high and narrow it looks, which is just the way it felt screaming down.

8.3 As you pass some concrete guardrails on your left, look over the edge and you'll find a cool railroad tunnel that runs right underneath you.

9.1 Pass another white gate and continue straight on old US 70.

9.4 As you finally finish climbing, watch for the pair of dogs who live at the trailers on the left: The small one likes to bark and chase you, and you'll be surprised how fast the little bugger is. The big, gentle pitbull just keeps a quiet eye from atop his wrecked car throne.

10.0 Turn left at this intersection onto King George Road and follow it to the end.

10.3 Return to the trailhead.

Mo' Heinous

Location: Bent Creek Research Forest, 20 minutes south of Asheville.

Distance: 9.9-mile loop.

Time: 1.5 to 2.5 hours.

Tread: 5.2 miles of singletrack, 2.1 miles of old Forest Service road and doubletrack; 2.6 miles of gated gravel road.

Aerobic level: Strenuous. The only climb in Bent Creek worse than the Sidehill/IFG Connector/Ingles Field Gap route is straight up Ingles Field Gap the whole way. It's the kind of climb that will bring tears of pain and frustration to your face on the way up and tears of relief once you finally hit the summit. The adrenaline factor on the way back down Mo' Heinous is possibly more debilitating than the climb up, if that's possible.

Technical difficulty: Tech 3+ overall. Initial drop on Mo' Heinous is a tech 4+: It's extremely steep and loose, perhaps the toughest move in this section of the forest and is not for the faint of heart. Just Plain Heinous is extremely fast (30+ miles per hour) over loose gravel and wicked water bars. Lower Sidehill offers a festival of tech 3 rooty hops to gradually bring your pulse back down into the normal range. This is a black diamond run; make no mistakes.

Highlights: Wretched, unforgiving climb; incredibly steep eroded descent; horrendous water bars; steep rocky drops; high-speed, contour-hugging singletrack and doubletrack.

Land status: Experimental forest.

Maps: USGS Dunsmore Mountain; USDA Forest Service Pisgah District Trail Map; National Geographic Trails Illustrated Pisgah Ranger District.

Access: From Asheville, take Interstate 26 East (south, actually) to North Carolina Highway 191 South. Go about 2 miles, then turn right at the light onto Bent Creek Ranch Road (from here, you'll just follow the signs for Lake Powhatan). This road soon runs into a development and branches; bear left onto Wesley Branch Road. Go another 2 miles and look for the Hardtimes Trailhead sign on your left along with a dirt parking area. Get out, get geared up, and get ready to ride.

Notes on the trail

This downhill should be attempted only by riders who are either very secure in their bike-handling skills or don't mind crashing and bleeding (I'm still carrying the scars from this one). The locals rated the entry to Mo' Heinous a tech 4+ on a scale of 5, which should give you reason to pause right there. The initial drop-in requires total commitment; this deep, steep-sided gully offers only one choice of lines and no exit except out the bottom. After the initial scare, the trail slips through some very tight and sudden switchbacks, over a number of major water bars, then starts to drop again. The next few miles are insanely fast, down old Forest Service road doubletrack, around blind corners, and over more water bars. This ride is brutal, sick, and pounding, and will have even the most jaded of hammerheads working to unclench their brake hands and clean that wide-eyed, post-trauma look from their faces.

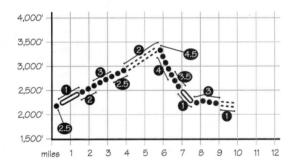

The Ride

0.0 Begin from Hardtimes Trailhead. Obvious entrance to Expresso Trail is straight across Wesley Branch Road (the paved road you just drove up on). Expresso will wake you up quickly with a short tech 2+ rocky climb and an uphill log pyramid.

0.2 Bear right at the Y.

0.4 Trail drops you out onto Ledford Branch Road (gravel), just past the gate. Turn right and head uphill.

1.3 Sharp left turn back onto Sidehill, just in the middle of a curve in the road. Trail entrance is clearly signed, but it's still easy to miss. Watch for a picnic area just across from the entrance. Sidehill starts with some easy tech 1+ cruising and a gorgeous 3-foot-tall berm. Climb that follows is long but not too tough if you stay in the clear line.

2.0 Top a rise and hit a funky intersection of trails. Take the first available right, a sharp turn back that starts climbing up the Ingles Field Gap (IFG) Connector Trail (signed). Another right farther on is the continuation of Sidehill. If you didn't like the last bit of climbing, you'll hate this next section. It's a good bit

Mo' Heinous

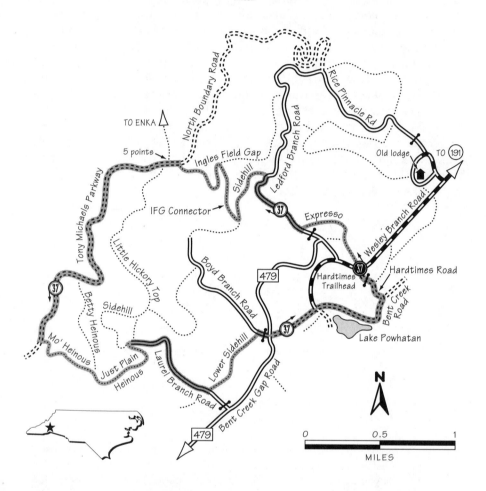

steeper with a number of tech 2 and tech 3 rock sections to grind and twist your way through.

2.7 Turn left as the connector trail intersects Ingles Field Gap Trail. Now the climbing gets *really* steep, though at least it's fairly smooth and buff. Serious pain potential here. Watch for riders screaming on the way down, who won't believe you're climbing IFG.

3.6 Drag yourself up the last pitch of IFG, and fall into an exhausted heap at 5 Points. After your medic has resuscitated everyone in your group, turn left onto the dirt doubletrack that is the Tony Michaels Parkway. Don't take the singletrack to your immediate left signed for Little Hickory Top, and definitely do not go straight across onto the lost trail to Enka. This next bit of climbing, while long, will seem like a picnic compared with the torture of climbing IFG.

4.2 Pass through a gap and dive into a really bad poison ivy (or is it poison oak?) section. Either way, don't stop here for a rest or bathroom break. Trail gets very rocky after this (tech 2+), which makes for even more miserable climbing.

5.0 Continue straight past the left turn for Betty Heinous. This spot is usually marked with a small cairn of stones. Do not mistake this for Mo' Heinous. If it doesn't look incredibly sketchy at the beginning, it's not Mo' Heinous.

5.7 Turn left for the entrance to Mo' Heinous, the big kahuna of Bent Creek. Initial entry is an eroded gully that pitches about 55 degrees down, switches back and forth a few times, then really starts to get ugly. We're talking big loose rocks, tight switchbacks, steep water bars, and way, way too much speed for such tight, rocky stuff. This trail can be a serious meat grinder, so watch it.

6.2 Though you probably didn't notice, Betty Heinous fed in from the left. And now kiddies, we really start to go fast: 30+ miles per hour on some steep, sketchy track that we call Just Plain Heinous. Tread fades into old dirt doubletrack, littered with big rocks and water bars; generally, there's only one clear line, unless you can bunny hop a long, long way.

7.0 Watch for a big stinky mudhole filled with rocks that lurks on the inside corner. It's a serious faceplant waiting to happen.

7.1 Turn right at the four-way intersection onto Laurel Branch Road (gravel). Watch your speed on the run-out from here, 'cause you'll still be high on adrenaline and the gravel is really loose.

7.5 Sharp left turn back onto Lower Sidehill Trail (signed). Trail climbs a bit, tops out in a little meadow, then descends over a bone-jarring series of water bars and root drops into a tight, twisty rhodo tunnel.

Most of the rides in the Bent Creek area begin at the Hardtimes Trailhead.

8.6 Turn right as Lower Sidehill dead-ends onto Boyd Branch Road (gravel). Go straight past the big rocks and the gate at the end of Boyd Branch, cross Bent Creek Gap Road (gravel; watch for cars), and pick up dirt doubletrack on the other side.

9.1 Cross Lake Powhatan Road (paved) and continue straight on dirt/gravel doubletrack past Lake Powhatan and a small water treatment plant.

9.7 Turn left onto Hardtimes Road (gravel).

9.9 Pass gate and return to Hardtimes Trailhead.

Little Hickory Top

Location: Bent Creek Research Forest, 20 minutes south of Asheville.

Distance: 10.3-mile loop.

Time: 1 to 2.5 hours.

Tread: 3.2 miles of singletrack; 6.7 miles of gated Forest Service road; 0.2 mile of gravel road; 0.2 mile of pavement.

Aerobic level: Easy to moderate. Climbing the North Boundary Road seems to take days. It's never very steep, but it just keeps on coming. The return run back from 5 Points is almost all downhill.

Technical difficulty: Tech 2 overall. Little Hickory Top throws a few tech 2+ and 3.5 rocky sections in your way, and Lower Sidehill is littered with tech 3 roots. Otherwise, it's either gravel road or wide-open singletrack cruising.

Highlights: Streams; roots; some large rocks; relatively easy climb to the top; Lake Powhatan for a dip after the ride.

Land status: Experimental forest.

Maps: USGS Dunsmore Mountain; USDA Forest Service Pisgah District Trail Map; National Geographic Trails Illustrated Pisgah Ranger District.

Access: From Asheville, take Interstate 26 East (south, actually) to North Carolina Highway 191 South. Go about 2 miles, then turn right at the light onto Bent Creek Ranch Road (from here, you'll just follow the signs for Lake Powhatan). This road soon runs into a development and branches; bear left onto Wesley Branch Road. Go another 2 miles and look for the Hardtimes Trailhead sign on your left along with a dirt parking area. Get out, get geared up, and get ready to ride.

Notes on the trail

Little Hickory Top is an excellent ride for someone who wants to venture up onto the high trails, but who isn't up for the speed of Ingles Field Gap or the technical challenges of Betty and Mo' Heinous. This loop gives you a long warm-up with plenty of time to build your courage for the trip back down. Enough rocks, roots, berms, and hops to still make it feel like an adventure.

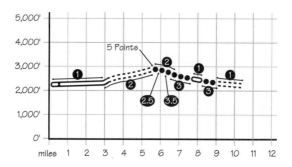

The Ride

0.0 Start from Hardtimes Trailhead. Turn left onto Wesley Branch Road (the paved road you drove in on).

0.2 Continue straight onto Bent Creek Gap Road (gravel), as Wesley Branch Road enters Lake Powhatan Park.

0.4 Continue straight again past the metal gate onto Ledford Branch Road (gravel) as Bent Creek Gap Road bears left. Tread is hardpacked gravel doubletrack.

2.7 Turn left at this intersection onto the North Boundary Road (gravel). This old forest doubletrack is a combination of dirt and pea-gravel. Several unmarked trails and old roads peel off of this road; ignore them all until you reach 5 Points. "Shelterwood" sign explains selective logging techniques used to encourage secondary growth of birch and ash.

3.8 North Boundary Road narrows to tech 2, dirt singletrack. Track is eroded and loose in many spots, making for tough climbing. And it keeps on climbing.

4.2 Nice view to right—if you can pick your weary head up.

5.4 A short, fun descent brings you to the clearing known as 5 Points. From here, bear ahead to the left onto Little Hickory Top Trail (signed). Ingles Field Gap falls back to the left, the Tony Michaels Parkway continues straight, and the lost trail to Enka turns right. Now all your climbing pays off. After just a tad more uphill, Little Hickory Top starts to drop, a hardpacked tech 2 singletrack. You'll run through a big dip, then hop onto some sweet track that hugs the contours as it drops through the forest.

5.7 Big berm to zoom around. Don't be afraid; just let go of the brakes and zip around the edge.

Little Hickory Top

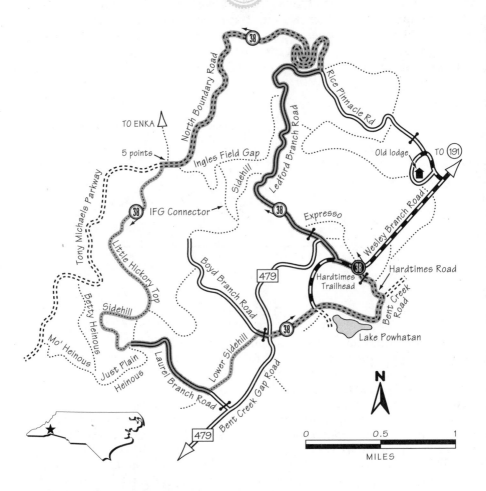

6.1 Watch for a section of tech 2+ rocks, a big switchback, then some big, nasty tech 3+ rocks. Novices should use some caution here.

6.4 Trail narrows and runs a tight edge through a cool rhododendron tunnel.

6.7 Two choices for Sidehill Trail at the Y. Stay straight for a bit of climbing.

6.9 Continue straight past this unsigned branch to the left. Trail starts to drop again, getting fast and a bit sketchy through some loose, tech 3+ rocks. Careful of the slick rocks when crossing the streams.

7.3 Little Hickory Top really hits its stride, switching back and forth, with some root drops, small water bars, and several more big berms.

7.5 Continue straight through this four-way intersection onto Laurel Branch Road (gravel). This is a good spot to catch your breath and make sure your friends all make it down in one piece.

7.9 Sharp left turn back onto Lower Sidehill Trail (signed). Trail climbs a bit, tops out in a little meadow, then descends over a bone-jarring series of water bars and root drops into a tight, twisty rhodo tunnel. The last section of Lower Sidehill is a continual tech 3, so novices need to stay on their toes.

9.0 Turn right as Lower Sidehill dead-ends onto Boyd Branch Road (gravel). Go straight past the big rocks and the gate at the end of Boyd Branch, cross Bent Creek Gap Road (gravel; watch for cars), and pick up dirt doubletrack on the other side.

9.5 Cross Lake Powhatan Road (paved) and continue straight on dirt/gravel doubletrack past Lake Powhatan, up over the curb, and down past a small water treatment plant.

10.1 Turn left onto Hardtimes Road (gravel).

10.3 Pass gate and return to Hardtimes Trailhead.

Timm soars on Little Hickory Top. DAVID TOLLERTON PHOTO

Ingles Field Gap

Location: Bent Creek Research Forest, 20 minutes south of Asheville.

Distance: 11.5-mile loop.

Time: 1.5 to 2.5 hours. You may want to allow some extra time because a single run around One Dog just won't be enough, and the jumps at the bottom of Ingles Field Gap (IFG) will call you back like a siren's song (quite possibly to your destruction).

Tread: 9.6 miles of singletrack; 1.8 miles of gravel road; 0.1 mile gravel doubletrack. Singletrack is extremely buff hardpack in most places, loose and rocky in a few others.

Aerobic level: Moderate. The climbs along Sidehill are slow and not a lot of fun but are fairly clear for the most part. Little Hickory Top is long and painfully steep at times, but ridable. The pure adrenaline factor descending IFG can also take its toll.

Technical difficulty: Tech 2+ overall. This loop runs a wide gamut of technical requirements. Ledford Branch and North Boundary Roads are tech 1. Sidehill and IFG are buff, tech 2 roller-coaster runs, but they throw a few dicey, tech 3 rocky sections at you that require finding that one clean line to prevent dabbing (or dashing). Nothing too tough overall, but a number of spots that can really leave you tweaked if your attention wanders (or if you panic and grab a handful of brake) at the wrong time.

Highlights: Incredibly smooth swooping descents; huge berms; big water bars and whoop-dee-doos; fast gate runs.

Land status: Research and demonstration forest.

Maps: USGS Dunsmore Mountain; USDA Forest Service Pisgah District Trail Map; National Geographic Trails Illustrated Pisgah Ranger District.

Access: From Asheville, take Interstate 26 East (south, actually) to North Carolina Highway 191 South. Go about 2 miles, then turn right at the light onto Bent Creek Ranch Road (from here, you'll just follow the signs for Lake Powhatan). This road soon runs into a development and branches; bear left onto Wesley Branch Road. Go another 2 miles and look for the Hardtimes Trailhead sign on your left along with a dirt parking area. Get out, get geared up, and get ready to ride.

Notes on the trail

This is a superb adrenaline run that will slap a grin on your face to last the rest of the day. There are downhills that score about a 9 on the fun factor and sweet, swooping descents, surprisingly smooth, with several 3- to 4-foot-high inside berms. Lots of bunny hopping potential and some huge air potential near the end of IFG. Advanced riders can crank this entire ride with plenty of time to warm up before hitting the steeps. Intermediates (and even really determined beginners) will find the climbs doable (if painful) and the descents exhilarating and will probably declare this their favorite ride so far.

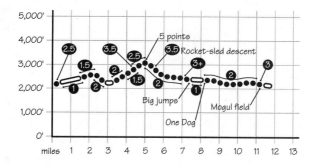

The Ride

0.0 Begin from Hardtimes Trailhead. Obvious entrance to Expresso Trail is straight across Wesley Branch Road (the paved road you just drove up on). Expresso will wake you up quickly with a short tech 2+ rocky climb and an uphill log pyramid.

0.2 Bear left at the Y.

0.3 Trail drops you out onto Bent Creek Gap Road (gravel; watch for cars). Turn right.

0.4 Go straight past gate onto Ledford Branch Road (gravel).

1.3 Sharp left turn back onto Sidehill, just in the middle of a curve in the road. Trail entrance is clearly signed, but it's still easy to miss. Watch for a picnic area just across from the entrance. Sidehill starts with some easy tech 1+ cruising and a gorgeous 3-foot-tall berm. Climb that follows is long but not too tough if you stay in the clear line.

2.0 Top a rise and hit a funky intersection of trails. Choices are straight for a hiking-only trail, sharp right back uphill for the IFG Connector, and another right for Sidehill; the trails are clearly signed. Take the second right turn to continue on Sidehill and start descending immediately. This downhill is fast and very smooth if you stay in the line. However, the line switches back and forth, and if you get out of it, you'll be in some nasty tech 3 rocks at an unhealthy speed, so pay attention. This run is about an 8 on the fun scale.

2.5 Sidehill ends and runs straight into Boyd Branch Road (gravel).

Ingles Field Gap

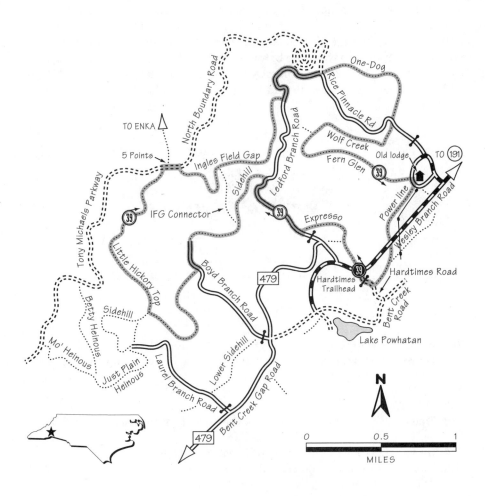

TO ENKA

5 Points

North Boundary Road

Ingles Field Gap

Sidehill

Ledford Branch Road

One-Dog

Rice Pinnacle Rd

Wolf Creek

Fern Glen

Old lodge

TO 191

39

Tony Michaels Parkway

39

IFG Connector

Little Hickory Top

Boyd Branch Road

39

Expresso

Power line

Wesley Branch Road

39

Hardtimes Road

Hardtimes Trailhead

479

Bent Creek Road

Betty Heinous

Sidehill

Mo' Heinous

Just Plain Heinous

Laurel Branch Road

Lower Sidehill

Bent Creek Gap Road

Lake Powhatan

479

N

0   0.5   1

MILES

2.6 Turn right off of Boyd Branch onto continuation of Sidehill. Two entrances here, only one of which is signed, that join back together shortly. Tread here is old dirt doubletrack.

2.8 Doubletrack starts to fade, and clear singletrack breaks to the left. Turn left to follow the fun stuff.

3.4 Continue straight on Sidehill. Faint singletrack breaks to the left, which is the Upper/Lower Sidehill connector.

3.9 Continue straight at the intersection onto Little Hickory Top. The sharp left back is a continuation of Sidehill. Unfortunately, now it's climb time. Little Hickory Top is probably the easiest climb to 5 Points, but you've still got to gain about 400 feet vertical, so be prepared for some grinding. Starts off with some contour running through a rhododendron tunnel.

4.5 Nasty, slippery tech 3 + rocks to navigate. Particularly in the middle of a climb, these guys are a bear. After, you get a tough uphill switchback to grunt through, then some more rocks.

5.0 Some relatively easy (tech 1 +) contour running brings you to a big dip, with a large drainage pipe in the bottom. The climb up the far side will be a pusher for just about everyone.

5.2 Finally, a short downhill run brings you to an intersection of five trails, known locally as 5 Points or Four Corners. Ingles Field Gap is ahead to the right and breaks immediately downhill. If it looks like the entrance drop on a roller coaster, it's the right trail. This track starts off very steep, very fast, and very smooth (tech 2, tops), launching you through a 4-foot-high berm. Beginners and cautious riders should keep a good check on their speed; otherwise, they chance gaining terminal velocity, then completely wigging when they zoom up on a nasty rock section or off-camber turn.

5.8 Continue straight on IFG. Trail back right is the IFG Connector down to Sidehill. This section of IFG is even sweeter than the first, if that's possible. Some sections seem almost polished, they're so buff, while several stream crossings on the inside corners are hairy tech 3 moves through large, loose, sharp rocks. Some sections are wide open, and others hold only a single 2-inch line through the rocks. All of it though is gut-wrenchingly fast. Watch for another one of those magnificent inside berms, followed by a rare outside-corner berm.

6.4 Watch for set of three 10-inch tombstones grouped together in the middle of a steep, descending curve. Excellent launching potential for the vertically inspired. Great faceplant potential for the overly cautious or maneuverability challenged.

6.6 Zip through a small opening that contains a short wooden bench (useful after the climb up IFG, but that's another ride). Final descent down IFG back to the road is exceptionally steep and fast (tech 3 +) with three serious whoop-dee-doos tacked onto the very end.

7.1 Exit off IFG and turn left on Ledford Branch Road (gated; gravel).

7.8 Continue straight through four-way intersection, up over the embankment for the entrance to One-Dog Trail (unsigned). Left is the North Boundary Road, and right is Rice Pinnacle Road. What lies ahead is perhaps the most enjoyable mile of singletrack I've ever discovered. The first descent on One-Dog gains speed steadily, switching through the trees, then the bottom drops out for a magnificent brakes-free zone. Easy climb after, with a respectable tech 3 suspended log to climb, jump, or avoid. Then another high-speed slalom run through the trees; big, sweeping right turn at bottom of hill can slingshot you

Tony slips along Wolf Creek. DAVID TOLLERTON PHOTO

into next section if you nab the line just right. (Note: Just across from the big turn lives a *big* black dog, for which the trail is named. Though he's supposedly fenced, this escape artist has twice come out of the trees at me like a hairy cruise missile. Doesn't seem mean, just touchy about unannounced visitors. Keep an eye out for him.)

8.6 Trail slips and twists through a dark, mysterious pine forest, on a track as smooth as poured concrete. Several nice bunny hops in here, but beware of the pine-branch spears. Bear left at T just after pines.

8.9 Turn left as you T into Rice Pinnacle Road (gated; gravel). Take an immediate right onto the first singletrack you see (it's only about 50 feet or so) then up and over a knee-high dirt hump.

9.1 Turn right at the T onto Wolf Creek Trail (unsigned).

9.3 Three intersections follow close together; turn left at each one. Last turn puts you onto Fern Glen Trail (unsigned), which slips and twists tightly through the trees for a gradual downhill.

10.3 Turn right as you T into an old logging road.

10.5 Bear right uphill onto a dirt doubletrack under some small power lines. This, of course, is called the Power Line Trail.

10.9 Turn right onto Wesley Branch Road (paved; beware of cars). After only 30 yards or so, turn left onto singletrack under some more small power lines. **Warning:** Do not jump the first jump under the lines, no matter how enticing it looks. The landing zone is a mogul field that will slap you down faster than you can say "Oh sh**!"

11.4 Turn right onto Hardtimes Road (gravel).

11.5 Pass the gate and return to Hardtimes Trailhead.

Sidehill Loop

Location: Bent Creek Research Forest, 20 minutes south of Asheville.

Distance: 7.6-mile loop.

Time: 1 to 1.5 hours.

Tread: 5 miles of singletrack; 1.3 miles of doubletrack; 1.3 miles of gravel road.

Aerobic level: Easy to moderate. No huge elevation gains, though there's a lot of up and down. While the climbs along Sidehill are slow and not a lot of fun, they are fairly clear for the most part.

Technical difficulty: Tech 2. Mostly buff singletrack with some tech 3 rocks along the descents on Sidehill and some tech 3 roots and water bars on Lower Sidehill.

Highlights: Smooth swooping descents; berms; water bars; tricky root drops.

Land status: Research and demonstration forest.

Maps: USGS Dunsmore Mountain; USDA Forest Service Pisgah District Trail Map; National Geographic Trails Illustrated Pisgah Ranger District.

Access: From Asheville, take Interstate 26 East (south, actually) to North Carolina Highway 191 South. Go about 2 miles, then turn right at the light onto Bent Creek Ranch Road (from here, you'll just follow the signs for Lake Powhatan). This road soon runs into a development and branches; bear left onto Wesley Branch Road. Go another 2 miles and look for the Hardtimes Trailhead sign on your left along with a dirt parking area. Get out, get geared up, and get ready to ride.

Notes on the trail

A fun loop for someone who isn't up for the climb to the top of the ridge. Also a good introductory run for beginners who want to try their hand at some true singletrack. Descents vary from rail smooth to loose and sketchy. Water bars and roots on Lower Sidehill will have you hopping whether you like it or not. An excellent, fun ride that doesn't cost you a lot.

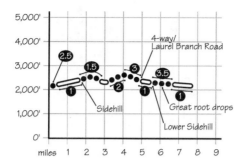

The Ride

0.0 Begin from Hardtimes Trailhead. Obvious entrance to Expresso Trail is straight across Wesley Branch Road (the paved road you just drove up on). Expresso will wake you up quickly with a short tech 2+ rocky climb and an uphill log pyramid.

0.2 Bear right at the Y.

0.4 Trail drops you out onto Ledford Branch Road (gravel), just past the gate. Turn right and head uphill.

1.3 Sharp left turn back onto Sidehill, just in the middle of a curve in the road. Trail entrance is clearly signed, but it's still easy to miss. Watch for a picnic area just across from the entrance. Sidehill starts with some easy tech 1+ cruising and a gorgeous 3-foot-tall berm. Climb that follows is long but not too tough if you stay in the clear line.

2.0 Top a rise and hit a funky, but clearly signed, intersection of trails. Choices are straight for a hiking-only trail, sharp right back uphill for the IFG Connector, and another right for Sidehill; take the second right turn to continue on Sidehill and start descending immediately. This downhill is fast and very smooth if you stay in the line. However, the line switches back and forth, and if you get out of it, you'll be in some nasty tech 3 rocks at an unhealthy speed, so pay attention. This run is about an 8 on the fun scale.

2.5 Sidehill ends and runs straight into Boyd Branch Road (gravel).

2.6 Turn right off of Boyd Branch onto continuation of Sidehill. Two entrances here, only one of which is signed, that join back together shortly. Tread here is old dirt doubletrack.

2.8 Doubletrack starts to fade and clear singletrack breaks to the left. Turn left to follow the fun stuff.

3.4 Continue straight on Sidehill.

3.9 Intersection with Little Hickory Top Trail. Turn sharply left back uphill to continue on Sidehill. Trails are clearly signed, but be sure not to miss the turn since your head will be hanging as you drag yourself up the last climb.

4.1 Continue straight on Sidehill. Unsigned singletrack breaks to the left, marked by a cairn of stones. From here Sidehill starts descending fast, alternating smooth buff sections with hairy tech 3 fields of chicken heads. Hold the line, stay off the brakes, and scream yourself silly.

Sidehill Loop

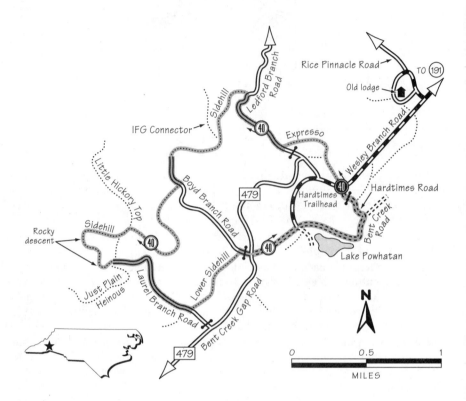

Rice Pinnacle Road

TO 191

Old lodge

Ledford Branch Road

Sidehill

IFG Connector

Expresso

Wesley Branch Road

40

Little Hickory Top

Boyd Branch Road

479

Hardtimes Trailhead

40

Hardtimes Road

Bent Creek Road

Rocky descent

Sidehill

40

Lower Sidehill

40

Lake Powhatan

Just Plain Heinous

Laurel Branch Road

Bent Creek Gap Road

479

N

0	0.5	1

MILES

4.8 Continue straight at this four-way intersection onto Laurel Branch Road (gravel). Watch your speed on the run-out from here, 'cause you'll still be high on adrenaline and the gravel is really loose.

5.2 Sharp left turn back onto Lower Sidehill Trail (signed). Trail climbs a bit, tops out in a little meadow, then descends over a bone-jarring series of water bars and root drops into a tight, twisty rhododendron tunnel.

6.3 Turn right as Lower Sidehill dead-ends onto Boyd Branch Road (gravel). Go straight past the big rocks and the gate at the end of Boyd Branch, cross Bent Creek Gap Road (gravel; watch for cars), and pick up dirt doubletrack on the other side.

6.8 Cross Lake Powhatan Road (paved), and continue straight on dirt/gravel doubletrack. As you pass Lake Powhatan itself, the gravel track turns into Bent Creek Road.

7.4 Turn left onto Hardtimes Road.

7.6 Pass gate and return to Hardtimes Trailhead.

"Everything out here is Sidehill."—A common quote heard in Bent Creek

Betty Heinous Loop

Location: Bent Creek Research Forest, 20 minutes south of Asheville.

Distance: 12.8-mile loop.

Time: 1.5 to 2.5 hours.

Tread: 8.9 miles of singletrack; 1.4 miles of old Forest Service road/doubletrack; 2.5 miles of gated gravel road.

Aerobic level: Strenuous. The climb up Ingles Field Gap is a killer. No one will make this climb without a serious amount of pain. The run out Tony Michaels Parkway is flatter, but still doesn't give you much of a break. Descent down Betty and Just Plain Heinous are fast and sketchy, with no chance to catch your breath. The final climb up Sidehill will take the last bit of juice you've got left. Then finally you get a long downhill run back to the trailhead.

Technical difficulty: Tech 3 overall. Betty and Just Plain Heinous are a surly lot, and can slap down even the most confident of riders with a nasty combination of speed, tech 3 rocks, and a tech 4 erosion gully. Lower Sidehill is a tech 3 root-fest. Ingles Field Gap isn't too technical; it's just one mean mother of a climb.

Highlights: Screaming contour running; heart-breaking climb; big berms; stream crossings.

Land status: Experimental forest.

Maps: USGS Dunsmore Mountain; USDA Forest Service Pisgah District Trail Map; National Geographic Trails Illustrated Pisgah Ranger District.

Access: From Asheville, take Interstate 26 East (south, actually) to North Carolina Highway 191 South. Go about 2 miles, then turn right at the light onto Bent Creek Ranch Road (from here, you'll just follow the signs for Lake Powhatan). This road soon runs into a development and branches; bear left onto Wesley Branch Road. Go another 2 miles and look for the Hardtimes Trailhead sign on your left along with a dirt parking area. Get out, get geared up, and get ready to ride.

Notes on the trail

Betty Heinous, while not quite in the same league as her big brother Mo', is a fast, hair-raising run that will have you alternately grabbing all the brakes you can and letting them go to hope for the best. This loop includes a brutal climb up Ingles Field Gap, the bonzai run down Betty, root-hopping along Lower Sidehill, then a final grind up one side of Sidehill and a bobsled run down the other. Don't make the mistake of thinking this is a girly run, no matter what the name says.

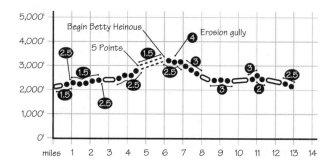

The Ride

0.0 Start from Hardtimes Trailhead. Go past gate at bottom of parking area onto Hardtimes Road.

0.1 Turn left onto the second singletrack you see, which is the Warm-up Trail. This little tech 1+ track offers a bit of everything including a short climb, a stream crossing, a couple of fun logs to work over, and a zippy descent back and forth down through a gully.

0.8 Continue straight across Wesley Branch Road (paved). Trail on this side is much rockier (tech 2+).

0.9 Turn left onto a paved walkway. Small wooden bridge back to right.

1.0 Continue straight past the ruins of an old Boy Scout lodge. Track turns into a wide tech 1 gravel doubletrack.

1.2 Turn left onto the first true singletrack you see, which is known as Fern Glen. Tread is somewhat soft clay and pine mix; smooth tech 1+ track with some tech 2 roots.

1.9 Turn left at the T, up and over a series of small, slippery water bars. Track quickly turns into an old logging road, filled with large egg-sized gravel. Steep switchbacks are a bear to climb.

2.4 Turn right onto Ledford Branch Road. Tread is hardpacked gravel doubletrack.

2.6 Turn sharply left back onto Ingles Field Gap (IFG) Trail (signed). This first section of climbing is brutally steep, running up over several big whoop-dee-doos. **Warning:** Watch for riders coming down this trail, as they'll have little chance to slow down before flattening you.

3.1 Hit a tiny clearing with a small wooden bench. You can say a prayer of thanks to the builder as you rest here. Following track teases with some flats through an old clearcut, then starts climbing again.

3.9 Continue straight and continue climbing. Branch left is the signed IFG Connector down to Sidehill.

Betty Heinous Loop

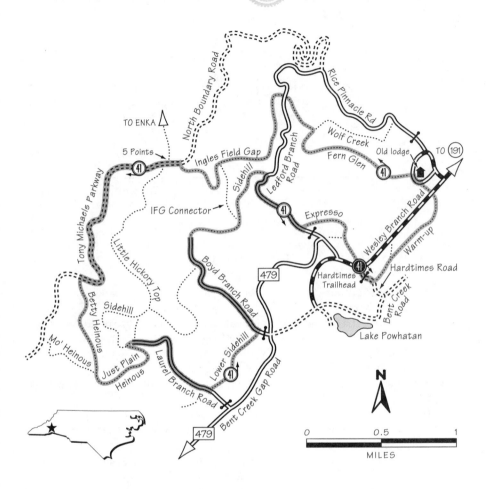

4.3 Again, continue straight past this left branch (another connector to Sidehill, this one unnamed and unsigned). The next climb is again brutally steep, but it's very smooth, and—more important—it's the last one.

4.5 Finally reach 5 Points. After a long rest and a search for your missing lung, saddle back up and bear left onto the unsigned doubletrack, which is known as the Tony Michaels Parkway. Do not take the immediate left onto Little Hickory Top, and whatever you do don't take the unsigned singletrack straight ahead, which is the lost trail to Enka. It'll be a long ride home if you do.

5.1 Pass through a gap and enter a really bad poison ivy field. Trail gets rockier and more eroded, always climbing a slight grade.

5.9 Turn left at the entrance to Betty Heinous. This turn is usually marked with a small cairn of stones. Initial drop is very steep, with a tech 2.5 covering of loose chicken heads. Serious speed here carries you abruptly into a sharp right turn at the bottom, so pay attention.

6.2 A little flat contour running and even a dash of uphill. But don't fret, because the bottom is just about to drop out.

6.3 Fast, steep contour running through some tech 3 rock fields and an extremely sketchy tech 4 erosion gully. You won't be able to stop in time for the gully, so just try to bounce from one side to the other and hop over the cracks.

6.9 Mo' Heinous peels in from the right, though you probably didn't see it. Now Just Plain Heinous takes over with crazy speed (30+ miles per hour) over some tech 3+ rocks and a number of big water bars. You'll be getting air whether you want it or not, so just relax and hold on.

7.7 Watch for a big stinky mudhole filled with rocks that lurks on this inside corner. It's a serious faceplant waiting to happen.

7.8 Turn right at this four-way intersection onto Laurel Branch Road (gravel). Watch your speed on the run-out from here, 'cause you'll still be high on adrenaline and the gravel is really loose.

8.2 Sharp left turn back onto Lower Sidehill Trail (signed). Trail climbs a bit, tops out in a little meadow, then descends over a bone-jarring series of water bars and root drops into a tight, twisty rhodo tunnel.

9.3 Turn left as Lower Sidehill dead-ends onto Boyd Branch Road (gravel). Follow Boyd Branch to the end.

10.3 As Boyd Branch Road ends, continue straight onto the entrance for Sidehill Trail (signed). Climbing Sidehill this direction is a test of grit and handling skills, as you slowly grind your way up the slope, dodging loose baby heads and downhill-bound riders.

10.8 Finally top a rise and hit intersection with the IFG Connector Trail. Take the second left to continue on Sidehill. This run down Sidehill is fast and sweet, a smooth tech 2 run with a huge 3-foot berm on one inside corner for some serious screaming fun. IFG Connector cuts sharply back left and starts climbing.

11.5 Sidehill drops you out onto Ledford Branch Road (gravel). Turn right to descend back to the trailhead.

12.4 Just before you hit the gate at the end of Ledford Branch, turn left onto a short section of singletrack, which is a spur off Expresso.

12.6 Bear left at the Y to continue on Expresso and return to the trailhead. Watch for a tech 3 pyramid and some dicey tech 3 rocks just before you drop down to the hardtop.

12.8 Trail drops you out onto Wesley Branch Road, just across from Hardtimes Trailhead.

Into the big woods. DAVID TOLLERTON PHOTO

Explorer

Location: Bent Creek Research Forest, 20 minutes south of Asheville.

Distance: 8.7 miles.

Time: 45 minutes to 1.5 hours.

Tread: 4.9 miles of singletrack; 0.6 mile of gravel road; 3.2 miles of doubletrack.

Aerobic level: Easy to moderate. The hills are sometimes a little long and sometimes a little steep. Ridable by almost everyone, but even advanced riders will stand once or twice.

Technical difficulty: Overall, tech 2+. Lots of easy contour cruising both up and down with some respectable water bars and a few hungry rocks to avoid.

Highlights: Excellent 2-mile downhill; stream crossing; water bars; rhododendron tunnel.

Land status: Experimental forest, USDA.

Maps: USGS Dunsmore Mountain; USDA Forest Service Pisgah District Trail Map; National Geographic Trails Illustrated Pisgah Ranger District.

Access: From Asheville, take Interstate 26 East (south) to North Carolina Highway 191 South. Go about 2 miles, then turn right at the light onto Bent Creek Ranch Road (from here, you'll just follow the signs for Lake Powhatan). This road soon runs into a development and branches; bear left onto Wesley Branch Road. Go roughly 1 mile and look for the North Carolina Arboretum on your left. Enter the gates, hang an immediate right, and follow this paved road around to the greenhouse parking lot. By the way, the greenhouse is usually open for visitors and has clean restrooms, a hose, and a water cooler. Just be considerate and don't track lots of crud in after your ride.

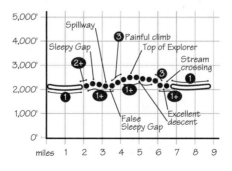

Explorer

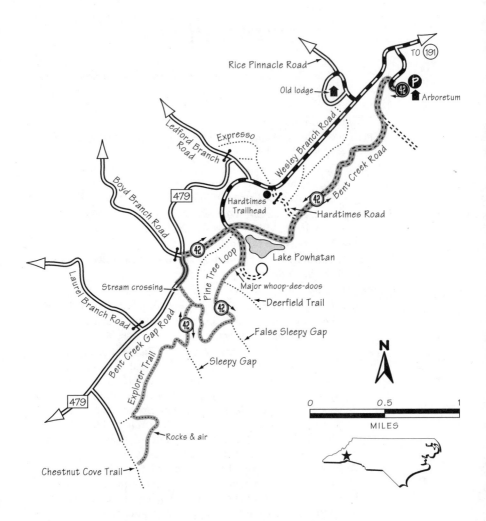

Rice Pinnacle Road

TO (191)

Old lodge

(42) (P)

Arboretum

Ledford Branch Road

Expresso

Wesley Branch Road

Bent Creek Road

Boyd Branch Road

479

Hardtimes Trailhead

(42)

Hardtimes Road

(42)

Lake Powhatan

Laurel Branch Road

Stream crossing

Pine Tree Loop

Major whoop-dee-doos

Deerfield Trail

(42)

Bent Creek Gap Road

Explorer Trail

(42)

False Sleepy Gap

Sleepy Gap

479

Rocks & air

Chestnut Cove Trail

N

0   0.5   1

MILES

Notes on the trail

Another fine intermediate ride from Bent Creek's tamer south side. Explorer is a perfect choice for introducing someone to the exquisite pleasure of zooming downhill (someone you like and want to enjoy the ride, that is. Otherwise, ship 'em off to Mo' Heinous). It doesn't require too much effort to gain the top, then you get a gorgeous run back down that could vary from mild to wild, depending on your speed and aeronautics. A stream crossing at the bottom is the perfect way to end the run before an easy return trip back to the arboretum. This is an excellent ride overall if you just want to spin for an hour and still get a little downhill time in.

Note that Explorer is a seasonal trail and is only open to mountain biking from October 15 through March 15.

The Ride

0.0 Head back out from the arboretum parking lot and look for a gravel path on the left (it's only 50 feet or so). Then hang another immediate left onto Wolf Branch Road, a gated gravel doubletrack.

0.2 Turn right onto Bent Creek Road (gated gravel doubletrack). Use small pedestrian door set beside large vehicle gate to get through the arboretum fence.

1.0 Bear left at the Y to continue on Bent Creek Road.

1.2 Continue straight on Bent Creek Road, past the water treatment, up over the curb, and past Lake Powhatan on your left.

1.6 Turn left onto paved campground road. Surface immediately changes to gravel, and you cross a small stone bridge. Just past bridge, continue straight past the first entrance to Pine Tree Loop.

1.8 Now turn right onto the second Pine Tree Loop entrance, which is clearly signed. Trail starts off as a rocky tech 2 + singletrack and immediately begins climbing up over a long set of monster water bars (see Pine Tree Loop, Ride 43, for a chance to come down these puppies).

2.1 Go straight on Pine Tree, past the left for Deerfield Trail. Flat, easy contour climbing.

2.4 Continue straight past the sign for Sleepy Gap Trail (actually, another trail at the other end is signed Sleepy Gap as well, with no connection between the two). After the gap, you'll roll into a fine buffed downhill old doubletrack that has faded to singletrack in most spots. It's fast and polished with several smooth water bars that can convince even first-timers to reach for a little air. Pretty much a tech 1 + run with a few eroded spots in the middle.

3.0 Turn left onto the signed connector trail to Explorer. Trail wanders up through a gorgeous green meadow.

3.1 Turn left again as you intersect Explorer Loop Trail.

3.3 Trail crosses a concrete spillway. Yellow blazes on the trees.

3.5 Continue straight past another signed left for Sleepy Gap Trail. (See? What's up with that?)

4.1 Sharp turn left uphill to continue on Explorer Trail. Brutal, steep climb, lots of rocks and roots, tech 3. Track straight goes to unnamed gravel road leading to Bent Creek Gap Road.

4.4 Once the painful stuff stops, you get rewarded with some easy, tech 1 + contour climbing.

4.7 Here's the turn-around spot, as Explorer dead-ends into Chestnut Cove Trail (hiking only). The return run back down Explorer starts off building speed quickly and easily, until you suddenly realize you're just *cranking* through the woods. Then, just after your confidence settles in and you start to kick back, the bottom drops out and the rocks pop up, and you find yourself wrestling an angry, bucking bicycle down the trail. Just hang on and enjoy the ride.

5.9 Straight past the turn for Sleepy Gap Trail. Zip across the concrete causeway.

6.3 Hammer on past the connector trail. Now you gets lots of small but sweet root drops, a rhododendron tunnel, and some big mud.

6.6 Zoom through a wide tech 1 + stream crossing for an excellent cool-down as you catch your breath. Trail after stream forks with both choices leading up to Bent Creek Gap Road. One fork gradually climbs to a gate, and the other claws its way straight up the side of a big embankment to reach the road.

6.7 Turn right onto Bent Creek Gap Road (gravel; open to traffic).

7.1 Turn right, across from the gated entrance to Boyd Branch Road. Cross a few humps, and find yourself on smooth tech 1 doubletrack.

7.5 Cross Lake Powhatan Road (paved) and continue straight on dirt/gravel doubletrack past Lake Powhatan. Keep going straight, up over the curb, and down past the water treatment plant.

7.7 Bear right at the Y to continue on gravel doubletrack (Bent Creek Road).

8.5 Go through the door in the arboretum fence, then immediately turn left onto Wolf Branch Road.

8.7 Turn right onto the short gravel path that leads you back to the arboretum parking lot.

Pine Tree Loop

Location: Bent Creek Research Forest, 20 minutes south of Asheville.

Distance: 5.4-mile loop.

Time: 30 minutes to 1 hour.

Tread: 2 miles of singletrack; 3.4 miles of gravel Forest Service road.

Aerobic level: Easy. One of the flattest rides in Pisgah that still offers you some singletrack.

Technical difficulty: Tech 1+ if ridden clockwise and pushed up the climb. Tech 3 if ridden counterclockwise and bombed down the rocky descent and water bars. Several tech 3+ root moves scattered throughout will have novices and some intermediates wisely choosing to dismount.

Highlights: Excellent introductory or warm-up trail; fun swooping track through beautiful rhododendron tunnels; choice of fast and fun or fast and furious downhill.

Land status: Experimental forest, USDA.

Maps: USGS Dunsmore Mountain; USDA Forest Service Pisgah District Trail Map; National Geographic Trails Illustrated Pisgah Ranger District.

Access: From Asheville, take Interstate 26 East (south) to North Carolina Highway 191 South. Go about 2 miles, then turn right at the light onto Bent Creek Ranch Road (from here, you'll just follow the signs for Lake Powhatan). This road soon runs into a development and branches; bear left onto Wesley Branch Road. Go roughly 1 mile and look for the North Carolina Arboretum on your left. Enter the gates, hang an immediate right, and follow this paved road around to the greenhouse parking lot. By the way, the greenhouse is usually open for visitors and has clean restrooms, a hose, and a water cooler. Just be considerate and don't track lots of crud in after your ride.

Notes on the trail

I'd consider this trail the perfect sampler for a novice rider who has bellied up to Pisgah's fat tire feast for the first time. Pine Tree offers up enough fun to get friends hooked on riding, and enough scary stuff to keep them humble. It also makes a fine appetizer for advanced riders before moving on to the main course in the mountains above.

Pine Tree can be a bit two-faced. Ridden clockwise, the trail starts with a steep rocky climb that will have you out of the saddle one way or the other. Then, like a transformed ugly duckling, it melts into a long, swooping descent that runs over some gentle humps before returning to the flatter track below. Riding Pine Tree counterclockwise though, shows a bit of its darker face. While the climb to False Sleepy Gap is a piece of cake, the descent (particularly at speed) can get a bit ugly, with roots and rocks setting up unexpected ambushes. Directions are given for the counterclockwise trip only.

The Ride

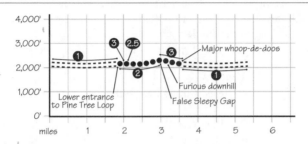

0.0 Heading back out from the arboretum parking lot, look for a gravel path on the left (it's only 50 feet or so). Then hang another immediate left onto Wolf Branch Road, a gated gravel road.

0.2 Turn right onto Bent Creek Road (gravel). Use small pedestrian door set beside large vehicle gate to get through the arboretum fence.

1.0 Bear left at the Y to continue on Bent Creek Road.

1.2 Continue straight on Bent Creek Road, past the water treatment and Lake Powhatan on left.

1.6 Turn left at the intersection with paved campground road. Surface changes to gravel and crosses a small stone bridge. Then make an immediate right onto Pine Tree Loop. The lower entrance is clearly signed.

2.0 Trail parallels the road; tight slipping and dipping through a beautiful rhododendron tunnel. Tunnel is laced with some difficult roots in spots with at least one tech 3 move along the way.

2.2 Tech 2+ stream crossing with roots lacing the far bank.

2.4 Pass through a small grassy meadow with a beautiful ribbon of singletrack snaking across it. Continue straight up Pine Tree Loop and begin some easy climbing. Branch right is a connector trail that leads to Explorer Loop Trail.

2.8 Big sweeping climb up to left will leave even some intermediates pushing. Some more easier climbing, then the trail flattens out.

3.0 Continue straight past sign for Sleepy Gap. Following downhill is fast and treacherous, with small rooty drops, respectable rocks, washouts, and some big whoop-dee-doos. Call it a tech 3 descent. (Note: The Sleepy Gap sign is incorrect. The true Sleepy Gap Trail breaks off from Explorer Loop and

Pine Tree Loop

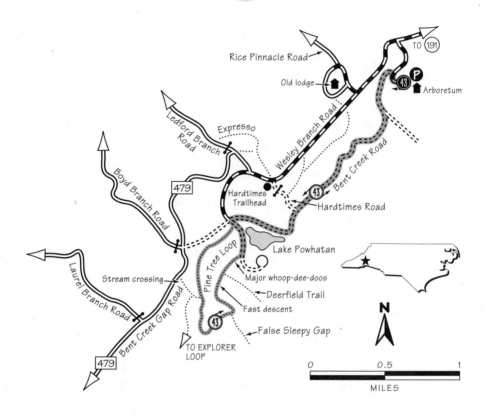

continues up past South Ridge Road to the Blue Ridge Parkway. Locals call this trail False Sleepy Gap.)

3.3 Intersection with Deerfield Trail; continue straight on Pine Tree Loop. Beware of major whoop-dee-doos on steep return to the road.

3.6 Turn left as trail feeds out onto the same gravel road you came in on.

3.8 Pass the lower entrance to Pine Tree. As gravel turns into pavement, make an immediate right back onto Bent Creek Road (gravel).

4.2 Continue straight on Bent Creek Road, past the water treatment plant and Lake Powhatan.

4.4 Bear right at the Y to continue on Bent Creek Road.

5.2 Go through the door in the arboretum fence, then immediately turn left onto Wolf Branch Road.

5.4 Turn right onto the short gravel path that leads you back to the arboretum parking lot.

Lower Sidehill

Location: Bent Creek Research Forest, 20 minutes south of Asheville.

Distance: 8.2 miles.

Time: 1 to 1.5 hours.

Tread: 5.1 miles of tasty singletrack; 2 miles of doubletrack; 1.1 miles of gravel road.

Aerobic level: Moderate. The initial climb onto Lower Sidehill is brutal, particularly after the painful grinder to get there. After that though, it's almost all downhill.

Technical difficulty: Tech 3 overall. The entry runs on Pine Tree and Explorer aren't too technical, but Lower Sidehill offers a tech 3+ climb and a long rock-spiked descent that rates a 4 for sheer pounding.

Highlights: Sweet contour running; crazy hairball descent; mud; lots of rocks; beautiful coves.

Land status: Research and demonstration forest.

Maps: USGS Dunsmore Mountain; USDA Forest Service Pisgah District Trail Map; National Geographic Trails Illustrated Pisgah Ranger District.

Access: From Asheville, take Interstate 26 East (south) to North Carolina Highway 191 South. Go about 2 miles, then turn right at the light onto Bent Creek Ranch Road (from here, you'll just follow the signs for Lake Powhatan). This road soon runs into a development and branches; bear left onto Wesley Branch Road. Go another 2 miles and look for the Hardtimes Trailhead sign on your left along with a dirt parking area. Get out, get geared up, and get ready to ride.

Notes on the trail

Get ready for a preeminent ride with an easy singletrack warm-up, one big dose of pain on the way up, then nothing but fun for the rest of the ride. This is one of the most enjoyable descents in Bent Creek (if you like it rocky, that is) and certainly the most underridden. Seems like most riders don't want to venture up the road that far. Believe me though, their loss is your gain. Once you get past the bone-breaking entrance climb, Lower Sidehill offers more than 2.5 miles of almost pure descending. It's sketchy, fast, and unpredictable, just like a good trail should be.

Note that the Pine Tree and Explorer Trails, which are used as part of this ride, are seasonal trails and are open to bikes only from October 15 through March 15. During off-season you'll have to either ride Bent Creek Gap Road all the way up to the Lower Sidehill entrance or find someone to shuttle you (a lazy but awfully tempting alternative).

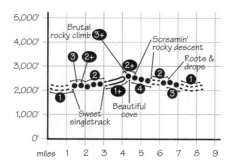

The Ride

0.0 Start from Hardtimes Trailhead. Go past gate at bottom of parking area onto Hardtimes Road (doubletrack).

0.2 Turn back right at the Y onto Bent Creek Road (gated doubletrack).

0.4 Continue straight on Bent Creek Road, past the water treatment plant and Lake Powhatan on left.

0.8 Intersection with paved campground road. Turn left; surface changes to gravel and crosses a small stone bridge. Take an immediate right onto Pine Tree Loop. This lower entrance is clearly signed.

1.2 Trail parallels the road; tight slipping and dipping through a beautiful rhododendron tunnel. Tunnel is laced with some difficult roots in spots with at least one tech 3 move along the way.

1.4 Tech 2+ stream crossing with roots lacing the far bank.

1.6 Pass through a small grassy meadow, then turn right onto the connector trail to Explorer Loop Trail.

1.7 Turn right again at T with Explorer Loop. Now you get lots of small but sweet root drops, a rhododendron tunnel, and some big mud.

2.0 Zoom through a wide tech 1+ stream crossing. Immediately after, turn left up into the rhododendron thickets to follow the lower section of Explorer Loop. A painful tech 2+ climb awaits, then lots of smooth contouring.

3.0 Turn right as trail dead-ends into an unnamed gated gravel road.

3.1 Cross gated bridge (or take the stream option), then turn left onto Bent Creek Gap Road (gravel; open to traffic). Now for a bit of unpleasantness: a long gravel road climb that gets steeper as it goes.

4.1 Turn right onto the signed entrance for Lower Sidehill (notice the "Most Difficult" sign). Turn is just past a gated road on the left. Good news is you get to leave the road. Bad news: The climbing gets a whole lot uglier. Long, excruciating tech 3+ rocky climb. Not especially steep, but it's a killer all the same; just wait and see.

Lower Sidehill

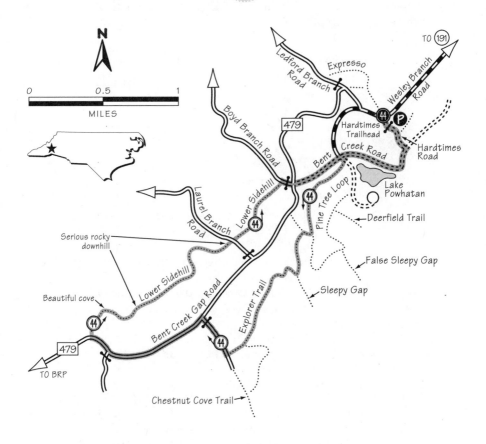

4.3 Turn right again out of the rocks by another sign for Lower Sidehill. Sweet, tech 2+ singletrack takes over for a bit.

4.5 Exceptionally cool track hangs along the side of a steep slope with log underpinnings beneath the curves. One of the most beautiful sections of singletrack you'll ever see anywhere. Track gradually picks up speed along some downhill contouring.

4.8 Now the Lower Sidehill shows you its ugly side. The bottom just drops out, and you're making a double black diamond run down through serious rocks and drops, often running along only 8 inches from a long drop off the side. Call it a tech 4 if you run it at warp speed.

5.7 Continue straight past unmarked connector trail (excellent side trip for anyone who loves big water bars).

5.8 Bust through a major set of mudholes, then turn right as trail T's into Laurel Branch Road (gated; gravel). In less than 50 yards watch for sharp left back onto signed continuation of Lower Sidehill. Trail climbs a bit, tops out in a little meadow, then descends over a bone-jarring series of water bars and root drops into a tight, twisty rhododendron tunnel.

6.9 Turn right as Lower Sidehill dead ends onto Boyd Branch Road (gated; gravel). Go straight past the big rocks and the gate at the end of Boyd Branch, cross Bent Creek Gap Road (gravel; open to traffic) and pick up dirt doubletrack (Bent Creek Road) on the other side.

7.4 Cross Lake Powhatan Road (paved), and continue straight on dirt/gravel doubletrack past Lake Powhatan and water treatment plant.

8.0 Turn left onto Hardtimes Road (doubletrack).

8.2 Pass gate and return to Hardtimes Trailhead.

Ned grinding up Lower Sidehill trail.

Trace Ridge

Location: Pisgah National Forest, Trace Ridge Trailhead area; 25 minutes south of Asheville.

Distance: 7.2-mile loop.

Time: 1 to 2 hours.

Tread: 4.5 miles of singletrack; 2.7 miles of gravel road.

Aerobic level: Moderate. The climb up Forest Road 5000 seems to go on forever and is a real grinder near the top. Spencer Gap gets steep in spots but throws in plenty of flat contouring for a chance to catch your breath.

Technical difficulty: Tech 3 overall. The gravel roads are tech 1, and Spencer Gap averages about tech 2+. The run back down Trace Ridge hits tech 3+ for most of the descent with lots of loose baby heads and chicken heads and numerous eroded lines. Be aware that the extreme speed you'll experience dropping Trace Ridge can push the technical requirements up a notch or two and means that busting will carry some severe penalties.

Highlights: Screaming descent; beautiful contour running; huge whoop-dee-doos.

Land status: Pisgah National Forest.

Maps: USGS Dunsmore Mountain; USDA Forest Service Pisgah District Trail Map; National Geographic Trails Illustrated Pisgah Ranger District.

Access: From Asheville, take Interstate 26 East (south) to North Carolina Highway 280 South. After about 5 miles, watch for a right on to North Mills River Road. Just before the entrance to North Mills River Campground, turn right onto FR 5000. After about 2 miles, look for FR 142 on the left; you'll know you're okay if you drive over a small concrete spillway. Trace Ridge Trailhead and parking area are at the end of the road.

Notes on the trail

Trace Ridge is one of the must-do classic descents in Pisgah National Forest. It's the kind of run that can shock you, rock you, melt your brakes, and leave you with scars to remember it by. The climb up to Spencer Gap is painful at times but well worth the payback. And the drop will simply

take your breath away with scary amounts of speed over loose rocks, following tracks that twist, disappear, and skirt the edges of eroded, rocky
disaster areas. Keep your eyes glued to the line, don't look at the nasty
stuff, and just hang on. It's great fun, if you like your riding loose and
crazy. Oh, and pay proper respect to the five (used to be three, but they've
multiplied) huge whoop-dee-doos at the end of Trace; they're known to
exact a high toll in broken bones and shattered weekends from those who
take them too lightly.

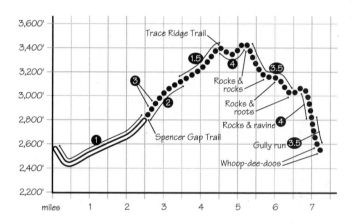

The Ride

0.0 From the Trace Ridge Trailhead, ride back down FR 142 and across the concrete
causeway.

0.5 Turn left onto FR 5000 and start a long gradual climb. The road is narrow and
windy, and the locals are known to blast down it, so keep an eye out and be
ready to dive for the ditch.

2.3 Continue straight past a gated road down to the left. This is *not* the entrance to
Spencer Gap, and if you take it, you'll be lost for days, believe me. FR 5000
starts to steepen, and you start to wonder if the descent will be worth it. It is,
so just keep spinning.

2.7 Turn left, just as the road makes an inside curve, onto Spencer Gap Trail (sign
exists, but it's planted way back in there). First real trail payment, in the form
of a rocky, tech 2+ climb.

2.9 Turn right to follow the rocky singletrack. Old doubletrack continues straight
into a grassy field.

3.0 Turn right again, as trail runs up a steep rocky bank and into a small meadow.
Track crosses meadow, then hits you with some tech 3 rocks and roots as you
reenter the woods.

3.5 Flat tech 1+ contour running.

3.9 Wind your way through some huge boulders, and cross a small rocky stream
as trail bends through an inside corner.

Trace Ridge

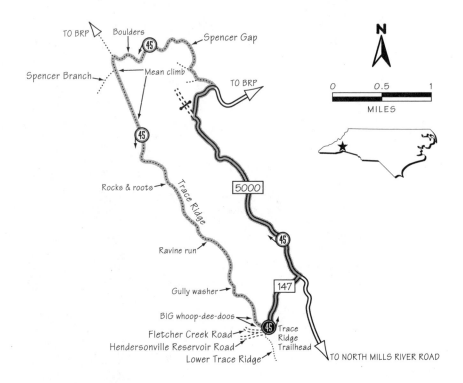

TO BRP
Boulders
45
Spencer Gap

Spencer Branch
Mean climb
TO BRP

N

0   0.5   1
MILES

45

Rocks & roots
Trace Ridge
5000

Ravine run

Gully washer
147

BIG whoop-dee-doos
Fletcher Creek Road
Hendersonville Reservoir Road
Lower Trace Ridge
45
Trace
Ridge
Trailhead
TO NORTH MILLS RIVER ROAD

4.6 Turn left at this T, onto Trace Ridge; trail is clearly signed. You get a short drop, pass the sign for Spencer Branch Trail 50 feet down on the right, then your final payment: a mean, heart-breaking, rock-filled climb that ranks a tech 4 to clean the whole mess.

4.9 Hit the top of the ridge, and now it's time for payback. Trail drops quickly, and before you're ready, you're sailing at speed down a treacherous rocky track. Some hops along the way, though the landing zones are very sketchy.

5.8 Trail flattens for a bit, rolling through a rhododendron thicket. Catch a quick breath, then dive back in for more warp speed running over more tech 3+ terrain, this time with some roots thrown into the mix. Remember that sometimes you've just got to ride over whatever's in front of you.

6.3 Short flat along a finger, then dropping again. Trail feeds into a shallow ravine, which may also be a stream depending on weather conditions. Dicey tech 4 run over loose, clattering rocks.

7.1 Short climb, then the last drop. Track skirts the edge of a steep gully. Hold the right line near the trees or face sliding into the gully's belly, which is a place you don't want to be.

7.4 At the end of Trace Ridge, like silent guardians, sit five massive whoop-dee-doos, ready to defend the trail's honor against any riders foolish enough not to be humbled. This spot is notorious for claiming victims, so pay proper respect or be able to handle 10 to 15 feet of air, five times over. Return to earth and slide back into the Trace Ridge Trailhead. Don't be ashamed of your wide eyes or shaking limbs—anyone down ahead of you will understand.

Looking down onto Trace Ridge.

Wash Creek

Location: Pisgah National Forest, Trace Ridge Trailhead area; 25 minutes south of Asheville.

Distance: 1.8-mile loop.

Time: 10 to 20 minutes.

Tread: 1.4 miles of singletrack; 0.4 mile of gravel road.

Aerobic level: Easy. Ride seems almost all downhill. You'll just break a sweat as you return to the trailhead.

Technical difficulty: Tech 1+. Probably the easiest true singletrack that Pisgah has to offer. Very buff, though initial descent after turning onto Wash Creek may be a little scary for first-timers.

Highlights: Roller-coaster contour running; forest tunnels; easy return.

Land status: Pisgah National Forest.

Maps: USGS Dunsmore Mountain; USDA Forest Service Pisgah District Trail Map; National Geographic Trails Illustrated Pisgah Ranger District.

Access: From Asheville, take Interstate 26 East (south) to North Carolina Highway 280 South. After about 5 miles, turn right onto North Mills River Road. Just before the entrance to North Mills River Campground, turn right onto Forest Road 5000. After about 2 miles, look for FR 142 on the left; you'll know you're okay if you drive over a small concrete spillway. Trace Ridge Trailhead and parking area are at end of the road.

Notes on the trail

This trail is a perfect warm-up—or cool-down—for any of the other trails off the Trace Ridge Trailhead. Fun, frisky, a good chance to stretch your legs a little to get the blood flowing. And most folks will tell you that this trail violates some law of physics, because it's a loop that's all downhill.

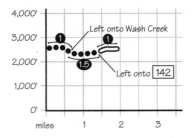

Wash Creek

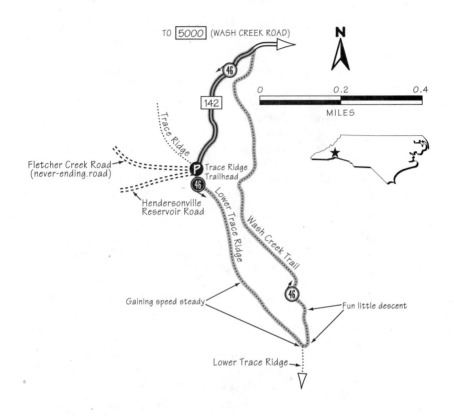

TO 5000 (WASH CREEK ROAD)

46

142

N

0   0.2   0.4

MILES

Trace Ridge

Fletcher Creek Road
(never-ending.road)

P Trace Ridge
Trailhead

46

Hendersonville
Reservoir Road

Lower Trace Ridge

Wash Creek Trail

Gaining speed steady

46

Fun little descent

Lower Trace Ridge

The Ride

0.0 Enter just to the left of the information station onto Lower Trace Ridge. Tread starts off as wide hardpacked clay and pine-needle surface—singletrack XXL.

0.2 Trail begins to narrow and drop, gaining speed and a certain zippy quality that will bring a smile to the face of any rider.

0.5 Take a sharp left back onto Wash Creek Trail. Brown Forest Service sign is broken off at knee height. Keep an eye out for this one, 'cause it's easy to miss, and you'll be sorry if you follow Lower Trace out. Wash creek starts a little steep, but it's easy and fun and smooth as can be. Tech 1+, slight downhill contour cruising through the hemlocks.

0.8 Old road to left. Continue straight on Wash Creek.

1.1 Little ups, little downs, slipping through a dark forest.

1.4 Turn left onto FR 142 (gravel road). Watch for cars.

1.8 Return to Trace Ridge Trailhead.

Little Pisgah Ridge (Big Creek)

Location: Pisgah National Forest; Trace Ridge Trailhead area; 25 minutes south of Asheville.

Distance: 6.6 miles one way.

Time: 45 minutes to 2 hours, depending on your level of speed or foolishness.

Tread: 4.6 miles of primo, hardpacked forest singletrack; 1.8 miles of Forest Service road.

Aerobic level: Moderate. You could actually coast down most of this trail, but the fear and adrenaline factor will wipe you out way more than you'd expect. The high-speed descents will force several stops just to let your forearms rest.

Technical difficulty: Tech 4 overall. The contour running is insanely fast. Several tech 4 switchbacks, rocks, and root crossings. High-speed, off-camber turns with little (sometimes no) margin for error. Stream crossings ranging from tech 3 to tech 5. If you could go really slow, this trail would drop back to a tech 2+ in many stretches, but it's just not an option.

Highlights: Incredibly fast downhill singletrack; major rock/root moves; multiple stream crossing; logs; reservoir; serious adrenaline run.

Land status: Pisgah National Forest.

Maps: USGS Pisgah Forest; USDA Forest Service Pisgah District Trail Map; National Geographic Trails Illustrated Pisgah Ranger District.

Access: Since this is a one-way ride, you'll need to drop off a car at the Trace Ridge Trailhead or con some poor soul into ferrying you to the top and missing out on the ride of the day! Note that I do not recommend riding this trail alone because the chance of someone discovering your sorry mangled body 80 feet down in some cove before the raccoons start gnawing on you is pretty slim.

From Asheville, take Interstate 26 East (south) to North Carolina Highway 280 South. After about 5 miles, turn right on North Mills River Road. Just before the entrance to North Mills River Campground, turn right onto Forest Road 5000. After about 2 miles, look for FR 142 on the left; you'll know you're okay if you drive over a small concrete spillway. Trace Ridge Trailhead and parking area are at the end of road. Leave one vehicle here.

From Trace Ridge Trailhead, take FR 142 back out to FR 5000. Turn left onto FR 5000 and follow it all the way up to the Blue Ridge Parkway. Turn left (south) on the Blue Ridge Parkway, go about 10 miles, and watch for the Little Pisgah Ridge Tunnel (*not* the Young Pisgah Ridge Tunnel). Go through the tunnel, then hang an immediate left onto a small, dirt service road that doubles back around the outside of the tunnel. Proceed to the end of a short road, park, and look for a faint trail through bushes, over rock piles, and up a 6-foot rooty embankment. *Carry* bikes approximately 0.2 mile along the trail through a twisty rhododendron tunnel and down stairs to the trail marker. From this point downward, the trail is legal to ride. Please obey trail signs and carry to this point.

Notes on the trail

Dropping 1,800 feet in 2 miles insists that there'll be insane amounts of speed over some awfully scary terrain, regardless of your personal level of comfort. This is, quite simply, a downhill by which all others should be measured. After hiking 0.2 mile off the Blue Ridge Parkway to get to the bike-legal track, you'll find 2 miles of solid, sick, crazy speed over steep contour runs, lots of it incredibly buff with some extremely nice berms tossed in here and there. Washouts, off-camber turns laced with snaky roots, and short rocky patches generally come up too quick to be scared over (which is probably the safest way to handle it). In some areas, a 1-inch mistake is going to send you bouncing off trees down a 60-degree drop for 100 feet, so be careful. A flatter, streamside track offers a chance to pedal for a change, rather than just hang on and pray, with lots of wood, stone, and water obstacles. Some extremely hairy stream crossings for those emboldened to idiocy by the downhill. Ugly surprise drop at mile 4.5 requires total commitment and health insurance. Easy ride out gives you time to quit shaking before you get back to the car.

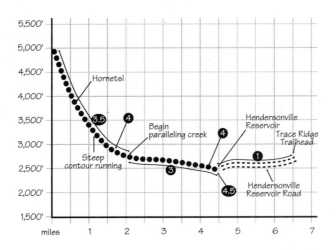

Little Pisgah Ridge (Big Creek)

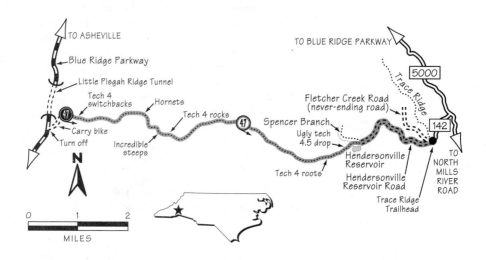

The Ride

0.0 Start riding at sign for Big Creek Trail. Notice the "Most Difficult" rating, and keep it in mind when you start to get too cocky later. Remember to carry bikes from car to here; it's not far and will guarantee that the rest of the trail stays open to us.

0.3 Fairly smooth track, gradually faster and faster, much cleaner track than expected. Several tech 4 switchbacks.

0.5 Contour running gets fast, then faster, then insane. Hands and feet begin cramping at this point from high-speed pounding and instinctive desire to slow down. Some logs and fast rock sections.

0.7 Large downed tree crossing trail forces portage. **Caution:** The base of this tree is inhabited by big, fat, ill-tempered hornets, who *do not* grant the right-of-way. Give it a wide berth, or sneak underneath real quick and pray they go for your buddy behind you.

1.0 Beautiful contour running. Fast through the rhododendron thickets. Watch for unexpected water bars.

1.2 Steep! Steep! Steep! Fastest contour running you've ever seen, stuck somewhere between a dream and a nightmare. Big berms and extremely tight switchbacks. Here the world is just kick-ass fast, no way around it. Simply an amazing downhill run.

1.5 Serious tech 4 washout/rock crossing at speed. Sudden off-camber left turn filled with chicken heads and bordered by a respectable drop, for serious damage potential. Brakes could be the death of you here, causing a major slideout and a drop off the side. Either keep a heads-up and creep through it, or hold a tight inside line and pray the speed carries you through.

2.0 Trail flattens and starts to parallel Big Creek. Typical Pisgah streamside ride, always slightly downhill, allowing you to go as fast as you can pedal. Tech 3 overall. More frequent root and rock gardens. Multiple steep-sided stream crossings, some ridable, some not, with a few extremely dicey tech 4+ drops.

2.5 Nasty mudhole, deep and long, filled with old, rotten corduroy. Good place for a faceplant.

2.7 Stream crossing via a huge, 20-foot-long log. Long drop into the stream below. Not that tough of a move technically, but it carries an extremely high payment for failure.

3.2 Tasty rock garden, followed by a tech 3 stream crossing.

3.8 Long boulder head territory. Trail splits; bear uphill to left for a short hike-a-bike.

4.1 Nasty off-camber root crossing (tech 4) appears out of nowhere with a 25-foot drop on the side. Requires speed, belief, and a line on the high side to get you through. Anything less than total commitment here will leave you broken at the bottom. If you're not really sure about your skills (or aren't going way too fast to either stop or care), walk this one and save yourself a trip to the ER.

4.3 Beautiful rhododendron tunnel.

4.5 Very sudden, eroded, and rocky tech 4+ drop back to stream level. This spot is really mean, and it comes up really fast. Last opportunity for a serious bust before hitting the easy ride out.

Watch for the tunnel at Little Pisgah Ridge. DAVID TOLLERTON PHOTO

4.6 Climb up steps and cross old double-log bridge. Bear right at intersection with Spencer Branch Trail. Drop down a tough series of log steps to come out at the Old Hendersonville Reservoir. Beautiful old stone dam, nice and cool down below. Unfortunately, the lake itself looks pretty skanky and was definitely *not* inviting for a swim. From the dam, turn right and follow Hendersonville Reservoir Road back up to the Trace Ridge Trailhead.

5.1 Nice double waterfall on left.

5.8 Begin your only bit of climbing.

6.6 Pass gate; return to Trace Ridge Trailhead and second vehicle.

Fletcher Creek

Location: Pisgah National Forest, Trace Ridge Trailhead area; 25 minutes south of Asheville.

Distance: 9.4-mile loop.

Time: 1 to 2 hours.

Tread: 2.4 miles of singletrack; 7 miles of gravel Forest Service road.

Aerobic level: Easy to moderate. The climb up the Never-Ending Road is a breeze, and you can almost coast the entire upper section of Fletcher Creek. The climb after the creek crossing is slow-motion technical torture, and the drop after is no place to sit down and take it easy. The climb back up Hendersonville Reservoir Road is a grinder.

Technical difficulty: Tech 1 (upper section) to tech 3+ (lower section). Upper section of Fletcher Creek Trail is buff to the point of being polished. Lower section more than makes up for it though, with a long tech 3+ rocky descent that will have even experienced riders paying very close attention.

Highlights: Technical rocky descent; meadows; old homesite.

Land status: Pisgah National Forest.

Maps: USGS Dunsmore Mountain; USDA Forest Service Pisgah District Trail Map; National Geographic Trails Illustrated Pisgah Ranger District.

Access: From Asheville, take Interstate 26 East (south) to North Carolina Highway 280 South. After about 5 miles, watch for a right on to North Mills River Road. Just before the entrance to North Mills River Campground, turn right onto Forest Road 5000. After about 2 miles, look for FR 142 on the left; you'll know you're okay if you drive over a small concrete spillway. Trace Ridge Trailhead and parking area are at end of the road.

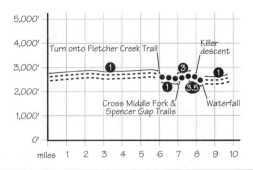

5,000'
4,000' — Turn onto Fletcher Creek Trail   Killer descent
3,000' — ❶   ❸
2,000'   ❶ ❸.❺   ❶
1,000' — Cross Middle Fork &   Waterfall
         Spencer Gap Trails
0'
miles 1 2 3 4 5 6 7 8 9 10

Notes on the trail

Fletcher Creek is a good ride for intermediates to hone their skills on. The long spin out the Never-Ending Road warms you up plenty, then gets you ready for the drop back along the singletrack. Although the upper section of Fletcher Creek starts off running smooth and easy, don't get fooled, 'cause once you cross the creek all hell breaks loose. A tough rocky climb leads into an adrenaline-inducing descent. If you like riding rocks—loose, sketchy rocks, at speed—do this trail. If you don't like rocks, bail out early off the Never-Ending Road onto Spencer Branch Trail instead, or you'll be really unhappy.

The Ride

0.0 Start at the Trace Ridge Trailhead. Enter past the right-most gate (the one next to the big humps of Trace Ridge) onto Never-Ending Road. This well-named gravel and dirt doubletrack winds on for a long, long way, and seems to go down as much as up.

The Fletcher Creek Trail leads you past the Hendersonville Reservoir.

Fletcher Creek

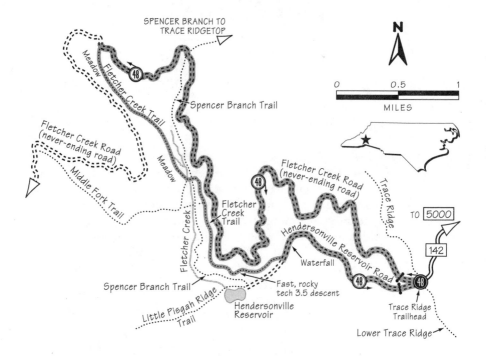

SPENCER BRANCH TO
TRACE RIDGETOP

Meadow

Fletcher Creek Trail

Spencer Branch Trail

Fletcher Creek Road
(never-ending road)

Middle Fork Trail

Meadow

Fletcher Creek Road
(never-ending road)

Fletcher
Creek
Trail

Fletcher Creek

Hendersonville Reservoir Road

Trace Ridge

N

0   0.5   1

MILES

TO 5000

142

Waterfall

Fast, rocky
tech 3.5 descent

Spencer Branch Trail

Little Pisgah Ridge Trail

Hendersonville
Reservoir

Trace Ridge
Trailhead

Lower Trace Ridge

2.7 The long, gradual climb on this section of the Never-Ending Road will have even seasoned riders grousing. Blooming dogwoods or rhododendron and some long-range views will help to distract you from the pain.

4.7 Continue straight on Never-Ending Road, past the turn for Spencer Gap Trail.

5.7 Turn left onto Fletcher Creek Trail. Easy, smooth descent rolls past several meadows and an old homesite.

6.9 Middle Fork Trail branches off to the right, but continue straight. After about 50 yards, cross Spencer Branch Trail. Continue straight on Fletcher Creek Trail, which crosses its namesake creek and clearly picks up on the other side.

7.5 Contour running, mixed with a bit of steep rocky climbing, brings you about 100 feet up above the creek. Now brace yourself for a half mile of white-knuckled descending through switchbacks, laurel thickets, bunny hops, berms, and lots and lots of rocks.

8.1 Turn left onto Hendersonville Reservoir Road.

8.4 Nice little waterfall just on the edge of the road. Singletrack drops down off the right to follow creekside for a while before joining back to the road later—always better than gravel, in my book.

9.4 Finish one long grinder of a climb, pass the gate, and return to the trailhead.

Spencer Branch

Location: Pisgah National Forest, Trace Ridge Trailhead area; 25 minutes south of Asheville.

Distance: 8.2-mile loop.

Time: 45 minutes to 1.5 hours.

Tread: 2 miles of singletrack; 6.2 miles of gravel Forest Service road.

Aerobic level: Easy to moderate. The climb up the Never-Ending Road is a breeze, and Spencer Branch descends for most of its length. Some of the technical climbs on the lower section are tiring, and the climb back up Hendersonville Reservoir Road is a grinder.

Technical difficulty: Tech 1+ overall. Singletrack is generally quite buff with light roots and a scattering of rocks. Stream crossings can be tricky, as are some of the climbs. Alternate drop down to the reservoir is a tech 4+ move down eroded water bar and stairs that will test your resolve, courage, and skills.

Highlights: Reservoir; ridable log bridge; views; tough stream crossings; sweet cruising.

Land status: Pisgah National Forest.

Maps: USGS Dunsmore Mountain; USDA Forest Service Pisgah District Trail Map; National Geographic Trails Illustrated Pisgah Ranger District.

Access: From Asheville, take Interstate 26 East (south) to North Carolina Highway 280 South. After about 5 miles, watch for a right on to North Mills River Road. Just before the entrance to North Mills River Campground, turn right onto Forest Road 5000. After about 2 miles, look for FR 142 on the left; you'll know you're okay if you drive over a small concrete spillway. Trace Ridge Trailhead and parking area are at end of road.

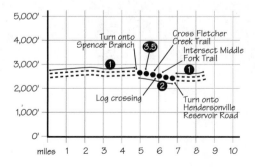

Keep your wheels straight on this bridge at Spencer Branch.

Spencer Branch

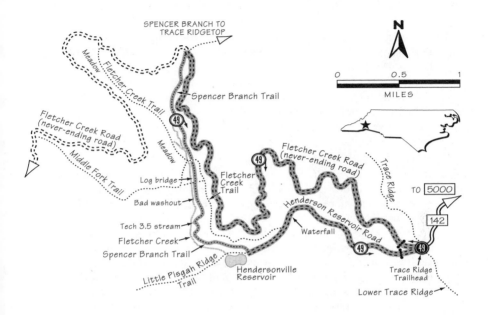

SPENCER BRANCH TO
TRACE RIDGETOP

Spencer Branch Trail

Meadow

Fletcher Creek Trail

Fletcher Creek Road
(never-ending road)

Middle Fork Trail

Meadow

Log bridge

Bad washout

Tech 3.5 stream

Fletcher Creek

Spencer Branch Trail

Fletcher
Creek
Trail

Fletcher Creek Road
(never-ending road)

Henderson Reservoir Road

Waterfall

Trace Ridge

TO 5000

142

Little Pisgah Ridge
Trail

Hendersonville
Reservoir

Trace Ridge
Trailhead

Lower Trace Ridge

N

0   0.5   1

MILES

Notes on the trail

This is a great ride for someone looking to do some spinning and have some technical fun without spending all day or working all that hard. It's also a perfect trail to give novice riders a chance to acclimate themselves to the wonders of singletrack. The Never-Ending Road is an easy up and down for a nice long warm-up, then Spencer Branch offers up a splendid lunch of buff, tech 1+ track sprinkled with some respectable technical challenges. The track can also be ridden as part of a loop linking the Fletcher Creek, Spencer Branch, and Middle Fork Trails.

The Ride

0.0 Start at the Trace Ridge Trailhead. Enter past the rightmost gate (the one next to the big humps of Trace Ridge) onto the Never-Ending Road. This well-named gravel and dirt doubletrack winds on for a long, long way and seems to go down as much as up.

2.7 The long, gradual climb on this section of Never-Ending Road will have even seasoned riders grousing. Blooming dogwoods or rhododendron and some long-range views will help to distract you from the pain.

4.7 Turn left onto Spencer Branch Trail. Brown wooden sign points the way to some prime tech 2 Pisgah singletrack: smooth, twisty, and turny with enough roots, rocks, logs, and mudholes to make it interesting.

5.1 Tech 3+ stream crossing with a tough rock/root combo on the far bank. This move earns you a bit of a break afterward with a long stretch of tech 1 singletrack cruising.

5.6 Intersection with Fletcher Creek Trail. Continue straight on Spencer Branch.

5.7 Trail turns right to cross feeder stream over a 12-inch-wide, 12-foot-long log bridge. This move is only about a tech 2, but the drop to the stream looks *really* scary. Just after the log, a signed shortcut to Middle Fork Trail peels off to the right. Continue straight on Spencer Branch, up a funky tech 3 climb, then into some fun contour running through the rhododendron.

6.2 Challenging tech 3+ section with multiple stream crossings, quick ups and downs, and snaky playgrounds of roots and rocks. Log bridge requires walking.

6.5 Big Creek Trail joins in from the right. Continue straight on Spencer Branch.

6.7 Trail splits. Spencer Branch continues up to the left for a gradual return to Hendersonville Reservoir Road. Big Creek Trail drops down to the right over a series of steep water bars, bringing you out at the old Hendersonville Reservoir. Note that these eight to ten steps combine for a tech 4+ maneuver, one that will slam you down hard and maybe toss you in the drink if you get too cocky or sloppy about it (believe me; it's not deep, but it's damned embarrassing). If you're not *really* sure, best to walk this one. (If you end up taking Spencer Branch to the end, just double back down the gravel road to get to the reservoir. I highly recommend the visit to the bottom of the dam: It's really gorgeous, and the spray is just the ticket after a hot ride. Once you've cooled off enough, start up Hendersonville Reservoir Road for the return trip to the trailhead.)

6.9 Pass the signed entrance to Spencer Branch Trail back to the left. Pass Fletcher Creek Trail marker shortly afterward. Continue straight up Hendersonville Reservoir Road.

7.2 Nice little waterfall just on the edge of the road. Singletrack drops down off the right to follow creekside for a while before joining back to the road later— always better than gravel, in my book.

8.2 Finish one long grinder of a climb, pass the gate, and return to the truck for those cold drinks you remembered to pack.

Middle Fork

Location: Pisgah National Forest, Trace Ridge Trailhead area; 25 minutes south of Asheville.

Distance: 12.1-mile loop.

Time: 1.5 to 2.5 hours.

Tread: 2.6 miles of singletrack; 9.5 miles of gravel doubletrack. Never-Ending Road is somewhat loose gravel that gets sparser and harder packed the farther you go. Middle Fork is hardpacked singletrack. Lower Fletcher Creek is often loose and rocky. Hendersonville Reservoir Road is an old Forest Service road.

Aerobic level: Easy to moderate. The Never-Ending Road provides an easy entrance for this loop. You could coast for most of the descent down Middle Fork. Climbing the lower section of Fletcher Creek is a pain though, and the climb back up Hendersonville Reservoir Road is still a grinder.

Technical difficulty: Tech 2 overall. Middle Fork is generally a smooth track, though a good bit steeper and rootier than the other drops off the Never-Ending Road. Lower section of Fletcher Creek is full of loose melon-sized rocks, running rampant over several fast eroded downhill sections.

Highlights: Long warm-up ride; fast tight singletrack; nice stream views; stream crossings; rocky downhill.

Land status: Pisgah National Forest.

Maps: USGS Dunsmore Mountain; USDA Forest Service Pisgah District Trail Map; National Geographic Trails Illustrated Pisgah Ranger District.

Access: From Asheville, take Interstate 26 East (south) to North Carolina Highway 280 South. After about 5 miles, watch for a right on to North Mills River Road. Just before the entrance to North Mills River Campground, turn right onto Forest Road 5000. After about 2 miles, look for FR 142 on the left; you'll know you're okay if you drive over a small concrete spillway. Trace Ridge Trailhead and parking area are at end of road.

Notes on the trail

If you like a long warm-up, then want to spice up things a bit, this is a good trail for you. Never-Ending Road gives you plenty of time to work the kinks out. A quick descent over small rocks and roots down Middle Fork starts to wake you up. Then the descent out on Lower Fletcher Creek will have you either walking or working all the body English you've got just to stay up-right and intact.

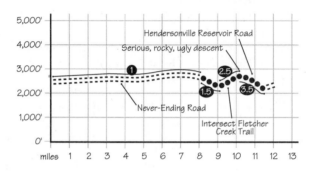

The Ride

0.0 Start at the Trace Ridge Trailhead. Enter past the rightmost gate (the one next to the big humps of Trace Ridge) onto Never-Ending Road. This well-named gravel and dirt doubletrack winds on for a long, long way and seems to go down as much as up.

4.7 Continue on Never-Ending Road. Spencer Branch Trail breaks off left and right.

5.7 Continue on Never-Ending Road. Fletcher Creek Trail breaks off down to the left.

7.9 Pretty, 6-foot waterfall on inside corner of road. Good place to cool your head.

8.2 Turn left onto Middle Fork Trail. Sweet tech 1+ trail zips along a wide little valley, dancing over lots of small root drops just perfect for hopping. Beautiful creekside running with some tech 2+ rocks and a few easy stream crossings.

9.3 Nice swimming hole in the stream down beside the trail.

9.5 Sign for shortcut down right to Spencer Branch Trail. Continue straight on Middle Fork Trail.

9.6 Turn right onto Fletcher Creek Trail and cross the creek.

10.2 Contour running, mixed with a bit of steep, rocky climbing. After topping, get ready for a frightening, or exhilarating, descent (tech 3+) over lots of loose rocks and wicked water bars.

10.8 Turn left onto Hendersonville Reservoir Road.

11.1 Nice little waterfall just on the edge of the road. Singletrack drops down off the right to follow creekside for a while before joining back to the road later— always better than gravel, in my book.

12.1 Finish one long grinder of a climb, pass the gate, and return to the trailhead.

Middle Fork

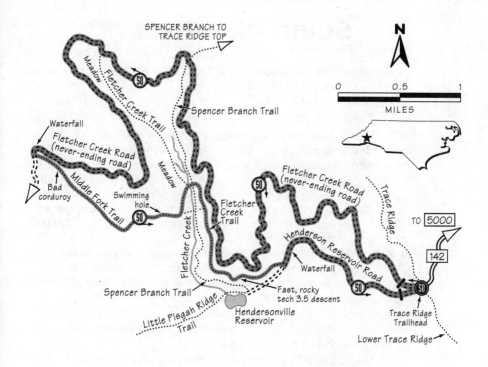

SPENCER BRANCH TO
TRACE RIDGE TOP

N

0   0.5   1
MILES

Meadow

Fletcher Creek Trail

50

Spencer Branch Trail

Waterfall

Fletcher Creek Road
(never-ending road)

Meadow

Bad
corduroy

Middle Fork Trail

Swimming
hole

50

Fletcher
Creek
Trail

Fletcher Creek Road
(never-ending road)

50

Trace Ridge

TO 5000

142

Fletcher Creek

Henderson Reservoir Road

Waterfall

50

Spencer Branch Trail

Little Pisgah Ridge Trail

Hendersonville
Reservoir

Fast, rocky
tech 3.5 descent

50

Trace Ridge
Trailhead

Lower Trace Ridge

South Mills River

Location: Pisgah National Forest, South Mills River area; 30 minutes south of Asheville.

Distance: 19.2-mile lariat.

Time: 4 to 7 hours.

Tread: 9.8 miles of singletrack; 9.4 miles of doubletrack.

Aerobic level: Strenuous. The first 5 miles or so you'll just be rolling along, singing a song. The next 4 or 5, your legs will be talking to you as you muscle through the rocks and mud. Then you get 5 miles of serious pain, both up and down hill. And finally, you crawl back up all those jumps you enjoyed on the way in. The length and severity of this trail are factors to be reckoned with.

Technical difficulty: Tech 1 to tech 4. Initial doubletrack is an easy tech 1. Later riverside running is a tech 2, with tough river crossings and mudholes. Horse's Gap and Cantrell Creek run from tech 3 to tech 4.

Highlights: River crossings; rhododendron tunnels; cliff faces; beautiful fern gardens; long, treacherous descent; lots of mud.

Land status: Pisgah National Forest.

Maps: USGS Pisgah Forest; USDA Forest Service Pisgah District Trail Map; National Geographic Trails Illustrated Pisgah Ranger District.

Access: From Asheville, take Interstate 26 East (south) to North Carolina Highway 280 South and follow it for about 8 or 9 miles. Just past the sign for Etowah (whatever that is), watch carefully for Turkey Pen Gap Road on the right. Follow this rough, single-lane gravel road all the way to the end to the Turkey Pen Gap Trailhead.

Notes on the trail

We affectionately call this loop the Bataan Death Ride; it's not especially fun, but it will test your mettle. Once fooled into believing it was a 3-hour cruise (yeah, I know, us and Gilligan), a crew of us spent the next 7 hours trying to escape from the forest's clutches. This is the kind of trail that can crush your will to live, so bring plenty of water and food, and most important, a good attitude. Smooth sections running along the river can lull you into an easy cruising frame of mind, then slap you down with some nasty rock/mudhole combinations. Then, after you're already worn down, you get a brutally steep climb and a descent that's just plain hateful. Plan to get very wet, as you've got to ford, ride, wade, or swim across the South Mills River no fewer than 14 times. Start the ride early or take a chance on spending a cold, wet night in the woods.

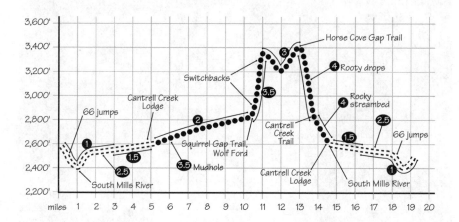

The Ride

0.0 From the Turkey Pen Gap Trailhead, go straight past the gate at the end of the parking area and onto 66 Jumps, a long, dirt and gravel doubletrack. You open the trail with a smile as you launch yourself over one perfect water bar after another, all the way to the bottom. Enjoy this trip down, because you'll be dragging by the time you come back this way. Control your speed, particularly over those bars located in corners or covered with new gravel, and watch for hikers, fishermen, horses, and other riders grinding their way back up.

1.0 Cross the South Mills River and continue straight onto the South Mills River (SMR) Trail on the other side. Tread is still gravel doubletrack with white blazes.

1.4 Bear left and down at this Y to stay on SMR and continue following white blazes. Track straight is the bottom of Mullinax.

1.5 Continue straight on SMR past a turnoff to the river. Tread gradually changes to hardpacked dirt doubletrack, tech 1+.

2.4 Pass several gorgeous campsites as trail wanders along this heavily wooded river bottom. Just continue following the white blazes, ignoring any turnoffs. Hit a respectable tech 2+ rock garden for your first taste of things to come.

2.6 Continue straight on SMR past the turn for Pounding Mill Trail (hiking only) on the right.

3.6 Trail turns left and crosses the river on a cool swinging bridge that's great fun to wobble across. Turn right after you cross the bridge and pick up SMR and the white blazes again.

Daniel table-tops in 66 Jumps on the South Mills River Trail.

South Mills River

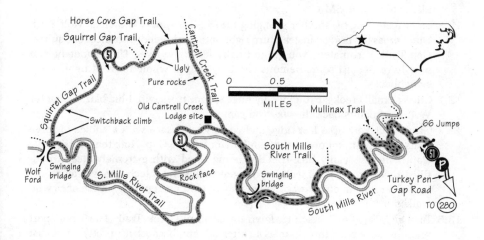

4.3 Turn right just before an old washed-out bridge and cross the river again. This one's generally ridable, but you'll still get wet.

4.7 Cross a pair of streams and enter a clearing with the remains of the old Cantrell Creek Lodge. Only the chimney of the lodge still survives; the rest (built in 1890) was moved to the Cradle of Forestry. Continue straight at the split after the lodge, staying on SMR as it changes to more of a wide singletrack. Cantrell Creek Trail cuts off to the right and is your return leg of the loop.

5.0 Bear left to continue on SMR and follow the white blazes.

5.4 Cross the river again and fight your way up the steep-sided ravine on the other side. Anyone seriously *not* enjoying themselves by this point in the ride should turn back now, 'cause it only gets worse, and dragging some waterlogged whiner another 14 miles could be grounds for a spontaneous human sacrifice.

5.5 Nasty corduroy-filled mudhole. Excellent faceplant opportunity.

5.7 Cross the river again. This crossing is deep, with big slick rocks, and can be a bit daunting to the uninitiated. No one rides across this spot without the use of pontoons.

6.0 Super mudhole, steamy, skanky, and full of hidden rocks. Keep churning and keep the front wheel light, and you'll be the only one without shoes full of goo.

6.3 Cross the river three times in very short order. Tech 3 rock sections begin to appear with more frequency.

7.7 Trail turns sharply down right and crosses the river yet again. There's a deep hole in the middle of the river, so keep an eye out for each other—you don't want to miss an opportunity to help your buddies or at least laugh at them as they go under.

8.3 Cross the river again and begin to silently curse whoever decided on this trail.

8.8 Cross the river just as the trail bends around the base of a big rock face. Ride some more, then cross the river another two or three times (we've all lost count by now; just resign yourself to it).

10.1 Bear left at this unmarked fork, crossing a small creek and following the white blazes to stay on SMR.

10.3 Enter a clearing by another swinging bridge; this spot is known as Wolf Ford. Don't cross the bridge; instead turn right onto the (signed) entrance for Squirrel Gap Trail. Fortunately, you get to finally leave the river. Unfortunately, you now have to start some heinous climbing with a whole mess of tight, steep switchbacks.

12.1 Cross a small creek surrounded by huge spruce trees with blue blazes. Sign for Wolf Ford points back the way you came.

12.7 Grind your way up a last ridge and come face to face with a choice of three trails. Bear right, following the sign for Horse Cove Gap. Note that Horse Cove Gap is *not* especially bike-friendly, being filled with extremely steep, mud-filled rooty drops. It's a tech 3+ descent with several tech 4 moves along the way. Everyone in our crew of seven took at least one endo, even the ones who walked it.

13.5 Turn right at the T, heading down on Cantrell Creek Trail. The "trail" part seems to have been thrown in as an afterthought, because it's pretty much just a dry creekbed, a continuous tech 4 assault that will pound your legs, arms, and spine into mush. Busting along here somewhere is almost a certainty.

14.1 Follow the trail as it bears up and to the left, out of the creekbed.

14.5 Return to the clearing by the old Cantrell Creek Lodge site and turn left back onto the SMR Trail. This is a good spot to share that last bit of power food you've been hoarding because you've still got nearly 5 miles, a couple of river crossings, and a mile-long climb before you get back to the trailhead.

15.6 Turn left to cross the swinging bridge again, then right to continue on SMR. Ignore any turnoffs and slog through the river when necessary to follow the trail.

17.8 Continue straight on SMR past the turn for Mullinax. Not that you'll have the energy for such foolishness at this point, but there's 20 or more beautiful water bars between here and the river that you could sail off of, had you the notion.

18.2 Cross the South Mills River one last time. Continue straight across and start the long grind back up 66 Jumps.

19.2 Drag yourself back into the Turkey Pen Gap parking area. Wait to make sure that all of your crew manages to escape as well—unless you're the ride leader, in which case start worrying about a possible lynching.

Mullinax

Location: Pisgah National Forest, South Mills River area; 30 minutes south of Asheville.

Distance: 6-mile lariat.

Time: 1.5 to 2 hours.

Tread: 3.7 miles of singletrack; 2.3 miles of doubletrack.

Aerobic level: Moderate. The singletrack climb up to Pea Gap is steep and rocky but not that long. The return climb up 66 Jumps isn't much fun, particularly with all the water bars, but it isn't a heartbreaker either.

Technical difficulty: Tech 3 overall. 66 Jumps is a wide-open tech 1 run, though it's full of smooth, 2- to 3-foot water bars, as the name implies. Pea Gap is a painful tech 3+ climb, full of loose rocks and water bars. Mullinax itself is a tech 4 descent with a few deadly tech 4 and 4.5 rooty sections and another slew of jump-ready water bars. The South Mills River Trail drops it down to tech 1+ with 20 or so more water bars.

Highlights: A hopper's paradise with more than 100 water bar–induced soaring opportunities; river crossings; technical descent; mud runs; typical Pisgah rocks and roots.

Land status: Pisgah National Forest.

Maps: USGS Pisgah Forest, USDA Forest Service Pisgah District Trail Map; National Geographic Trails Illustrated Pisgah Ranger District.

Access: From Asheville, take Interstate 26 East (south) to North Carolina Highway 280 South and follow it for about 8 or 9 miles. Just past the sign for Etowah (whatever that is), watch carefully for Turkey Pen Gap Road on the right. Follow this rough, single-lane gravel road all the way to the end to the Turkey Pen Gap Trailhead.

Notes on the trail

Do you love to jump your bike and sail through the air off smooth, rounded water bars? Do you cherish those fleeting airborne moments when gravity no longer pins you to the earth? If you answered Yes! then you absolutely, positively must ride Mullinax. In 6 miles you'll hit more than 100 smooth-lipped, knee-high water bars, most of which provide excellent opportunities

Paying for Mullinax.

for some supreme air. Of course, those riders more fond of gravity's embrace can simply roll over them for the finest roller-coaster action this side of Six Flags. But don't think this is some kiddy ride because the upper section of Mullinax is a mine field of tech 4 and 4.5 root drops and erosion gullies that can chew up even the most experienced rider.

In the midst of a scorching Carolina summer, the best part of the ride may just be zooming into the South Mills River at the end of the ride.

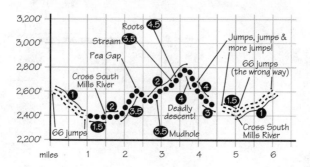

The Ride

0.0 From the Turkey Pen Gap Trailhead, go straight past the gate at the end of the parking area and onto 66 Jumps. Brace yourself for some nonstop water bar action for the next mile with perfectly sculpted launching pads every 15 or 20 feet on a wide, hardpacked, gravel and dirt doubletrack. Watch for hikers, fishermen, horses, and other riders grinding their way back up.

1.0 Turn right *before* the river onto Riverside Trail. Tread changes to tech 1+ sandy hardpack with some tech 2 rocks and occasional mudholes.

1.4 At your first opportunity, bear left and cross the South Mills River. Crossing may be ridable depending on recent rains and your waterdog status. Riverside Trail picks up on the other side with red blazes, rockier track, and some serious mudholes. Don't miss this turn, or you're going to be hopelessly lost.

1.8 Bear left onto Pea Gap Trail and start climbing up away from the river. There's no sign, but it's a very clear split. You'll know you're on the right course if you're hating life within the first 100 yards; it's a mean tech 3+ climb over water bars and lots of loose baby heads.

2.3 Cross over Pea Gap and past a small campsite. Trail immediately begins to descend afterward over some steep water bars.

2.5 Cross a stream (Pea Branch) and turn left at the T onto Squirrel Gap Trail. Track is fairly flat, tech 1+ with blue blazes.

2.7 Tech 3+ rock-filled mudhole, then a ridable—but scary—log bridge crossing.

3.2 Tech 3+ steep-sided stream crossing with some tech 4 root lace on the far side. Just after stream, turn left at the T onto Mullinax Trail. Squirrel Gap Trail continues to the right.

3.5 Mullinax abruptly changes from easy toodling to life-threatening. Starts off with a long twisty section of heinous tech 4+ roots, then a bunch of old log

Mullinax

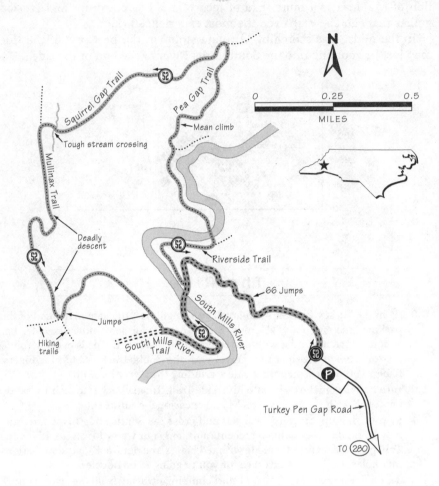

water bars with steep washouts on their back sides. A short rooty climb is your only rest, then you dive back in for some more mean water bars. This is a tech 4 descent that will leave you quivering at the bottom and thankful to have survived unscathed.

4.1 Cut sharply back left at this four-way intersection to stay on Mullinax and follow the yellow blazes (straight and right are hiking-only trails). As a reward for riding that heinous upper section, Mullinax now dishes out 20 or so smooth water bars of the dirt-hump variety. It's a quick descent and a little dicey at times with some loose chicken heads scattered about, but it pegs the fun meter.

4.6 Continue straight as Mullinax merges with the South Mills River Trail. Trail flattens and changes to hardpacked doubletrack, but the water bar action continues with at least another 25 smooth-topped beauties just waiting to launch you as high as you care to fly. Watch for gravel on some of the bars, along with other trail traffic.

5.0 Splash straight into the South Mills River. You get an official River MacDaddy patch if you make it across without dabbing. In warm weather you'll probably want to stop and roll around in the river awhile before continuing. In cold weather, you'll be hustling your freezing carcass back to the car as fast as your little legs will carry you.

6.0 Climbing back up 66 Jumps isn't especially fun, but it'll give you a chance to appreciate just how big some of those puppies are that you were sailing off of on the way down. Return to the parking area, and decide if you have enough juice left for one more trip down to the bottom of 66 Jumps and back.

Big Avery Loop

Location: Pisgah National Forest; Davidson River Campground area; 45 minutes south of Asheville.

Distance: 12.9-mile loop.

Time: 3 to 5 hours. However long it takes, you'll have nothing left at the end of it.

Tread: 11.6 miles of butt-stomping Pisgah singletrack; 1.3 miles of gravel road.

Aerobic level: Strenuous. The constant climbing will just flat-out tear you down. Some descents in the saddles, but they always ask for more than they give. Surviving the trip back down will take all the energy you've got left, and then some.

Technical difficulty: Tech 4 overall. Brutally steep rocky climbs and long, pounding rock gardens that go on for miles. If you don't like rocks, stay away.

Highlights: Incredible rocky descents; water bars (both up and down); ascent up Satan's Staircase; rhododendron tunnels; tons of stream crossings; long-range views of Looking Glass Rock.

Land status: Pisgah National Forest.

Maps: USGS Pisgah Forest; USDA Forest Service Pisgah District Trail Map; National Geographic Trails Illustrated Pisgah Ranger District.

Access: From Asheville, take Interstate 26 East (actually south) to North Carolina Highway 280 South. Follow NC 280 for about 15 miles to the town of Brevard. Turn right onto U.S. Highway 276, which leads up into the heart of Pisgah National Forest. Go about 5 or 6 miles and watch for the Coontree Gap Picnic Area on the left. Park here; the trail begins just down the road.

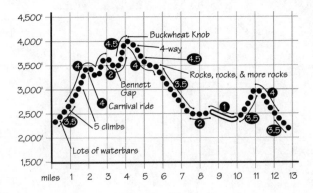

Notes on the trail

In some parts the trail is a smooth dirt highway; in other parts it's frame-buckling, rocky madness and wheel-wide cliff ledges. There are climbs that an alpaca would struggle with and descents that will plaster a rictus of thrill and terror across your face. An imposing ride, this thing will humble you, thrill you, kiss you, maybe kill you. Pay the insurance premium, then go enjoy yourself.

"I ain't too proud to call for m' granny." —Author

"No Timm, there is no top." —David T, victim of Satan's Staircase

The Ride

0.0 From the Coontree Gap Picnic Area, turn right and head down US 276 just 20 or 30 yards. The entrance for Coontree Mountain Trail is clearly marked on the left. Track immediately hits you with a climb up some loose rocks and respectable log water bars, tech 2 + .

0.5 Cross a log bridge, then bear right at the Y (hiking-only trail to the left). Cross another bridge, then hunker down for a tougher climb, up and over no less than eight major water bars. Plenty of time to admire the beautiful stream and magnificent trees along the trail, as you'll probably be pushing somewhere along the way.

1.0 Double log, then a knee-high single. Trail starts to look and feel like a seasonal streambed, steep and full of tech 3 + moves.

1.2 Massive 3-foot water bars that are just about undoable on the way up (but a heck of a lot of fun on the way down). Long, painful climb follows, a rooty assault that requires a lot of spinning and a lot of pain to conquer. Four more climbs follow, like the most foul-tempered quintuplets in Mother Earth's nursery. All five are steep, rooty, rocky, washed out, and most other uncomplimentary adjectives.

2.0 Bear left as you intersect Bennett Gap Trail.

2.4 Top Coontree Mountain and commence contour running fast and narrow, like an evil carnival ride. Zip through a dark rhododendron tunnel, pop out onto track only as wide as your tire, no margin for error, with a 50- to 80-foot drop off the side. Toss in one of those chest-to-seat switchback turns, and you've got some white-knuckle stuff. Tech 4 descent, pegging the adreno-meter.

2.6 Continue straight, past Perry Cove Trail down to the right. And now face the first step in Satan's Staircase: huge rock stairs that laugh at puny mortals who attempt to surmount them. These monsters continue now and again, mixed in with some hellish steeps, all the way to Buckwheat Knob. Just think about what it'd be like to come down it.

2.7 In the midst of a raging rock garden, check out the phenomenal view of Looking Glass Rock, off to the left. After the appropriate amount of appreciation, get ready for more of Satan's Staircase.

3.2 Pass through a beautiful mountaintop meadow, then on to a campsite with a gorgeous view. Afterward, you get a chance to hit warp speed as you dash down a long clear track into Bennett's Gap.

Big Avery Loop

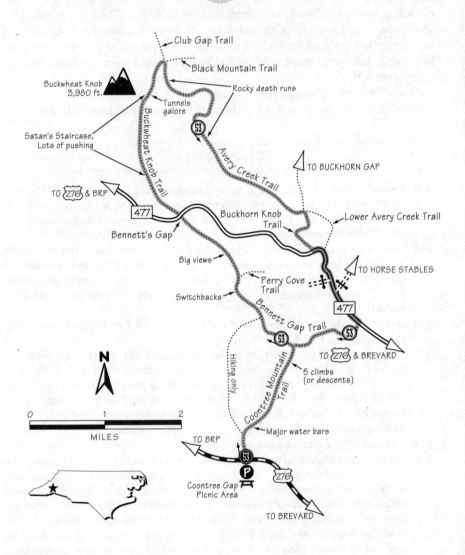

Club Gap Trail

Black Mountain Trail

Buckwheat Knob
3,980 ft.

Rocky death runs

Tunnels
galore

Satan's Staircase,
Lots of pushing

Buckwheat Knob Trail

Avery Creek Trail

TO BUCKHORN GAP

TO 276 & BRP

477

Bennett's Gap

Buckhorn Knob
Trail

Lower Avery Creek Trail

Big views

TO HORSE STABLES

Perry Cove
Trail

Switchbacks

477

Bennett Gap Trail

53

53

N

Hiking
only

Coontree Mountain Trail

TO 276 & BREVARD

5 climbs
(or descents)

0   1   2
MILES

Major water bars

TO BRP

53

P

276

Coontree Gap
Picnic Area

TO BREVARD

3.5 Hit Forest Road 477 (gravel road). Jag left just for bit, then pick up Buckwheat Knob Trail on the other side. Now for the last of Satan's Staircase: long, rooty climbs, one after another after another. It's a tech 4+ slice of trail hell.

4.2 Finally crest Buckwheat Knob, just below 4,000 feet. Take note as to how you feel after 1,600 feet of climbing. As you drop off the upper side of the knob, you get a chance to work the kinks out as you soar along buff tech 2 track through dark, silent rhododendron tunnels.

5.0 Drop down into Club Gap and a four-way intersection. Turn right onto Avery Creek Trail. (Note the name: Avery Creek Trail. Called this perhaps because for some of its length, it *is* Avery Creek. Imagine a continual, tech 4 barrage of rocks and deep holes. Picking the right line here is essential for survival.)

5.2 Hug trail left; sudden washout on right could swallow bike and rider alike.

5.3 Steep staircase of rocks 10 to 15 feet long, a tech 4+ move requiring total commitment. Trail pounds through a rocky stream that follows, then cruises through a deep emerald cove with a high-banked berm in the corner.

6.0 Cross a Forest Service road and zip past a 5-foot double waterfall. Track is rocky and loose, ugly through and through, but not quite as bad as up top, more like a tech 3+.

6.6 Long, fast downhill with a bad drop off the right side of the trail. Root drops start to appear in the trail at an alarming rate, growing from respectable 12-inchers to wide-eyed, 3-foot hungry beasts ready to make you or break you.

7.2 Track smooths out to a tech 2, granting you a breezing brakes-free section down through a couple of streams and over a string of easy root drops.

7.6 Bear right just after the "Horse Ford, People Ford" sign onto Buckwheat Knob Trail. For some mysterious reason, this trail is inaccurately signed "Upper Avery Creek Trail" at this point, which makes little sense 'cause you just came down Avery Creek Trail. Whatever you call it, follow this trail and it will take you back to the road. Smooth tech 2 cruising, some of the smoothest stuff you'll find anywhere in Pisgah.

8.5 Turn left as you pop out onto FR 477. Watch for cars.

9.2 Keep rolling as you pass the gated road on your right for Perry Cove.

9.8 Turn right at the sign for Bennett Gap Trail. Brace yourself for some more pain in the form of a brutal steep climb studded with big old water bars every 50 feet or so. And this goes on for a long time.

10.8 Turn left onto Coontree Mountain Trail. Now, remember those five brutal climbs at the beginning of the ride? Well, you get to salvage your ego a bit and take a shot at trouncing them on the way back down. They're tech 4 descents, and any one of them will be happy to blood-type you if you're not careful. But it's a hoot, make no mistake.

12.8 Drop back down onto US 276 and turn right to return to the Coontree Gap Picnic Area.

12.9 Return to the picnic area.

Laurel Mountain

Location: Pisgah National Forest; 8 miles west of North Mills River Campground; about 45 minutes south of Asheville.

Distance: 12.4 miles out and back.

Time: 1.5 to 2.5 hours.

Tread: 12.4 miles of pure, prime Pisgah singletrack.

Aerobic level: Moderate to strenuous. The climb up Laurel Mountain starts off fairly easy then gets steeper as you go. Descents through the saddles are only teases to set you up for the climbs to follow.

Technical difficulty: Tech 2 with a number of tough, off-camber tech 3 and 3.5 rock moves. The tech 4+ move at the cave is a bike (or rider) breaker, so use caution.

Highlights: Roller-coaster descent; smooth track; rhododendron tunnels; wildlife (that you'd just as soon miss).

Land status: Pisgah National Forest.

Maps: USGS Dunsmore Mountain; USDA Forest Service Pisgah District Trail Map; National Geographic Trails Illustrated Pisgah Ranger District.

Access: From Asheville, take Interstate 26 East (south) to North Carolina Highway 280 South. Drive about 6 miles, pass the airport and the fairgrounds, then turn right on North Mills River Road. After passing the North Mills River Campground, the road turns from pavement to gravel, becoming Forest Road 1206 or Yellow Gap Road. Go another 6 miles, and look for a small parking area on the left in the middle of an inside curve, just past a gated road. Trail sign is on the right.

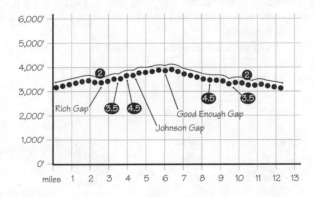

Laurel Mountain

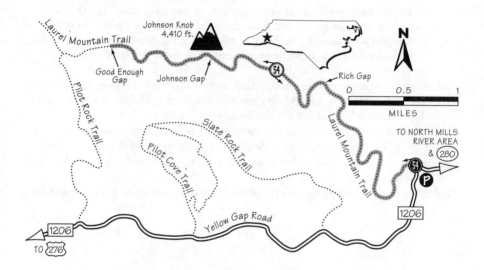

Notes on the trail

Though I generally don't like out-and-backs, this one rates up there as a great ride. It's a straightforward ride, with no turns to worry about, and a relatively easy climb—for 1,400-foot elevation gain, that is. Even determined beginners can make it up to Good Enough Gap, and the run back down is like a dirt-faced roller coaster that pegs the fun meter. You'll come back down the mountain like your ass is on fire and you like the heat. Just watch for the off-camber rocks and rattlesnakes.

The Ride

0.0 From the parking area at Yellow Gap, follow the brown trail sign across the road to begin climbing up Laurel Mountain. Trail begins with easy tech 2 track with occasional tech 3 rock moves.

1.0 Cool, beautiful rhododendron tunnel. Track begins to narrow with often only a 2-inch margin for error on the side.

2.8 Cross Rich Gap. Small campsite on the right.

3.0 Tech 3+ rock move. Last time through, we found a 5-foot timber rattler sunning itself here, so be careful.

3.5 Big rocky overhang, almost a cave. Tech 4+ rock move, or a wise carry.

4.7 Drop into Johnson Gap. Use caution as you drop through the saddles, as some of the off-camber curves could send you tumbling for a long, long way.

5.8 Small campsite to right. Trail curves left uphill (of course) for the nastiest climb yet up a steep, eroded rock-strewn slope. This is one of those climbs where you just take off your helmet, take a nice big drink, then start pushing. Take note of the beautiful huge oak trees (maybe 5 feet in diameter) as you trudge by.

6.2 Short descent into Good Enough Gap. Now's the time to rest and laugh away the pain. Then turn around and brace yourself for a wild, high-speed descent down narrow track and tight rhododendron thickets.

6.6 Watch it on this descent, as the rocks are loose and hungry for human flesh.

8.9 Pass the cave again. Don't be emboldened to foolishness by the descent-induced adrenaline rush. Walk your bike over this tech 4+ rock move, unless you cleaned it on the way up.

12.4 Return to the parking area and consider doing it all over again. It's that much fun.

Pilot Rock Loop

Location: Pisgah National Forest; 8 miles west of North Mills River Campground; about 45 minutes south of Asheville.
Distance: 14.5-mile loop.
Time: 3 to 5 hours.
Tread: 9.4 miles of singletrack; 5.1 miles of gravel road.
Aerobic level: Strenuous. The climb up Laurel Mountain starts off fairly easy, then gets steeper as you go. It never seems to end, and the final climb up to Turkey Spring is almost enough to make you turn back. The descent down Pilot Rock allows no chance to catch your breath.
Technical difficulty: Climb, tech 2; descent, tech 4+. The trip up Laurel Mountain is fairly smooth (except for the last climb) with only a handful of tech 3 rock moves and one tech 4+. The descent down Pilot Rock is extremely challenging with incredibly tight switchbacks, huge rock slabs, big erosion gullies, and dozens and dozens of water bars.
Highlights: 1,400-foot descent; long-range views; rocky switchbacks; rhododendron tunnels; water bars; wildlife.
Land status: Pisgah National Forest.
Maps: USGS Dunsmore Mountain; USDA Forest Service Pisgah District Trail Map; National Geographic Trails Illustrated Pisgah Ranger District.
Access: From Asheville, take Interstate 26 East (south) to North Carolina Highway 280 South. Drive about 6 miles, pass the airport and the fairgrounds, then turn right on North Mills River Road. After passing the North Mills River Campground, the road turns from pavement to gravel, becoming Forest Road 1206 or Yellow Gap Road. Go another 6 miles, and look for a small parking area on the left in the middle of an inside curve, just past a gated road. Trail sign is on the right.

Notes on the trail

This ride contains what may be the most technically challenging descent in the entire forest. Dropping more than 1,400 feet in just over 2 miles is the easy part. You feel like you're riding on the bones of the mountain, as you descend over huge rock slabs and pick your way through tight, 180-degree switchbacks that are simply solid boulders and chicken heads. Sometimes the tight rhododendron thickets on either side are all that keep you from flying off into space. And if the rocks up top weren't bad enough, the lower part of the descent is just one knee-high water bar after another, like some sick suspension torture test. I recommend this ride only for advanced riders and really game intermediates.

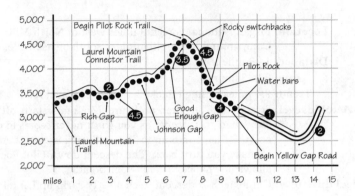

The Ride

0.0 From the parking area at Yellow Gap, follow the brown trail sign across the road to begin climbing up Laurel Mountain. Trail begins with easy tech 2 track with occasional tech 3 rock moves.

1.0 Cool, beautiful rhododendron tunnel. Track begins to narrow with often only a 2-inch margin for error on the side.

2.8 Cross Rich Gap. Small campsite on the right.

3.0 Tech 3+ rock move. Last time through, we found a 5-foot timber rattler sunning itself here, so be careful.

3.5 Big rocky overhang, almost a cave. Tech 4+ rock move, or a wise carry.

4.7 Drop into Johnson Gap. Use caution as you drop through the saddles, as some of the off-camber curves could send you tumbling for a long, long way.

5.8 Small campsite to right. Trail curves left uphill (of course) for the nastiest climb yet up a steep, eroded rock-strewn slope. This is one of those climbs where you just take off your helmet, take a nice big drink, then start pushing. Take note of the beautiful huge oak trees (maybe 5 feet in diameter) as you trudge by.

6.2 Short descent into Good Enough Gap.

6.5 Watch carefully for a trail split here as it's not marked and is easy to miss; a landmark is another small campsite. Turn sharply uphill left onto the Laurel Mountain Connector Trail, which will take you up to Pilot Rock. This is an extremely steep and painful climb.

6.8 Final climb leads you up to Pilot Rock Trail. Turn left at this clearly marked intersection, but not before checking that all of your crew made the

Pilot Rock Loop

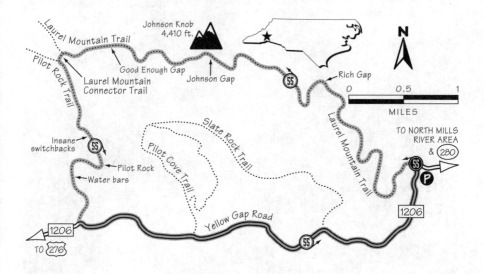

connector trail. Check your brakes, lower your seat, tighten up your suspension, and cough up some courage because here begins one hair-raising descent. Starts off with a fairly level ridge run. Then begins the nastiest switchbacks you've ever seen: These things are filled with solid rocks, like riding down the side of a quarry. It feels like you're coming down a cliff face, which basically you are. Call it a continuous tech 4+ nightmare.

8.0 Trail turns back into some semblance of hardpack, then drops into a big erosion gully. You'll probably curse the tight thicket, until you realize it's protecting you from the 600-foot drop on your left.

8.4 When you notice nothing but air to the left, you'll know you're at Pilot Rock. Stop for a break and some pictures, as this 180-degree view is not to be missed. Valley floor lies 800 feet below.

8.5 Now that the rocks have stopped, the water bars take over: Big tech 3 and 4 monsters that just never seem to end. We're talking dozens of big hits here, over and over again. Some you can slalom around, but most you just need to either jump or eat.

9.2 Old road to the left. Do *not* make the mistake of thinking this is a shortcut; you'll regret it, believe me.

9.4 Finally, just as the last drop of oil leaks from your shocks and your hands fall useless by your side, you return to Yellow Gap Road. Turn left and begin the long haul back to the start. If you were really smart, you left a shuttle vehicle here, 'cause the last mile of the return leg is a bitch.

14.5 Return to the Laurel Mountain Trailhead at Yellow Gap.

What a line! DAVID TOLLERTON PHOTO

Slate Rock–Pilot Cove Loop

Location: Pisgah National Forest; 8 miles west of North Mills River Campground; about 45 minutes south of Asheville.

Distance: 3.9-mile fat lariat (that feels like 12 miles).

Time: 45 minutes to 3 hours. No kidding. If you're a fresh, strong rider, you'll grind up the switchback climbs then fly back to the start. If you're already gassed or out to just take in the scenery, you'll probably push (and cuss) up the climbs, then hang out at the overlook until your camera is empty.

Tread: 100 percent Carolina singletrack.

Aerobic level: Strenuous. This is the toughest 4-mile ride I've seen yet. The climb up Slate Rock will explode your quads, and the numerous false tops will have you almost crying in despair. The drop back into Pilot Cove is steep and furious and takes a lot out of you both mentally and physically.

Technical difficulty: Tech 2 + overall but with some big spikes. The switchbacks are agonizingly tight and numerous but ridable. Downhill begins with some serious speed over roots, rocks, and water bars, mixed well for a knuckle-clenching tech 4 descent. Two large tech 3 + rock slabs spice up the return trip along the creek.

Highlights: Lots of mud, roots, twists and turns, and short surprising climbs.

Land status: Pisgah National Forest.

Maps: USGS Dunsmore Mountain; USDA Forest Service Pisgah District Trail Map; National Geographic Trails Illustrated Pisgah Ranger District.

Access: From Asheville, take Interstate 26 East (south) to North Carolina Highway 280 South. Drive about 6 miles, pass the airport and the fairgrounds, then turn right on North Mills River Road. After passing the North Mills River Campground, the road turns from pavement to gravel. Go another 6 miles, and look for a small parking area on the left in the middle of an inside curve. Trail sign is on the right.

Notes on the trail

The view—ohmygod, the view! Slate Rock perches 500 feet or so above the cove floor, with a breathtaking 180-degree view of the cove and an incredible profile of Pilot Rock across the way. Certainly one of the top three views in Pisgah Forest, with a hawk drifting on the thermals 100 yards out in front of you if you're as lucky as me. About 80 percent of this trail runs through rhododendron thickets and tunnels, with brutal, heartbreaking climbs up a number of false tops, a descent down through Pilot Cove that screams for the first mile, and several challenging technical moves tossed in throughout the return leg.

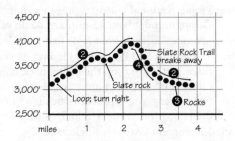

The Ride

0.0 Start at sign for Pilot Cove–Slate Rock Loop. Nice, easy tech 1 riding along stream through gorgeous rhododendron tunnels.

0.2 Trail splits to begin loop. Turn right uphill over set of rock/log steps. If you get to a narrow log bridge, you missed the turn.

0.3 Trail gets rockier. First tough climb is only a mild annoyance, compared with the pain ahead.

0.4 Ugly root crossing. First set of tough switchbacks; ridable but by no means easy.

0.7 Topping first climb. Don't get excited—it's only a finger, and the real top is still way above you.

0.9 Steep switchbacks, climbing to top of actual knob. Heavy rhododendron thickets.

1.0 Nice view off to right. Sweet little descent through saddle, slipping and dipping with no effort but lots of smiles.

1.2 Saddle ends too quickly; begin climbing again.

1.4 Tough climbs that always seem just about to top out, but only flatten out on a finger for a short while before throwing some more at you.

1.5 Trail breaks out of the brush and dumps you right on top of Slate Rock for one of the most spectacular view on these trails. Though it's early in the ride, no one will complain about stopping here for a break. Turn right as soon as you come out on Slate Rock to pick up the trail again. Incredible rhododendron tunnel just after leaving the rock. **Warning:** Do not ride straight out onto rock, as it curves away off into space. Also beware of walking too close to edge wearing cleated shoes, unless you have a desire to test out a new theory on unpowered human flight.

1.7 After drop through saddle, pump up a long, steep climb only to meet five (count 'em, five) steep-ass switchbacks in a row. Any one or two is doable, but five in a row is a righteous challenge. Tech 3 move on toughness alone.

1.9 Top another false peak, then drop through saddle past large rock outcropping and well-used campsite.

Slate Rock–Pilot Cove Loop

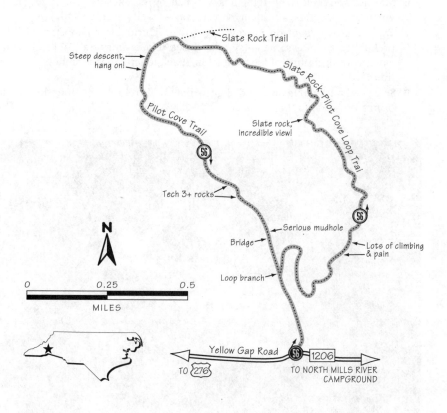

Slate Rock Trail

Steep descent, hang on!

Slate Rock–Pilot Cove Loop Trail

Pilot Cove Trail

Slate rock, incredible view!

56

Tech 3+ rocks

56

N

Serious mudhole

Bridge

Lots of climbing & pain

Loop branch

| 0 | 0.25 | 0.5 |

MILES

Yellow Gap Road

56

1206

TO 276

TO NORTH MILLS RIVER CAMPGROUND

2.2 Top last peak, then a quick, steep descent off back of knob. Seems to drop for a long time, and you'll be grinning the whole way. Watch for water bars and super bunny hop potential.

2.4 Sign marks intersection of Slate Rock and Pilot Cove Trails. Turn left to follow Pilot Cove Trail back to starting point. This begins a very steep and rocky tech 4 downhill assault. Lots of high water bars, and tight sections through some nasty rocks that must be maneuvered at speed. It's easy to gain dangerous amounts of speed through here. Beware that forearms may suddenly burst into flames from braking.

2.8 Tech 3+ move up and over ugly 2.5-foot rock ledge.

3.0 Tech 3 move over large rock slabs crossing stream. Looks intimidating but just loft the front wheel and keep pedaling.

3.3 Tough though short technical climb. Incredibly sweet twisting singletrack follows, slipping through the rhododendron.

3.5 Narrow path branches left, leading to large campsite. Stay straight on main trail.

3.6 Monster mudhole with tight heavy brush on either side. You'll get sloppy whether you walk it or ride it, so you may as well give it a shot!

3.7 Trail crosses stream on narrow log bridge. Unridable by mortal men (but probably doable by some gutsy gals). Track rejoins entry trail 100 feet farther along with beginning of loop branching back to left. Stay straight to return to trailhead.

3.9 Supremely easy, relaxing (and slightly downhill) return trip alongside stream brings you back to the trailhead.

Timm shows the only way to fly on Sliding Rock Falls near the Slate Cove Loop.

Buckwheat Knob Loop

Location: Pisgah National Forest; Davidson River Campground area; 45 minutes south of Asheville.

Distance: 11.3-mile loop.

Time: 4–6 hours. This is an epic, all-day ride; plan accordingly for food and water.

Tread: 9.3 miles of phenomenal Pisgah singletrack; 2 miles of gravel road.

Aerobic level: Strenuous. The climbing starts right from the beginning and doesn't end 'til you've gained 1,500 feet of elevation. Believe it or not, the descent is worse.

Technical difficulty: Tech 4. This trail is a supreme technical challenge. Long, continuous tech 3 and tech 4 sections. Many tech 4+ moves, with the first one within the first half mile of trail. And at least three sick tech 5 rock moves that will leave you broken and bleeding if you blow it.

Highlights: Water bars; rhodo tunnels; tough climbs; insane technical descents.

Land status: Pisgah National Forest.

Maps: USGS Pisgah Forest; USDA Forest Service Pisgah District Trail Map; National Geographic Trails Illustrated Pisgah Ranger District.

Access: From Asheville, take Interstate 26 East (actually south) to North Carolina Highway 280 South. Follow NC 280 for about 15 miles to the town of Brevard. Turn right onto U.S. Highway 276, which leads up into the heart of Pisgah National Forest. About 2 miles in, pass the Pisgah Ranger Station and turn right onto Forest Road 477 (gravel road), following the sign for the Pisgah Horse Stables. Go about another 2 miles, pass the gated road for the horse stables on your right, then look for another gated road immediately to your left. I like to park here, since it's your return leg for the loop. If this spot is taken, drive a little farther and park in the pullout at the Buckhorn Gap Trailhead (you can take Buckhorn Gap to the intersection at mile point 0.9, and the trail mileage will be just about the same).

Notes on the trail

Some of this trail is just simply insane. We rode up a waterfall; we rode down several small cliff faces. Sometimes you'll be afraid to continue, and sometimes you'll be too terrified to stop. The descent down from Buckwheat Knob is brutal and pounding with several ridable but life-threatening tech 5 moves along the way. This ride will test every limit you've got: endurance, technical skills, courage, fortitude, and strength. If you pride yourself on riding the hairy stuff, come to Buckwheat Knob, and come prepared to be humbled. This is the stuff that legends are made of.

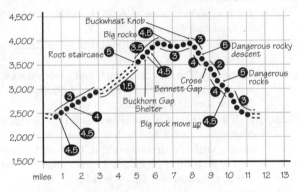

The Ride

0.0 Turn left and head up FR 477, the gravel road you came in on.

0.1 Turn right onto the signed lower entrance to Avery Creek Trail. It's a fast, slippery descent with a half-dozen mean water bars. Trail is mostly tech 1+ with some tech 2+ rocks and roots.

0.2 Bear left at the T, following the blue blazes. Trail right to Clawhammer Cove is hiking only.

0.5 Small but pretty waterfall to the left.

0.6 First major technical move, and it's a doozy: a tech 4+ stream crossing, with steep sides and some incredibly ugly roots on the back side. Of course, you could use the nearby log bridge, but where's the fun in that.

0.9 Bear right at this intersection toward the sign that says "Horse Ford, People Ford." Ignore the "Upper/Lower Avery Creek" signs, as they really don't make any sense. Trail back left is the beginning of Buckhorn Gap Trail and leads up to FR 477 and the alternate parking area.

1.0 40 feet of continuous tech 4+ roots. If this is too ugly for you, turn around now and find an easier trail to ride, because you won't enjoy the next 10 miles.

1.1 Buckhorn Gap Trail turns right and crosses creek over a log bridge, following orange blazes. Trail straight is the continuation of Avery Creek Trail.

1.4 Several tech 3+ stream crossings and some walking log bridges brings you to a miserable tech 4 rock garden and some unridable stairsteps and water bars. Trail hint: A puddle that's small isn't necessarily shallow.

Buckwheat Knob Loop

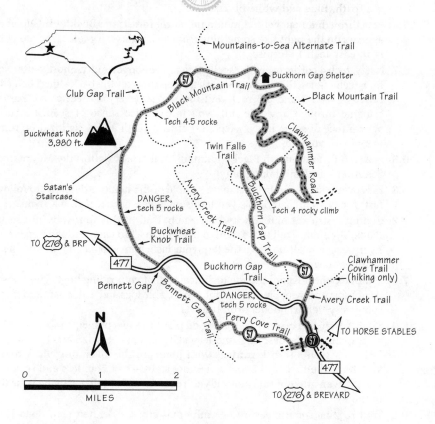

1.8 Turn sharply right and look for the orange blazes to continue on Buckhorn Gap Trail. Blue trail straight is the Twin Falls Trail (hiking only). These falls are very beautiful and definitely worth seeing, but please either stash your bike in the bushes (yeah, right!), carry it the quarter mile to the falls, or come back later with your hiking boots and a camera.

2.0 Long, continuous tech 4 rocky section. If the stream up top gets diverted, like it was for us, you'll find yourself floundering up a rushing stream and a small waterfall, for a truly unique riding experience.

2.3 Turn right, following blue blazes, as trail mellows to a tech 1+ (albeit uphill still). Track straight is clearly marked shortcut for hikers only (or cyclically challenged, as we call them).

3.2 A long, grinding tech 2 climb finally brings you to Clawhammer Road (gated gravel Forest Service road). Turn left onto the aptly named Clawhammer, which will tease you with a cool descent, then proceed to claw your lungs apart and hammer your body for the next mile or so.

5.1 Turn left at this five-way intersection onto Black Mountain Trail, which starts with a hideous tech 5 root-riddled staircase. Look carefully for the sign, because your mind may simply choose to ignore what your eyes say is an unridable goat path. Blue and white blazes.

5.3 Pass through an enchanted mountain laurel forest; the Buckhorn Gap shelter appears on the right like something from a Grimms fairy tale. Trail along here is an easy tech 1+ cruise.

5.7 Nasty, tech 4 corduroy, with excellent faceplant opportunity. Shortly after you'll hit a tech 4+ log that's cut out, with a steep drop off the back side. Then a long series of tech 3 and 3.5 rock and root moves every 30 feet or so. Easy flat cruising through a saddle lulls you into a false sense of security. Sudden appearance of some hungry tech 3+ dragonsteeth and a big log drop remind you where you are.

6.3 Bear left to continue on Black Mountain Trail. Track right is the Mountains-to-Sea Alternate Trail (hiking only).

6.8 Pass over a knob and begin a mere sample of the heinous descents to follow. A fast, rocky tech 3 run leads you into some even nastier tech 4+ rocks.

7.2 Continue straight onto Buckwheat Knob Trail at this four-way intersection. Black Mountain Trail turns right to head up to Club Gap, and the upper end of Avery Creek peels down to the left (your last chance to bail out before the real nastiness begins).

7.8 Top Buckwheat Knob, and the technical trial of your riding life begins. Descent begins fast and swooping over some respectable logs and water bars and through some very tight rhododendron tunnels.

8.4 Satan's Staircase begins. This is a good place to say a prayer, strap on any body armor you may be carrying, and leave all caution behind. Starts out steep and fast, over tech 3+ rock gardens with jumps in the midst of it all. **Warning!** Watch for the first tech 5 move, a 6-foot staircase of boulders and rock slabs. Do not even attempt this move if you're alone, as it could easily be your ticket to the ER.

9.0 Trail regains some measure of sanity and crosses Bennett Gap Road (gated; gravel). Jag left on the road then an immediate right to pick up Bennett Gap Trail on the other side. Short tech 2+ climb awaits.

9.1 Pass a beautiful high-alpine meadow and an ugly campsite with about 10,000 beer cans. Easy tech 1 grassy track.

9.5 Drop and climb through several small saddles, then run along a sharp ridgeline. Nice view of Looking Glass Rock to the right.

9.6 The nightmare continues with a number of tech 4 and tech 4+ rock slabs, leading you into another tech 5 move: a big rock garden staircase that requires two 90-degree turns in the middle. Big, big bust potential. Follow it up with a tech 4, 2-foot ledge drop that seems almost tame in comparison.

9.7 Satan's Staircase's final offering: a tech 4+ move *up* a 4-foot-high pile of rocks. Then a long continual barrage of tech 4 and 4.5 boulders and rock slabs. Get your butt so far back it's buzzing the rear tire, let go the brakes, and scream like a kid on his first trip to the carnival.

9.9 Sharp left turn back onto Perry Creek Trail, just after the insane rock garden above (it's easy to miss, so keep an eye out). Trail signs rate this trail as "Most Difficult," which is bull after what you've just been through. Tech 2 run at the most, though it's fast and off-camber in spots with lots of switchbacks.

10.6 Cross a ridable log bridge, and pass through a gorgeous fern garden. Then drop through some wickedly fast swooping turns with some great smooth water bar jumps.

11.2 Turn left as Perry Creek dumps you onto gravel doubletrack.

11.3 Pass the gate and you're back at the truck. Say a prayer of thanks to the protective divinity of your choice, and celebrate your survival. Now you can honestly tell folks you're a mountain biker.

"This is the way up Buckwheat Knob? You must be kidding."

Thrift Cove Loop

Location: Pisgah National Forest, Davidson River Campground area; 45 minutes south of Asheville.

Distance: 3.7-mile loop.

Time: 30 minutes to 1 hour.

Tread: 3.3 miles of singletrack; 0.4 mile of gravel Forest Service road.

Aerobic level: Moderate. Climb is a bit steep and long in places, but it's generally clear and easy to ride. You can coast back down most of Black Mountain if you so desire.

Technical difficulty: Tech 1 +. Some of the rock gardens on the return down Black Mountain rate a tech 3 and 3.5, but most of the track is wide, smooth, and fast. One avalanche jumble of rocks and trees across the trail throws up a tech 4+ for a serious challenge. Know that some riders make this move (though not me, not yet).

Highlights: Relatively easy climb; zippy return; big berms; fun run for little cost.

Land status: Pisgah National Forest.

Maps: USGS Pisgah Forest; USDA Forest Service Pisgah District Trail Map; National Geographic Trails Illustrated Pisgah Ranger District.

Access: From Asheville, take Interstate 26 East (actually south) to North Carolina Highway 280 South. Follow NC 280 for about 15 miles to the town of Brevard. Turn right onto U.S. Highway 276, which leads up into the heart of Pisgah National Forest. Just a mile or so in, watch for the brown Art Loeb Trail sign on the right. Just after the sign, turn right into a service area parking lot by a big metal power line tower. If you get to the ranger station, you've gone too far. Gated gravel road at back of lot is the beginning of Black Mountain.

Notes on the trail

Think of this trail as Black Mountain Extra, Extra Light. It's got a respectable (if smooth-surfaced) climb up Thrift Cove, then returns along the lower section of Black Mountain. The descent back down is either a lazy roller coaster (with a few surprise rock gardens) or a scorching, teeth-chattering run, depending on your choice of speed. It's a good alternate if anyone in your group isn't up to the challenge of a full assault on Black Mountain.

The Ride

0.0 Start in on old gravel doubletrack at back of parking lot. Sign for Black Mountain points the way.

0.2 Turn right at sign onto Thrift Cove Trail. This way up gives your legs a good warm-up before the real climbing begins.

0.4 Continue straight past a group campsite, as the gravel gives way to XXL dirt singletrack. The Mountains-to-Sea Alternate Trail breaks off to the right.

0.5 Thrift Cove turns up to the left, following red blazes, and starts making some serious elevation gain. An unmarked gravel road (Grassy Road Trail) breaks off to the right.

2.5 Continue straight at intersection onto the lower section of Black Mountain for the return. Track starts to drop right away, and you can easily gain scary amounts of speed. Two high inside corners offer 8-foot-tall berms or runaway ramps. Watch for sudden rock gardens and a huge tech 4+ log/rock obstacle.

3.5 Turn right as Black Mountain spills you out onto the gravel entrance road. Four or five nice rounded water bars to jump on the way out.

3.7 Return to parking lot.

Thrift Cove Loop

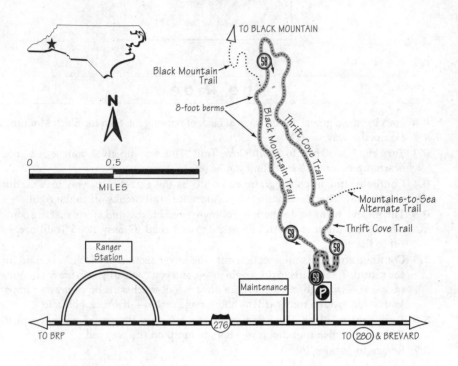

TO BLACK MOUNTAIN

Black Mountain Trail

8-foot berms

Black Mountain Trail

Thrift Cove Trail

Mountains-to-Sea Alternate Trail

Thrift Cove Trail

N

0   0.5   1

MILES

Ranger Station

Maintenance

TO BRP

276

TO 280 & BREVARD

Black Mountain

Location: Pisgah National Forest, Davidson River Campground area; 45 minutes south of Asheville.

Distance: 9.9 miles out and back.

Time: 2.5 to 4.5 hours, depending on how slow you push and how quickly you hammer back down.

Tread: 9.5 miles of rough-and-ready Pisgah singletrack; 0.4 mile of gravel Forest Service road.

Aerobic level: Strenuous. About 2,200 feet of elevation gain costs you dearly, whether you ride, push, walk, or crawl. This is a heart-breaking climb, and everyone will push it at some point. Descent will pound your tired limbs into putty and will cost you every bit as much as the climb.

Technical difficulty: Tech 4. Uncountable slippery water bars set at bad angles; big, loose rocks; serious drops—at speed—into even more serious rock gardens. This is the kind of trail where you just point the bike downhill, say a quick prayer, and try to hang on. A constant barrage of trail chaos will leave you battered and respectful at the bottom.

Highlights: Killer climbs; long-range views; no-holds-barred descent; insane bunny hops; wild irises along trailside.

Land status: Pisgah National Forest.

Maps: USGS Pisgah Forest; USDA Forest Service Pisgah District Trail Map; National Geographic Trails Illustrated Pisgah Ranger District.

Access: From Asheville, take Interstate 26 East (actually south) to North Carolina Highway 280 South. Follow NC 280 for about 15 miles to the town of Brevard. Turn right onto U.S. Highway 276, which leads up into the heart of Pisgah National Forest. Just a mile or so in, watch for the brown Art Loeb Trail sign on the right. Just after the sign, turn right into a service area parking lot by a big metal power line tower. If you get to the ranger station, you've gone too far. Gated gravel road at back of lot is the signed beginning of Black Mountain.

Notes on the trail

Simply put, this is one of the top three descents in the entire forest. It should be on the "A" list for any rider who requires enormous doses of heartbreak, challenge, and adrenaline. Make no bones about it: This descent is rough and treacherous, filled with high water bars and hungry rocks. Never mind what any of the signs or maps say: This is an advanced trail for advanced riders. I can't recall a more pounding descent.

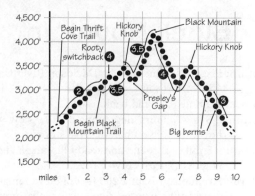

The Ride

0.0 Start in on old gravel doubletrack at back of parking lot. Sign for Black Mountain points the way.

0.2 Turn right onto Thrift Cove Trail. This way up gives your legs a good warm-up before the real climbing begins. You can go straight up Black Mountain, but you'll catch it on the way back down, and the surprise will be worth it.

0.4 Continue straight past a group campsite, as the gravel gives way to XXL dirt singletrack. The Mountains-to-Sea Alternate Trail breaks off to the right.

0.5 Thrift Cove turns up to the left, following red blazes, and starts making some serious elevation gain. An unmarked gravel road (Grassy Road Trail) breaks off to the right.

1.3 Trail smoothes out and flattens into an easy tech 1+ cruise. Don't be fooled— this is Mother Nature's idea of a joke.

2.5 Take a sharp right turn onto the Black Mountain Trail. Now begins one of the nastiest climbs you will ever experience. Just roots, rocks, and water bars disappearing into the woods above you for a long, long time. Blue and white blazes.

3.1 Tech 4, 180-degree switchback, with a choice of either the log stairs or the root-encrusted embankment.

3.6 Climb gets even steeper with water bars pitching up almost constantly. Pause for a moment to think about what the return down this slope is going to be like. Yep, that bad.

3.9 Top out on Hickory Knob at 3,560 feet. You just rode/pushed/crawled over 1,400 feet vertical, so rest a bit and enjoy the view. You even get a fun—if somewhat scary—downhill when you leave. Bad news though: It climbs another 1,000 feet from there. Watch for the racing turkeys.

4.3 Enter intersection at Presley's Gap. Continue straight on Black Mountain Trail. Forest Road 5098 heads left and right, and an unmarked grassy doubletrack cuts back to the right as well. March on, intrepid soul, for the climbing begins again here.

Black Mountain

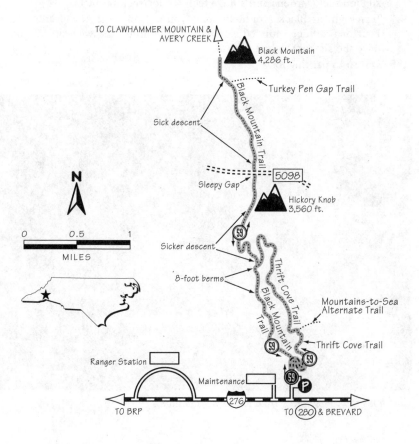

TO CLAWHAMMER MOUNTAIN & AVERY CREEK

Black Mountain 4,286 ft.

Turkey Pen Gap Trail

Sick descent

Black Mountain Trail

5098

Sleepy Gap

Hickory Knob 3,560 ft.

N

0   0.5   1

MILES

59

Sicker descent

8-foot berms

Thrift Cove Trail

Black Mountain Trail

Mountains-to-Sea Alternate Trail

59

Thrift Cove Trail

59

Ranger Station

59

P

Maintenance

276

TO BRP

TO 280 & BREVARD

4.9 Old unmarked logging road left and right. Continue straight on Black Mountain.

5.3 Continue straight on Black Mountain. Turkey Pen Gap Trail breaks off to the right and links up with trails in the South Mills River area.

5.6 Top out on Black Mountain, elevation 4,286 feet, and turn around. Rest well because the trip back down will test all your limits. It's fast and steep, covered with slippery water bars, loose baby heads, and dragonsteeth. You can get big bunny hops and bypass some of the real nasty stuff, but the landings are sketchy at best.

5.9 You never saw it, but Turkey Pen Gap Trail peeled back off to your left.

6.9 Straight through intersection at Presley's Gap. Here's a good place to check the health of your traveling companions and share a bit of hysterical laughter as you ride or push up a short stretch to Hickory Knob.

7.3 Top out on Hickory Knob. Believe it or not, this next descent is even worse than the top section. It's very steep with nothing even vaguely resembling a clean line.

8.7 Return to intersection with Thrift Cove. This time, turn right to follow Black Mountain back to the bottom. Trail changes to fairly wide, flat tech 2, and starts to gain the kind of speed that can melt the brakes right off your wheels. Two high inside corners offer 8-foot-tall berms or runaway ramps. Watch for sudden rock gardens and a huge tech 4+ log/rock obstacle.

9.7 Turn right as Black Mountain spills you out onto the gravel entrance road. Four or five nice rounded water bars to jump on the way out—if you don't have the shakes too bad, that is.

9.9 Return to parking lot.

Curt finds the yellow brick road to Black Mountain.

Daniel Ridge Loop

Location: Pisgah National Forest, near fish hatchery. About 35 miles south of Asheville.

Distance: 4.8-mile loop.

Time: 1 to 2 hours, depending on time spent just admiring the beauty.

Tread: 3.8 miles of singletrack; 1 mile of Forest Service road.

Aerobic level: Moderate. The climbs are difficult and steep; most riders will probably push somewhere along the way. Initial descent is pounding, whereas the lower section you can almost coast.

Technical difficulty: Tech 1+ for the climb and the lower descent. Tech 4 for the upper descent from Farlow Gap; it's a continual rock field.

Highlights: Spectacular waterfall and cascades; extremely technical descent.

Land status: Pisgah National Forest.

Maps: USGS, Shining Rock; USDA Forest Service Pisgah District Trail Map; National Geographic Trails Illustrated Pisgah Ranger District.

Access: From Asheville, take Interstate 26 East (actually south) to North Carolina Highway 280 South. Follow NC 280 about 15 miles to the town of Brevard. Turn right onto U.S. Highway 276, which leads up into the heart of Pisgah National Forest. Follow US 276 for roughly 4 miles, then turn left onto Forest Road 475 (paved at this point), which leads to the fish hatchery. About 1.5 miles past the fish hatchery, watch for the second gated road on the right. Trail entrance is signed.

Notes on the trail

The cove of Daniel Ridge Creek may just be the most peaceful, beautiful place you have ever seen. Words cannot do justice to the wonder of this place, where the air, the stream, the rocks, and the trees all sparkle as if freshly made by the Creator's hands. It touched me that strongly. Be sure to bring your camera, as the 60-foot waterfall at the beginning is only a prelude to the beauty of this place.

But be forewarned that this sylvan paradise is guarded by one of the meanest descents around. After leaving Farlow Gap, the next mile is nothing but rocks, more rocks, and gaping holes where the rocks used to be. In spots the trail narrows to 6 inches wide, running along an almost sheer fall line. This trail would scare most people to simply walk it in some places. Riding it seemed like insanity. I loved it.

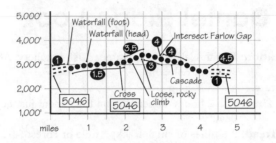

The Ride

0.0 Enter past the gate onto FR 5046.

0.1 Cross a wide concrete bridge and continue straight. Return leg of the trail enters from the left.

0.4 Turn left onto Daniel Ridge Trail. Trail starts out as tech 2 leafy hardpack, gaining some easy elevation as it climbs through a mountain laurel thicket. You can't miss the trailhead, since it starts at the foot of a gorgeous 60-foot waterfall.

0.7 Steep rocky switchback, tech 2 +.

0.9 Trail swings by the very top of the waterfall. You can't see much, but it sounds really cool. Don't be stupid enough to walk out onto it; the rocks are really slick, and it's a long way down. Cross a short wooden bridge just after the falls, then bear up to the right.

1.2 Four more wooden bridges in a row. Trail is pristine along here; just a clean dirt ribbon through the green.

1.3 Stream and log crossing, then edge along a small meadow.

1.5 Another wooden bridge, then a nasty tech 3 climb that's steep and rocky and littered with water bars. This one is probably a pusher.

1.7 Cross FR 5046 again. This is the same gated road you started the ride on. Trail picks up straight across with red blazes on the trees. Unfortunately, the climbing picks up again as well.

1.8 Nice long-range view to left. Track is extremely loose and rocky, which makes for one bitch of a climb.

2.0 Trail turns suspiciously smooth (tech 1 +) and begins contour running.

2.3 Continue straight. Unmarked singletrack breaks off uphill to the right, eventually leading to FR 225. Cross over saddle and begin some fast downhill contour running.

2.6 Pair of super-tight switchbacks, followed by some tech 3 + corduroy.

2.9 Turn left at intersection with Farlow Gap, down some nasty-looking stairs (tech 4). The gorgeous stream below is Daniel Ridge Creek, and it is truly a thing of beauty. The following descent is filled with peril in the form of big loose rocks and big rock-shaped holes. It's pounding and unrelenting and a good place for

Daniel Ridge Loop

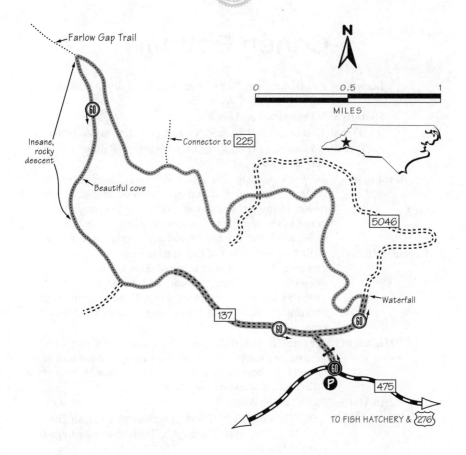

a bad bust. There are also two spots where the trail narrows to about 6 inches wide with a 75-degree fall line dropping 50 or 60 feet down the side. Don't even *think* about blowing your move there. I'd rate the next half mile a solid tech 4 descent.

3.5 Trail drops down alongside the creek. You'll find an awe-inspiring cascade here by the sound of its laughter.

3.6 Pass an old stone bridge to the right. Trail begins to run along an old roadbed, FR 137. Not doubletrack but maybe XXL singletrack. Smooth cruising in some places, sketchy running over loose chicken heads in others. Red blazes still on the trees.

4.2 Go straight, as another old road breaks to the right. Trail leads down a ferocious drainage ditch/stairs combination, tech 4+. Track afterward turns into true Forest Service road.

4.7 Track dumps you back onto FR 5046. Turn right to return to the parking area.

4.8 Pass the gate and return to your car.

Caney Bottom

Location: Pisgah National Forest, near fish hatchery. About 50 minutes south of Asheville.

Distance: 5.2 miles out and back.

Time: 45 minutes to 1 hour, depending on time at the waterfall.

Tread: 4.4 miles of primo Pisgah singletrack; 0.8 mile of Forest Service road.

Aerobic level: Easy to moderate. The climb up is surprisingly gentle, given the amount of speed generated on the way back down. In the right gear, any fleet-footed granny could crank to the top then turn around, bomb back down in style, and leave the rest of you mugs gasping in her dust.

Technical difficulty: Tech 2 overall. Most of this trail is smooth and well groomed. However, a number of tech 3 and 4 root maneuvers lurk along the way, and the unending root drops on the way back down can get you pogo-ing with amazing regularity and astounding results. Ridable and enjoyable by bikers of all ability levels.

Highlights: Spectacular waterfall; easy climb; gravity-defying berms; an amazing number of little root drops; and a 4-foot-high jump at the bottom of the extension for those who need a little more altitude in their lives.

Land status: Pigah National Forest.

Maps: USGS Shining Rock; USDA Forest Service Pisgah District Trail Map; National Geographic Trails Illustrated Pisgah Ranger District.

Access: From Asheville, take Interstate 26 East (actually south) to North Carolina Highway 280 South. Follow NC 280 about 15 miles to the town of Brevard. Turn right onto U.S. Highway 276, which leads up into the heart of Pisgah National Forest. Follow US 276 for roughly 4 miles, then turn left onto Forest Road 475 (paved at this point), which leads to the fish hatchery. Roughly 1 mile past the fish hatchery, look for gated road and sign on right for Cove Creek Group Camping Area. Parking area is across the road on the left.

Notes on the trail

This may well be the most purely fun trail available in all of Pisgah National Forest. The climb is relatively mild, the waterfall is spectacular, and the descent will have you waking up the next morning with a grin still stretched across your face. Novices will be spoiled by the sheer beauty and exhilaration of this ride. More advanced riders can take what's offered, add several healthy dollops of speed, then holler themselves hoarse over one massive jump, two waist-high berms that belong on a NASCAR track, and enough bunny hops to make you think your bike sprouted wings.

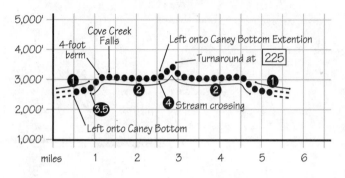

The Ride

0.0 Start at parking area across from gated road to the Cove Creek Group Campground area (on the road from the fish hatchery). Go around gate and up gravel road.

0.1 Cove Creek Road goes through a wide but doable creek crossing. Path to right ducks into a pretty rhodo tunnel crosses creek on short wooden bridge, then returns to road.

0.4 Turn left at trail entrance. Trail marker (Caney Bottom Loop) planted 20 feet in. Also brown sign: "Group Camping by Reservation Only."

0.5 Turn right across steep rocky tech 3+ stream crossing. Blue arrow mounted on tree. Trail straight is an ugly climb up to an uncharted fire road. Campground down to right.

0.6 Turn left uphill, following blue blazes. Right is shortcut back down to road. About 2 miles of easy climbing starts now.

0.8 Turn left (straight) to continue on bike trail. Hiking-only trail turns off to the right. Tech 3+ rocky stream crossing, followed shortly by a serious portage over a log bridge, then more climbing.

1.0 Three respectable root drop/water bars in a row, followed by beautifully carved 4-foot-high berm. Remember this spot for the trip back down; with a little speed, it pegs the fun meter.

1.2 Stop. Listen for the sound of rushing water and look for faint trail to the right. A very tough little track leads you through the rhododendron and right to the top of Cove Creek Falls, an incredible waterfall that rivals anything in Pisgah. *Do not* be a fool and attempt to walk or ride across the stone at the top; it'd either be your best move ever or your last. Look for branch trail that leads down to the bottom. The falls are 20 to 25 feet wide and drop 50 to 60 feet; easily as beautiful as Looking Glass Falls.

2.3 Nasty tech 4 descent through rocks and roots down to bridge with more roots on the climb up the other side. Definitely one of those all-or-nothing spots; do it right or walk it.

Caney Bottom

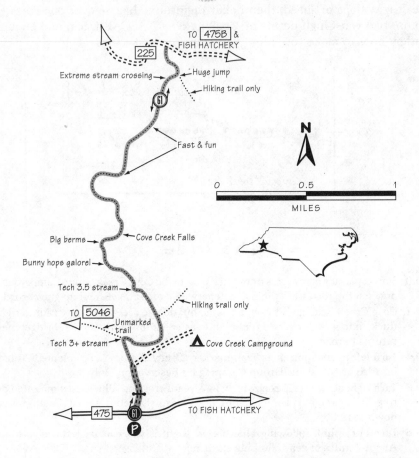

TO 475B & FISH HATCHERY

225

Extreme stream crossing

Huge jump

Hiking trail only

61

N

0   0.5   1

MILES

Fast & fun

Big berms

Cove Creek Falls

Bunny hops galore!

Tech 3.5 stream

Hiking trail only

TO 5046

Unmarked trail

Tech 3+ stream

Cove Creek Campground

475

61

P

TO FISH HATCHERY

2.5 Turn left onto Caney Bottom Extension Trail (yellow blazes). Blue trail to right is beginning of hiking-only leg. Climb up and over a sinister 4-foot-high erosion bar, which will be waiting patiently for your return.

2.6 Hit Forest Road 225 (gravel road). Turn around, rest, drink lots of water, and prepare yourself for what may just be the largest shot of straight fun this side of New Orleans. Very fast descent leads you back to that mammoth jump at the bottom of the extension. Even relatively sane levels of speed can send you soaring 6 feet or more, so either slow down and enjoy the ride or hit it hard, hang on, and pray for a safe landing.

2.7 Turn right at bottom of jump to stay on bike trail; straight is hiking only.

3.3 Track from here gets sweet and swoopy, with lots of long buff sections, fast curves, and short carpets of tech 3+ roots laid down in some of the corners. Oh, and those two magnificent berms lay somewhere along here for an opportunity to get horizontal with your bike without eating any dirt.

4.2 Unridable log across trail forces portage. Afterward watch for series of three good-sized root drops in a row that will have you doing more flying than rolling; I score this section a 9.5 for fun alone.

4.6 Bear right to stay on trail. Curve to left is shortcut back to Cove Creek Road.

4.7 Turn left after steep-sided tech 3+ stream crossing.

4.8 Turn right to put you back on Cove Creek Road for the return trip to the parking area.

5.1 Excellent cool-down opportunity crossing wide stream.

5.2 Return to parking area.

Pink Beds

Location: Pisgah National Forest, near the Cradle of Forestry. About 50 minutes south of Asheville.

Distance: 5.4 miles out and back.

Time: 45 minutes to 1.5 hours.

Tread: 4.6 miles of singletrack; 0.8 mile of gravel road.

Aerobic level: Easy. This is the flattest trail in Pisgah National Forest, even though it never dips below 3,000 feet. Perfect for just rolling along.

Technical difficulty: Tech 1+ overall. Most of this trail is wide-open XXL singletrack with minimal roots and rocks. There are a few respectable logs to cross, a long washed-out section to navigate, and a tech 3+ rock garden along the way.

Highlights: Long rhodo tunnel; easy cruising; logs; bridges; beaver dam.

Land status: Pisgah National Forest. Trail open to bikes October 1 through March 31.

Maps: USGS Shining Rock; USDA Forest Service Pisgah District Trail Map; National Geographic Trails Illustrated Pisgah Ranger District.

Access: From Asheville, take Interstate 26 East (actually south) to North Carolina Highway 280 South. Follow NC 280 for about 15 miles toward Brevard. At the first Brevard stoplight, turn right onto U.S. Highway 276. Follow US 276 for 10 or 12 miles, nearly to the Blue Ridge Parkway. Turn right at the sign for the Pink Beds Picnic Area, just past the Forest Discovery Center. Park in the lot. Trail picks up on the far side of the picnic area.

Notes on the trail

The Pink Beds is just about as easy a trail as you'll find in Pisgah. It doesn't drop more than 40 feet in elevation along its entire length. And yet, it's still Pisgah, with enough roots, rocks, and logs to keep you grinning. While you used to be able to loop this trail with Forest Road 1206, some industrious beaver families have claimed the bottom for themselves and thrown up a formidable moat around their property. So until our fat-tailed brothers decide to move on, this trail is an out-and-back ride or a swim, take your pick.

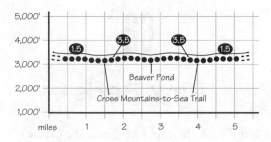

The Ride

0.0 From the parking lot, head toward the back of the picnic area by a gate that's signed "Road Closed."

0.1 Turn left at the Y to stay on the bike portion of the trail. Track starts out down an easy gravel doubletrack and crosses a wide but shallow stream. The stream is more than ankle deep and very cold, I can attest. Nearby bridge provides easy bypass.

Tony, Butchie, and Tom show us what "young at heart" really means.

Pink Beds

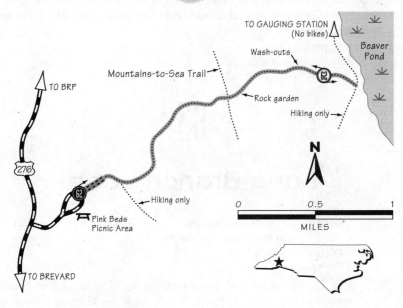

0.4 Tread changes to dirt singletrack, tech 1+. Nice descent through the woods and along the edges of several small meadows.

0.7 Cross two wooden foot bridges. Some twisting through the trees, then a swooping descent.

1.0 Ridable stream with accompanying footbridge. Trail then drops into a long rhodo tunnel so tight you can touch the ceiling. Orange blazes on the trees.

1.5 Pass between the cut halves of a huge fallen cedar tree. Continue straight as Pink Beds Trail crosses the Mountains-to-Sea Trail.

1.6 Tech 3+ rock garden covering both sides of a small ravine. Ridable, except for the fallen tree in the bottom.

2.2 Trail becomes very washed out and eroded. Enormous number of downed trees, some of which cross the trail for hopping opportunities.

2.5 Turn right at the T, following the orange blazes. Nice 18-inch log hop waiting around the corner.

2.7 Turn around when you reach a wide, unbridged stream and a four-way intersection. Trail used to continue straight, but the beavers decided against it. Even if you wade across, the beaver pond has flooded the trail on the other side as well. Trail left is signed "To Gauging Station—No Bikes at All." Trail right is the other end of the hiking loop, which is also flooded. So, it's time to either turn around or start swimming.

2.9 Turn left, following the orange blazes.

3.2 Washed-out section again.

3.8 Return to the rock garden. Big jumble of rocks stacked at odd angles with a bit of a stream running down the middle. Some of this may rate a tech 4 if you get the line wrong. Remember the downed tree at the bottom.

3.9 Cross the Mountains-to-Sea Trail. Several creeks and footbridges follow.

5.3 Tread changes back to gravel, crosses the wide stream, and drops you back at the picnic area.

5.4 Return to parking lot.

Long Branch Loop

Location: Pisgah National Forest, near fish hatchery; about 50 minutes south of Asheville.

Distance: 8-mile loop.

Time: 1 to 2 hours.

Tread: 4.3 miles of prime singletrack; 3.7 miles of gravel road.

Aerobic level: Easy to Moderate. Nearly all of the climbing is done on gravel road Forest Road 475, though it's long and loose, if not particularly steep. Singletrack descends for most of its length (with the exception of one long, rooty climb), though it's way too technical to be called relaxing.

Technical difficulty: Tech 3+ overall. Nearly every water bar on this trail rates at least a tech 3, and there are dozens of them along the way. Toss in an ill-tempered climb, a couple of tough stream crossings, and a mean tech 4 rooty drop. Be prepared to either fly well or land badly.

Highlights: Water bars; views of John's Rock and Cedar Rock; stream crossings; extremely tight rhodo tunnels; more water bars; fast slalom downhill; old cemetery; still more water bars.

Land status: Pisgah National Forest.

Maps: USGS Shining Rock; USDA Forest Service Pisgah District Trail Map; National Geographic Trails Illustrated Pisgah Ranger District.

Access: From Asheville, take Interstate 26 East (actually south) to North Carolina Highway 280 South. Follow NC 280 for about 15 miles to the town of Brevard. At the first Brevard stoplight, turn right onto U.S. Highway 276, which leads up into the heart of Pisgah National Forest. Follow US 276 for roughly 4 miles, then turn left onto FR 475 (paved at this point), which leads to the fish hatchery. Park in the hatchery visitor's lot.

Notes on the trail

There are only two words for this trail: water bars. They're big, they're ugly, and there's an entire army of them waiting along Long Branch Loop to test your suspension and your mettle. Sometimes you can slalom around them, sometimes you can set up a rhythm and just start pogo-ing from one to the next. And sometimes you hit one wrong or blow the line, and your bike starts bucking like a bee-stung bronco. The views of Cedar Rock and John's Rock are impressive, and the old McCall cemetery holds a sense of quiet respect for earlier times.

"Awesome! Just freakin' awesome!" —Curt Atkinson, crew member
"It's the best ride I know out here." —John Grout, local trail hound

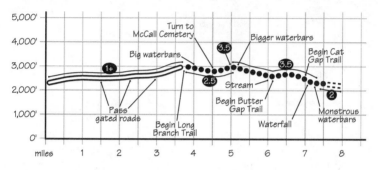

The Ride

0.0 Start from the fish hatchery parking lot. Leave the lot and turn left onto FR 475, which immediately turns to gravel.

1.4 Pass gated road to right, which leads to Cove Creek Group Campground and Caney Bottom Trail.

2.1 Pass gated road to right, which leads to Daniel Ridge Loop Trail.

2.7 Pass gated road (FR 5059) on left.

3.4 Pass trailhead for Cemetery Loop on left.

3.5 Turn left at dirt parking area and onto trailhead for Long Branch. Look for standard brown Forest Service trail sign. Trail starts fairly flat, though water bars grow wherever possible. Cool rhodo tunnels and hemlock groves to ride through. Watch for mega-mudholes if wet.

4.5 Turn right just before stream to stay on Long Branch Trail (orange blazes). Trail straight leads to McCall cemetery with tombstones from the mid-1800s. It's a beautiful, peaceful place; be respectful. To check it out, cross the stream, turn right at the T, and you're there.

4.6 Long Branch Trail runs straight through a small meadow. Keep an eye out for 30 feet of nasty corduroy shortly after.

5.1 Tough tech 3+ move up and over a big rock. Trail tops out, with an excellent view of Cedar Rock off to the right. Hitch up your britches and tighten your shoelaces here folks, because the following descent leads into the Land of the Wild Water Bars. Use caution: You'll pick up speed really quick, and most of

Long Branch Loop

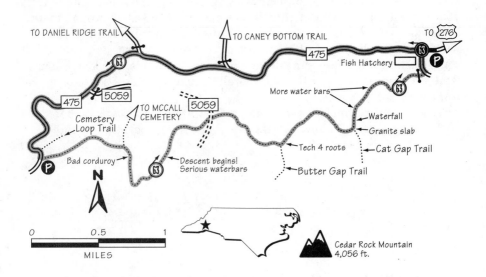

the bars drop at least 2 feet off the back side. The bars are generally too tall to ease over, so either slalom around them or keep the faith and just sail off the edge.

5.5 Good view of John's Rock off to right. Water bars up the ante even more, with some 3-footers in quick succession through incredibly dark rhodo tunnels. Watch for logs hidden in the depths of a large mudhole.

6.1 Cross Searcy Creek (tech 2 +). Left side of the stream is deceptively deep—stay right. Follows up with a tough short climb and a tech 3 + off-camber rock/log combination.

6.4 Steep descent drops down to intersection with Butter Gap Trail (blue blazes). Turn left. Watch for extremely nasty tech 4 root drop shortly after with a cool slalom section to follow.

6.9 Challenging tech 3 climb with a dozen or so tough root sections in a row. No one is undoable, but the difficulty seems to multiply exponentially when there's this many of them. Large clearing afterward.

7.0 Turn left onto Cat Gap Trail just as you ride over a huge slab of granite. You'll soon hear the sounds of a nice waterfall down to the right.

7.3 Really crazy through here. The waterbar/root/rock combos will shake the fillings out of your head. *Big* bunny hop potential in the middle of the descent.

7.5 Hit a gravel service road. Continue straight over the wooden bridge signed "To Fish Hatchery Parking Lot." Tough rooty climb and rocky, tech 2 + stream crossing.

7.8 Hit another gravel road. Immediate left across gated bridge takes you back into the fish hatchery parking lot.

8.0 Return to vehicles in parking lot.

Nantahala National Forest

Nantahala National Forest is the home of the famous Tsali trails. Tsali is the Autobahn of singletrack. Imagine 45 miles of smooth, undulating track that snakes along, high above the lake's edge, flaring out into huge carved berms in the corners. First-timers can ride Tsali and become enraptured by the sport. Hammerheads can just smoke through it all day long and still have enough left for a night ride. It's the closest thing to flying available on two wheels.

Nearby Fontana Village and the Nantahala Outdoor Center offer all the logistical support you'll need for outings in the area: lodging, rentals, repairs, supplies, and guided tours. Both facilities also host some more vertically inspired singletrack of their own for additional riding opportunities.

Tsali–Left Loop

Location: 12 miles west of Bryson City, about 1.5 hours from Asheville.
Distance: 12.2-mile loop.
Time: 1.5 to 2.5 hours.
Tread: 9.2 miles of singletrack; 3 miles of old gravel road.
Aerobic level: Easy. The Left Loop follows the contours pretty closely with only one or two painful climbs.
Technical difficulty: Tech 2 overall. Left Loop is probably the most technically challenging ride in Tsali, though most riders can still cruise through it. The trail is much more twisty than the other loops with some tough stream crossings and a number of off-camber tech 3 and 3.5 rock moves that can slap you down in a hurry.
Highlights: Big berms; stream crossings; fast twisty track; long-range view from overlook.
Land status: Nantahala National Forest and gameland. Entrance fee: $2 per rider per day.
Maps: USGS Noland Creek; *Tsali Mountain Bike Trails* by WMC Publishing, available at local outdoor centers.

Access: From Asheville, take Interstate 40 West and exit onto U.S. Highway 74 West to Dillsboro. Just after crossing a high bridge over the Little Tennessee River, turn right onto North Carolina Highway 28. Follow NC 28 for 5 minutes or so, and watch for right turn at brown sign: "Tsali Recreation Area." Follow this gravel road to the bottom and park in the parking area.

Notes on the trail

If you like some spice in your cruising, then Left Loop is the ride for you. It's just as fast as the other loops in Tsali, but it twists back and forth a good deal more with some excellent 4-foot berms laid in many of the inside corners. Outside corners often hide tricky off-camber rock sections just on the other side that can cost you big if you're not paying attention. The descent down from the overlook is fast and treacherous with a nasty switchback at the bottom over big rock slabs.

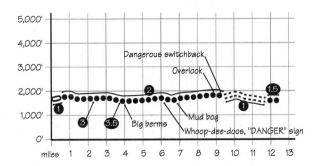

The Ride

0.0 Ride out the entrance to the parking lot, and hang an immediate right on the gravel road heading up to the horse stables, a small parking circle, and the end of County Line Road.

0.5 Turn left onto the Left Loop singletrack, following signs "To Stables and Left Loop." Trail starts with some big sweeping turns downhill and sweet contour running.

1.0 Trail wanders all the way down to the lake's edge. Wooden sign: "Mile marker 1.0."

2.4 Tech 3 stream crossing with some big rocks to avoid and a steep exit.

3.6 Tech 3+ off-camber rock move comes up with no warning around outside corner. Serious injury potential.

6.3 Short, brakes-free descent leads you into a painful climb. "Danger" sign lets you know there's some great whoop-dee-doos on the back side.

6.9 Major mud bog and a goopy stream crossing.

8.0 Sweet 4-foot berm, polished like a dirt roller coaster.

Tsali–Left Loop

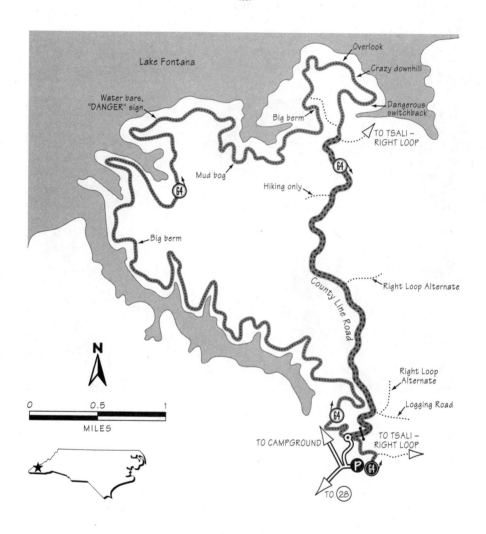

8.2 Continue straight for overlook. Trail back right is a shortcut to County Line Road.

8.7 Overlook. Gorgeous views and a prime resting spot. Descent afterward is loose and fast. When you hit some big rock slabs, drop speed quickly for a sharp switchback right. Missing this turn would be a really bad option, as it's a long drop to the lake.

9.4 Four-way intersection. Continue straight up County Line Road for the return trip.

9.8 Turn left at T, following sign "To Trailhead." Careful, 'cause you'll pick up speed easily on the ride back from here, and the gravel can be both fickle and unforgiving.

10.6 Continue straight. Alternate trail peels in back to left. You're probably really rolling by this point, so be careful of the whoop-dee-doos and the high-speed turns.

11.5 Pass by gate and roll into a small parking area. Turn left onto unmarked singletrack for a fun ride back to the trailhead. If you're too tired, you can follow the gravel road out, which drops you back at the parking lot entrance.

12.2 Intersect beginning of Right Loop. Hang a right, pass the bike wash station, and return to the parking area.

Three down in Tsali.

Tsali-Right Loop

Location: 12 miles west of Bryson City, about 1.5 hours from Asheville.

Distance: 12.6-mile loop.

Time: 1 to 2.5 hours.

Tread: 9.6 miles of singletrack; 3 miles of old gravel road.

Aerobic level: Moderate. Right Loop mixes in some long, loose climbs with the buffed, flat singletrack.

Technical difficulty: Tech 1 +. Typical flat high-speed, Tsali cruising. Some of the climbs are loose and eroded. The tech 3 + off-camber rock move on the way out to the overlook is doable, but the long drop off the side lends some serious consequences to failure.

Highlights: Prime cruising terrain; multiple water bars for big, big air; waist-high berms; nice views.

Land status: Nantahala National Forest and gameland. Entrance fee: $2 per rider per day.

Maps: USGS Noland Creek; *Tsali Mountain Bike Trails* by WMC Publishing, available at local outdoor centers.

Access: From Asheville, take Interstate 40 West and exit onto U.S. Highway 74 West to Dillsboro. Just after crossing a high bridge over the Little Tennessee River, turn right onto North Carolina Highway 28. Follow NC 28 for 5 minutes or so and watch for right turn at brown sign: "Tsali Recreation Area." Follow this gravel road to the bottom and park in the parking area.

Notes on the trail

The Right Loop is an excellent aerobic trail, where you can just cruise. It is also an aerialist's paradise with lots of dips for small bunny hops and mondo water bars on the downhills for major air. Use caution or land well. Contour running is fast and furious (or slow and reflective, if that's your preferred flavor), but use caution, because a 60-foot drop off a sudden off-camber turn is never a good thing.

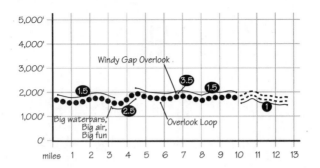

The Ride

0.0 From the Tsali parking lot, enter in past the information board and the bike washing station. Follow track straight in, ignoring turn back to the left. Sign: "Right Loop."

1.0 Exceptional cruising along super-smooth tech 1 hardpack, averaging 12 miles per hour. Big inside berms are a joy, though watch for off-camber outside turns.

2.0 Mile marker 2, followed by a tough climb up some big water bars.

2.3 Sign at top of climb: "Whoop-dee-doos. Danger. Stay in Control." Good advice. You've got six or seven serious water bars waiting on the downhill ahead, every one of which could launch the space shuttle. Enjoy.

2.6 Turn right to follow Right Loop; trail straight is hiking only. Now Tsali really starts to shine, with a high-speed mix of dips, twists and humps, little drops and huge water bars, big berms, rhodo tunnels, and long stretches where you can just flat out get it!

3.6 Continue straight on main trail. Right Loop Alternate turns back left for a quick return to County Line Road for those who feel that they've bitten off more than they can chew.

4.5 Old logging road back to left. Continue straight (and follow sign) for Right Loop.

5.6 Intersection with Right Loop Overlook Trail. Go straight to overlook (my recommendation) or turn left to follow the main track and miss out on the view.

5.8 Continue straight to the overlook. Alternate loop out to the overlook peels off here to the left and eventually brings you back to the overlook trail. It's very hard to spot but worth the effort if you like tight high-speed carving.

6.2 Be prepared for the tech 3+ rock move along overlook trail. While not too tough of a move, blowing this can result in a 60-foot fall off the side, so be *really* sure of your skills or walk it.

6.3 Windy Gap Overlook. Impressive view of lake and mountains. Excellent photo op. Once you're ready to ride again, saddle up and head back the way you came. Ignore any side trails.

7.1 Back at overlook intersection. Turn right to continue on Right Loop. Following descent is eroded and a bit shaky in spots. Leads into some more excellent cruising and big berms.

7.8 Continue straight. Alternate trail back to left for quicker return.

Tsali–Right Loop

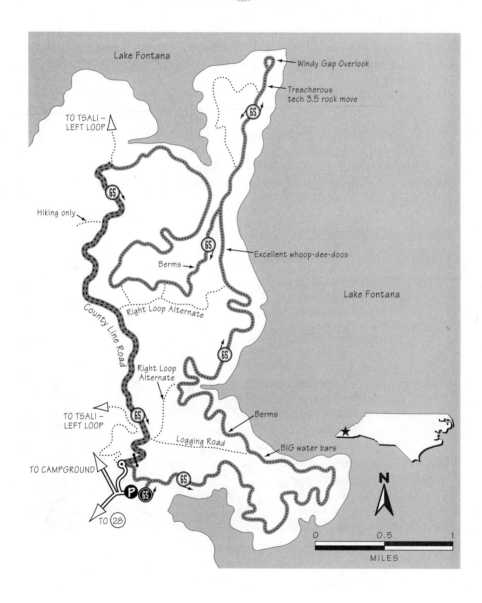

Lake Fontana

Windy Gap Overlook

Treacherous tech 3.5 rock move

TO TSALI – LEFT LOOP

65

Hiking only

65

Excellent whoop-dee-doos

Berms

Lake Fontana

Right Loop Alternate

County Line Road

65

Right Loop Alternate

TO TSALI – LEFT LOOP

65

Berms

Logging Road

BIG water bars

TO CAMPGROUND

P

65

65

TO 28

N

0   0.5   1

MILES

8.1 Continue straight. Second alternate trail back; this one leads over some huge water bars that occasionally hide small ponds behind them.

8.5 Enter an old clearcut area. Watch for snakes here, as it's a prime sunning spot.

9.8 Turn left onto County Line Road and begin a long, grinding climb. Sorry, but most of the fun ends here. This gravel track eventually leads back to the trailhead. Tracks straight and left are two legs of the Left Loop Overlook Trail.

10.2 Turn left at T, following sign "To Trailhead." Careful, 'cause you'll pick up speed easily on the ride back from here, and the gravel can be both fickle and unforgiving.

11.0 Continue straight. Alternate trail peels in back to left. You're probably really rolling by this point, so be careful of the whoop-dee-doos and the high-speed turns.

12.1 Pass by gate and roll into a small parking area. Turn left onto unmarked singletrack for a fun ride back to the trailhead. If you're too tired, you can follow the gravel road out, which drops you back at the parking lot entrance.

12.6 Intersect beginning of Right Loop. Hang a right, pass the bike wash station, and return to the parking area.

View from the right Loop Overlook. DEBRA MOYLAN

Tsali-Mouse Branch Loop

Location: 12 miles west of Bryson City, about 1.5 hours from Asheville.

Distance: 9.1-mile loop.

Time: 1 to 2 hours.

Tread: 7.6 miles of singletrack; 1.5 miles of gravel road.

Aerobic level: Easy to moderate. Mostly buff, flat contour running. Just depends how hard you want to hammer.

Technical difficulty: Tech 1+. Several tough switchback climbs; otherwise, smooth and buff singletrack all the way.

Highlights: Fast contour runs; perfect hardpack track; incredible views; blackberries in season.

Land status: Nantahala National Forest and gameland. Entrance fee: $2 per rider per day.

Maps: USGS Noland Creek; *Tsali Mountain Bike Trails* by WMC Publishing, available at local outdoor centers.

Access: From Asheville, take Interstate 40 West and exit onto U.S. Highway 74 West to Dillsboro. Just after crossing a high bridge over the the Little Tennessee River, turn right onto North Carolina Highway 28. Follow NC 28 for 5 minutes or so and watch for right turn at brown sign: "Tsali Recreation Area." Follow this gravel road to the bottom and park in the parking area.

Notes on the trail

Many riders call this their favorite Tsali trail; not me, but many others do. It's an excellent intro into what Tsali has to offer. For most of its length, Mouse Branch is a buffed dirt highway that slips and dips along the lake's edge. Completely ridable by novices, though the whoop-dee-doos on the downhills might throw a scare into them. The Mouse Branch Overlook is arguably the finest view from any of the trails.

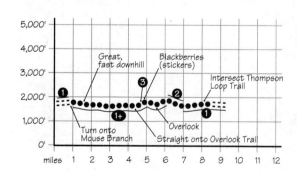

The Ride

0.0 Start from Tsali parking lot. Pay your fee first, then head back out of the parking lot entrance. As you leave the lot, the gated gravel road straight ahead is the entrance for both Thompson and Mouse Branch Loop. Follow it.

0.7 Turn right onto the signed entrance for Mouse Branch Loop. This is one of the finest opening sequences of any trail: big dips, fast contour running, perfect hardpack, and rhodo tunnels. Just the thing to get your morning started, together with that espresso.

1.3 Mile marker 0.6. The signmakers must have started their mileage from the turn-off above. All tech 1 track with lots of downhill action for seemingly little cost.

4.3 Tech 2 rock move. Tough outside climb. Ignore the unmarked trail to the left.

4.5 Go straight for Mouse Branch Overlook Trail (highly recommended). Gorgeous long-range views of mountains and lake frame several long swooping downhills. The Mouse Branch Alternate cuts back to the left and provides a bailout for anyone who really needs to shave 2 miles off the ride. You'll really miss out, though.

4.7 Sharp turn back to left to follow Mouse Branch Overlook Trail. Watch for this turn; it's not well signed, and judging from the tire tracks, a lot of folks miss it. False trail heads straight into a blackberry thicket, which is a wonderful thing only in July when the berries are ripe (and the bears are absent).

5.3 The Mouse Branch Overlook provides a simply spectacular view: gorgeous long-range mountain vistas, islands dotting the lake, occasional beavers, and other critters swimming far below.

Mouse Branch Loop rewards you with this view of Lake Fontana.

Tsali–Mouse Branch Loop

5.7 Trail turns fast, hard, and rutty after leaving overlook. Turn left at the T. Track fades from singletrack to old doubletrack for a high-speed descent. Make your own line, but watch for obstacles hidden in the deep grass. Getting air is just about a required course for this section.

6.7 Turn right to rejoin main trail.

6.9 Turn down to the right to continue on Mouse Branch; trail straight is hiking only. While you're enjoying the following contour running, try to ignore the 100-foot drop on your right.

8.3 Intersection with Thompson Loop and hiking trail. Follow track straight past arrowed sign: "To Trailhead." This puts you back on the gravel entrance road.

9.1 Back at Tsali parking lot.

Tsali–Thompson Loop

Location: Almond; Nantahala National Forest; 1.5 hours west of Asheville.

Distance: 7.6-mile loop.

Time: 1 to 2 hours.

Tread: 6.6 miles of singletrack; 1 mile of gated Forest Service road.

Aerobic level: Easy to moderate. Climb is tempered with plenty of downhills. That may not make much sense, but it sure makes for enjoyable riding.

Technical difficulty: Tech 2. Rootier than the other loops but still mostly just wide-open cruising.

Highlights: Slippery contour running; big berms; lots of bunny hops; one kick-ass downhill!

Land status: Nantahala National Forest and gameland. Entrance fee: $2 per rider per day.

Maps: USGS Noland Creek; *Tsali Mountain Bike Trails* by WMC Publishing, available at local outdoor centers.

Access: From Asheville, take Interstate 40 West and exit onto U.S. Highway 74 West to Dillsboro. Just after crossing a high bridge over the Little Tennessee River, turn right onto North Carolina Highway 28. Follow NC 28 for 5 minutes or so and watch for right turn at brown sign: "Tsali Recreation Area." Follow this gravel road to the bottom and park in the parking area.

Notes on the trail

While a bit more twisty than its longer cousins, Thompson Loop offers up what is probably the finest and fastest descent in Tsali. The singletrack starts off with sweet downhill cruising through the rhododendron. While the maps show that you start climbing from there, you'll swear that you're going down more than up. Then you'll want to check your brakes (particularly you Clydesdales!) before you climb onto the luge run back down to the road. This mile-long downhill puts any roller coaster to shame and will have you screaming with delight for the entire length.

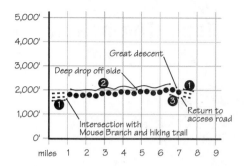

5,000'
4,000'
3,000'
2,000'
1,000'
0'

Great descent
Deep drop off side
Return to access road
Intersection with Mouse Branch and hiking trail

miles 1 2 3 4 5 6 7 8 9

The Ride

0.0 Start from Tsali parking lot. Pay your fee first, then head back out the parking lot entrance. As you leave the lot, the gated gravel road straight ahead is the entrance for both Thompson and Mouse Branch Loop. Follow it.

0.7 Pass entrance to Mouse Branch Loop on right.

0.8 Three-way intersection: turn left to follow "Thompson Loop" sign; straight is the return for Mouse Branch; right is a hiking-only trail. Trail leads into some sweet downhill running, with quick corners and well-angled hops.

1.5 Mile marker 1.5. Fabulous tunnel running, particularly during late spring. More stream crossings and some treacherous sinkholes. Sweet, sweet descents.

2.7 Trail snakes through several of the glassy-smooth berms for which Tsali is so revered.

3.0 Mile marker 3. Climbing starts to get a little more serious, but never gets too bad. Still the most fun you ever had going uphill.

5.0 As you round an outside corner and zip smartly along the buff Tsali singletrack, you may notice that 2 feet or so to the left of your front tire, the ground abruptly drops away into an emerald-cloaked canyon, 80 feet deep. It is a marvelous sight.

6.2 Turn left to follow Thompson Loop (right is Forest Road 2551). Here begins a descent, brothers and sisters, that at times may be considered transcendent. Huge waist-high berms, creekbed running, serious switchbacks, and big, big air if you want it.

7.3 Trail suddenly spits you back out on the entrance road—pointing the wrong way. Turn around and bear right to return to the trailhead.

7.6 Return to parking lot.

Tsali-Thompson Loop

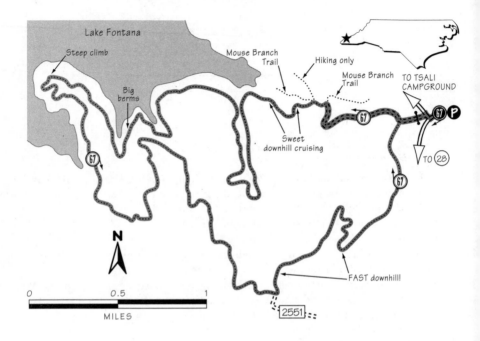

Lake Fontana

Steep climb

Mouse Branch Trail

Hiking only

Mouse Branch Trail

TO TSALI CAMPGROUND

Big berms

67

Sweet downhill cruising

67

67

67

P

TO 28

67

N

FAST downhill!

0   0.5   1

MILES

2551

Fontana–Hoor Hollow

Location: Fontana Village; 2 hours west of Asheville.
Distance: 6.3-mile loop.
Time: 1 to 1.5 hours.
Tread: 4.1 miles of singletrack; 0.2 mile of doubletrack; 2 miles of pavement (all inside the Village though, so few cars).
Aerobic level: Moderate. Almost constant up and down and back and forth. Most of the climbs are short but steep and rock-laden. The toughest part is probably the grind back up the paved road to the top of Turkey Shoot Trail.
Technical difficulty: Tech 3 overall. Some smooth contour running but not much. Mostly twists and turns, switchbacks, and lots of rocks. The Lunchbox is a serious tech 4+ rock garden, just waiting to mangle both the brave and the foolish alike.
Highlights: Tight, twisty track; big berms; fast, technical downhills; switchbacks; beautiful scenery.
Land status: Private land (Fontana Village) and Nantahala National Forest.
Maps: USGS Fontana Dam; trail map available at Fontana Village Adventure Center.
Access: From Asheville, take Interstate 40 West and exit onto U.S. Highway 74 West to Dillsboro. Just after crossing a high bridge over the Little Tennessee River, turn right onto North Carolina Highway 28. Follow NC 28 past the Tsali Recreation Area, then all the way out to Fontana Dam (about another 25 minutes). Turn left when the road makes a T and follow the signs to Fontana Village. All trail directions start from the Village Adventure Center.

Notes on the trail

This collection of trails is a solid intermediate ride, and beginners probably won't be happy if you haul them along. The switchbacks are killers—steep and rocky. The descents are fast, loose and rocky—the definition of "dicey." You'll thrill to several big water bar drops and some incredibly sweet berms. Once you've picked your favorite part, there's usually a return trail somewhere to let you ride it over and over again.

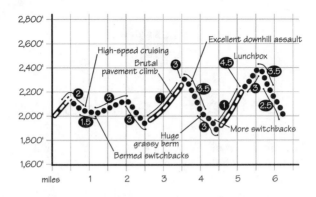

2,800'
2,600'
2,400'
2,200'
2,000'
1,800'
1,600'
miles 1 2 3 4 5 6

Excellent downhill assault
High-speed cruising
Brutal pavement climb — ③
Lunchbox — ④.⑤
②
③
③.⑤
①
③.⑤
③
①
③
②.⑤
①.⑤
③
More switchbacks
Huge grassy berm
Bermed switchbacks

The Ride

0.0 From the front of the Village Adventure Center, turn right and follow the blue arrows painted on the road. Continue straight, and arrows will eventually take you through a fence and up to NC 28.

0.4 Continue straight across NC 28 and up a short section of gravel doubletrack (sign on tree for Hoor Hollow Trail). Gravel quickly fades to grassy doubletrack, with green blazes on the trees.

0.6 Tread fades to hardpacked singletrack, climbing along the contours, then a fun, zippy downhill. All tech 2 stuff at this point.

0.8 Turn left just before a metal gate (there's a field on the other side you'll come to later), following the singletrack and green blazes. Do not hang a sharp left back down the gravel road. Get ready for some high-speed, singletrack contour cruising, a buffed tech 1+ run through the trees.

1.2 Incredibly sweet, sharp (as in 180 degrees), bermed switchbacks that you can just fly through if you bank it just right.

1.3 Turn right at the T onto Great Smoky Mountain Trail. The climb that follows is tough and rocky (tech 3), with a couple of brutal switchbacks to fight your way up.

2.2 Enter the meadow you saw at mile 0.8. Trail leads to a short section of old road/doubletrack that crosses the meadow. Turn left at a big stack of tires and follow a faint path through the grass and over a large pile of wood chips. Singletrack clearly picks up on the other side of the chip pile with some easy contour running.

2.6 Steep, rocky drop (tech 3) brings you out onto NC 28. Turn left toward the Texaco station. Turn right at the Texaco station, following the paved road back into Fontana Village.

2.9 Pass the Village General Store, then turn right at the round house onto another paved road. Turn right again onto Circle Road (paved), and begin a long uphill climb.

3.3 Pass a brown sign on your left for Yellow Creek Mountain Trail. Just keep climbing, and remember what you said about road riding never being as tough as singletrack.

3.7 Turn right at the sign onto Turkey Shoot Trail (brown sign) and bear right at the choice between Turkey Shoot and Piney Ridge. Make your way up a tech 3

Fontana–Hoor Hollow

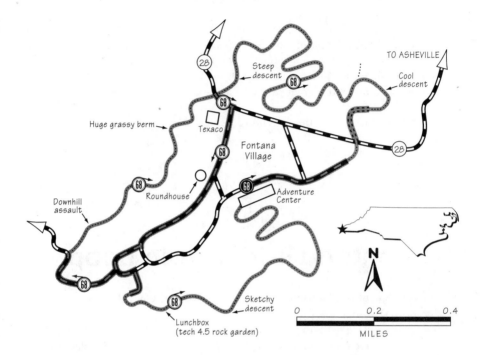

rooty uphill section, then get ready for a serious downhill assault. The run is fast and loose, with sharp, sudden turns, and water bars galore. Sign "Slow—Danger" warns you of a monstrous water bar and drop that sets you up for some supreme air time or one hell of a faceplant; be careful.

4.2 Some flat contour running brings you to a pair of nice, warm-up berms just above the maintenance shed. Then start cranking, because just around the corner lurks a 5-foot-tall monster berm that ought to be on a NASCAR track somewhere; it's big enough and fast enough for you to get completely horizontal.

4.5 Trail bears left uphill, drops you into a pair of steep switchbacks, then shoots you down across a wooden bridge. Be sure you thread this well; the bean bag chair strapped to the handrail ain't there just for looks.

4.6 Hit NC 28 again just below the Texaco. Turn right on NC 28, then right again at the Texaco. Same climb as before, though this time you don't have to grind all the way to the top.

4.9 Pass the Village General Store, then turn right at the roundhouse onto another paved road. Turn right again onto Circle Road (paved), and begin a long, uphill climb.

5.2 Bear left onto a gravel road just before the pavement really gets steep. Immediate right onto an older gravel road that quickly fades to singletrack: This is the entrance to Whitting Rail Trail.

5.3 Whitting Rail Trail ends with a choice of lefts: up or down. Head uphill for a tough climb and a tech 3 stream crossing.

5.4 Enter the Lunchbox. This is a serious tech 4+, bone-breaking rock garden that will have all but the most dialed (or foolhardy) riders dismounting in fear. After saddling back up, you get some cool contouring up and down on a really narrow track and a wide stream crossing.

5.8 Bear left as you hit the remains of an old road, then left again in short order. A tech 3+ descent, full of loose baby heads and razor-sharp chicken heads; a really nasty place to go down, so stay off those bloody front brakes!

6.0 Bear right at the Y, then right again at the four-way that follows.

6.2 Cool downhill with a great pair of back-to-back bermed switchbacks (left then right).

6.3 Drop out just behind the Adventure Center.

Fontana–Night Train Loop

Location: Fontana Village; 2 hours west of Asheville.

Distance: 12.1-mile loop.

Time: 1.5 to 2.5 hours.

Tread: 5.8 miles of singletrack; 5.5 miles of gravel doubletrack; 0.8 mile of pavement (mostly inside the Village, so few cars).

Aerobic level: Moderate. Like everything in this forest, it's a constant up and down. Not much room for resting, and the adrenaline factor definitely takes its toll.

Technical difficulty: Tech 3 overall. Numerous tech 3+ rock gardens, often located in the middle of a descent. Lots of buff contour running balances out the nasty stuff nicely.

Highlights: Stream crossings; rock gardens; high-speed gravel road descent; steep climbs; gorgeous scenery.

Land status: Private land (Fontana Village) and Nantahala National Forest.

Maps: USGS Fontana Dam; trail map available at Fontana Village Adventure Center.

Access: From Asheville, take Interstate 40 West and exit onto U.S. Highway 74 West to Dillsboro. Just after crossing a high bridge over the Little Tennessee River, turn right onto North Carolina Highway 28. Follow NC 28 past the Tsali Recreation Area, then all the way out to Fontana Dam (about another 25 minutes). Turn left when the road makes a T, and follow the signs to Fontana Village. All trail directions start from the Village Adventure Center.

Notes on the trail

This loop mixes together a wide selection of Fontana's trails: Smooth, buffed contour runs lead you into extremely technical stream crossings and rock gardens. The climbs are steep and challenging, and the descents will test both your courage and high-speed avoidance skills. Throughout it all, you're surrounded by the emerald Eden that is the Nantahala National Forest.

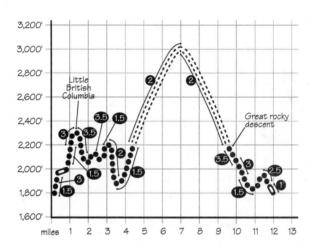

The Ride

0.0 Ride around to the parking area *behind* the Village Adventure Center. Squatter trail begins right at the edge of the parking lot with a fairly steep climb. Tech 1+, soft leaf, dirt singletrack.

0.1 Turn right at four-way intersection for some more climbing. Most beginners (and more than a few intermediates) will be pushing at this point.

0.2 Two tight uphill switchbacks in a row (tech 3). Track begins to follow an old roadbed.

0.3 Trail leads straight onto a short section of pavement.

0.4 Bear left at the Y and follow the pavement uphill, then an immediate right returns you to some singletrack and some tech 1+ contouring.

0.6 Cross a tech 2 stream, then another section of pavement. Continue straight onto a gravel doubletrack that quickly fades back into singletrack. Cross an old gravel road, then a short wooden bridge. Tech 3+ rocks and roots just after the bridge.

0.8 Turn left onto another paved road (this one has the normal yellow dividing lines) and head uphill for a bit.

1.0 Turn sharply back left onto Lookout Rock Trail (singletrack on old roadbed, slightly rocky, tech 1+).

1.1 Two stream crossing in quick succession, then a tough rocky, tech 3 climb.

Fontana–Night Train Loop

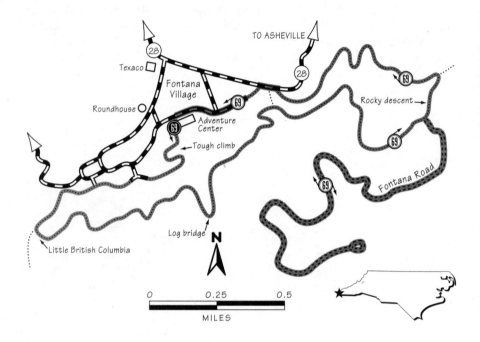

1.3 Bear left at the Y onto First Blood Trail (you'll understand the name in just a minute). Other branch is signed "To Lookout Rock," while trail back the way you just came is signed "To Village."

1.4 Now for a serious technical run, known as Little British Columbia: fast descending over some big rocks and dropoffs, in and out of a rocky creekbed that's slippery as eel snot, a tech 4 boulder field, and some formidable root drops.

1.7 Turn right at the T onto Elmer Hollow Trail for a bit of smooth contouring while you catch your breath after Little BC.

2.2 Another dicey descent, another stream crossing, and another tech 3+ rock garden. Narrow ridge running follows along some absolutely beautiful tech 1+ track.

2.7 Cross over stream on a log bridge. Dumps you onto an old rocky (tech 2+) logging road that's gradually decayed into XXL singletrack.

2.8 Turn right at this four-way. Some smooth cruising leads you into a pair of perfectly bermed 180-degree switchbacks.

3.4 Turn right onto Lewellyn Cove Loop Trail. Slight uphill contour running on this buff tech 1 + singletrack.

4.3 Nice view of Fontana Dam off to the left.

4.5 Cross over a cool little cascade.

4.6 Continue straight as track leads into Fontana Road, an old gravel doubletrack.

4.8 Bear right uphill to stay on Fontana Road. Relax and start spinning for this long, gradual climb.

7.3 Fontana Road ends. Rest up, then turn around for the scorching return run back down. You get to drop 800 feet in 2.5 miles and probably won't need to pedal a stroke. Just watch the loose gravel in the corners.

9.8 Return to mile marker 4.8. Turn left, following the sign for "Lewellyn Cove Trail."

10.1 Sharp right turn back onto singletrack, following sign for Loop Trail. Fast, rock-and-roll kind of descent with a couple small streams, a nice berm or two, and lots of rocks. Hit a tight, rocky switchback, then dive into some narrow rooty contour running. I'd call it a tech 3 + descent with about an 8 on the fun scale.

10.5 Sharp (180-degree switchback) left back (straight is the Nature Trail, hiking only). More dropping with some ornery tech 3 rocks stashed right in the middle of the drop and a big mudhole at the end.

10.6 Wide, wooden bridge carries you over a pair of rushing streams. Trail relaxes into a smooth tech 1 + forest cruiser.

11.4 Short, steep climb followed by a rocky tech 2 + descent, leading to another bridge.

11.6 Turn left as trail ends and drops you onto NC 28 (paved). Watch for cars! Another immediate left onto a short section of singletrack brings you through a gap in the Village fence. Trail leads you onto a paved resort road; just keep going straight to return to the Village Adventure Center.

12.1 Pull up in front of the adventure center. You'll probably need the bike washing station and a cold drink, not necessarily in that order.

Fontana–Lewellyn Cove Loop

Location: Fontana Village; 2 hours west of Asheville.
Distance: 3.6-mile loop.
Time: 30 minutes to 1 hour.
Tread: 2.7 miles of singletrack; 0.9 mile of pavement (mostly inside the Village, so few cars).
Aerobic level: Easy. The climbing is mostly gradual contour running. The adrenaline rush on the drop back down will have first-timers shaking, but that's what it's all about.
Technical difficulty: Tech 2 overall. Smooth buff track on the climb up. The descent can get a bit treacherous in places though, with some tech 3 and 3.5 rocks, streams, and switchbacks.
Highlights: Gorgeous forest cruising; stream crossings; rock gardens; adrenaline-inducing descent.
Land status: Private land (Fontana Village) and Nantahala National Forest.
Maps: USGS Fontana Dam; trail map available at Fontana Village Adventure Center.
Access: From Asheville, take Interstate 40 West and exit onto U.S. Highway 74 West to Dillsboro. Just after crossing a high bridge over the Little Tennessee River, turn right onto North Carolina Highway 28. Follow NC 28 past the Tsali Recreation Area, then all the way out to Fontana Dam (about another 25 minutes). Turn left when the road makes a T and follow the signs to Fontana Village. All trail directions start from the Village Adventure Center.

Notes on the trail

The easiest ride in Fontana's trail system, but still no greenway ride, has a little taste of everything: rocks, streams, cruising, speed, and danger (think of it as trail spice). Beginners can use this trail to gauge their fledgling skills. For more advanced rides, Lewellyn makes an excellent warm-up run, or a good loop to check out your bike setup while waiting on the rest of your crew to get their act together.

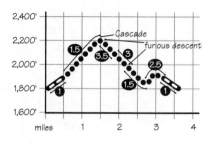

Fontana–Lewellyn Cove Loop

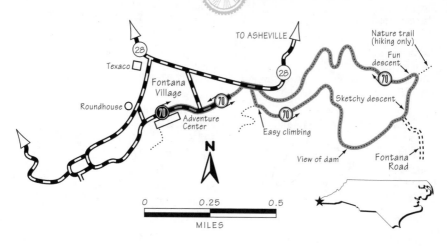

The Ride

0.0 From the front of the Village Adventure Center, turn right and follow the blue arrows painted on the road. Continue straight, and arrows will eventually take you through a fence and up to NC 28.

0.4 Turn right just before NC 28 and follow the sign for Lewellyn Loop Trail, which takes you to the trailhead. Begin with some slight uphill contour running on this buff tech 1+ singletrack.

0.5 Go straight past the turn for Whitting Rail Trail.

1.3 Nice view of Fontana Dam off to the left.

1.5 Cross over a cool little cascade.

1.6 Sharp left turn back downhill (sign: "Loop Trail"). Note that if the ride to this point has been a challenge, then you may want to turn around and go back the way you came. The descent that follows is fast and furious, with stream crossings, berms, and lots of rocks. Hang on, stay off the front brakes, and keep your front wheel (and eyes) pointed where you want to go. It's a tech 3+ run that will push most intermediates' skill limits and may terrify some beginners.

2.0 Sharp (180-degree switchback) left back (straight is the Nature Trail, hiking only). More dropping with some ornery tech 3 rocks stashed right in the middle of the drop and a big mudhole at the end.

2.1 Wide wooden bridge carries you over a pair of rushing streams. Trail relaxes into a smooth tech 1+ forest cruiser.

2.9 Short, steep climb, followed by a rocky tech 2+ descent, leading to another bridge.

3.1 Turn left as trail ends and drops you onto NC 28 (paved). Watch for cars! Another immediate left onto a short section of singletrack takes you through a gap in the Village fence. Trail leads you onto a paved resort road; just keep going straight to return to the adventure center.

3.6 Pull up in front of the Village Adventure Center. This short adrenaline run, if it hasn't scared them off, will have beginners begging for more.

Appendix A: Contacts

Bicycle Post
The Bicycle Post
919-756-3301, 919-757-3616

Biltmore Trails
Gina Elrod
  Biltmore Special Projects Coordinator
828-255-1785

Blue Clay
New Hanover County Parks and
  Recreation
910-343-3680

Cane Creek
Union County Parks and Recreation
704-843-3919

Country Park
Country Park
336-545-5342

Governor's Creek, Devil's Ridge
Fit To Be Tried
919-776-2453

Hobby Park
Paul's Schwinn
336-777-1002

Kitsuma
Epic Cycles
828-669-5969

Lake Crabtree
Lake Crabtree County Park
919-460-3390

Lake Fontana
Fontana Village
800-849-2258

Lake Johnson
Raleigh Parks and Recreation
919-831-6675

Pisgah, Asheville area
Pisgah District Ranger
336-877-3265

Pisgah, Boone area
Grandfather Ranger District
704-652-2144

San-Lee Park
San-Lee Park Office
919-776-6221

South Mountain
South Mountain State Park
828-433-4772

Uhwarrie—Supertree and Keyauwee
USDA Forest Service District Office
910-576-6391

Umstead Park
Umstead State Park
919-787-3033

UNCW
Chain Reaction
910-256-0828

UNC Outdoor Education
Carolina Adventures
919-962-4179

Watershed Trails
Bur-Mill Park
336-545-5300

Appendix B: Bike Shops

There are lots of good bike shops across the state, and I don't mean any disrespect by leaving any out. But here are the shops that went out of their way to help me out in the course of the book. They're good folks, who'll treat you right and help you spend as much time in the saddle as humanly possible.

The Adventure Center, Fontana Village
The Bicycle Post, Greenville
The Bike Arcade, Jacksonville
The Bike Shop, Elon
Chain Reaction, Wilmington
The Clean Machine, Carrboro
Cycle Center, Durham

Cycles de Oro, Greensboro
Epic Cycles, Black Mountain
Fit To Be Tried, Sanford
Magic Cycles, Boone
Paul's Schwinn, Winston-Salem
Ski Country Sports, Asheville

Appendix C: Ride Index

Sweet Singletrack

3 Bicycle Post
11 San-Lee Park
13 Governor's Creek
22 Beech Springs
25 Signal Hill
38 Little Hickory Top
49 Spencer Branch
61 Caney Bottom
66 Tsali—Mouse Branch Loop
67 Tsali—Thompson Loop
68 Fontana—Hoor Hollow

Water Bar Heaven (Jumper's Paradise)

4 Smith Lake
22 Beech Springs
24 South Mountain
26 Uwharrie—Supertree
31 Wilson Ridge–Schoolhouse Ridge Loop
52 Mullinax
55 Pilot Rock Loop
61 Caney Bottom
63 Long Branch Loop
65 Tsali—Right Loop

Screaming Descents

24 South Mountain
29 Long Yancey
36 Kitsuma
37 Mo' Heinous
39 Ingles Field Gap
45 Trace Ridge
47 Little Pisgah Ridge (Big Creek)
59 Black Mountain
67 Tsali—Thompson Loop

Murderous Climbs

24 South Mountain
29 Long Yancey
37 Mo' Heinous
41 Betty Heinous Loop
55 Pilot Rock Loop
57 Buckwheat Knob Loop
59 Black Mountain

Beginner's Banquet

1 UNCW
4 Smith Lake
7 Umstead Park
10 Southern Park
16 Reedy Fork
33 Patch Adams
46 Wash Creek
49 Spencer Branch
62 Pink Beds
66 Tsali—Mouse Branch Loop
70 Fontana—Lewellyn Cove Loop

Cruisers

1 UNCW
3 Bicycle Post
4 Smith Lake
17 Bald Eagle
50 Middle Fork
64 Tsali—Left Loop
65 Tsali—Right Loop
66 Tsali—Mouse Branch Loop
67 Tsali—Thompson Loop

Bruisers

9 UNC Outdoor Education Center
19 Hobby Park
24 South Mountain
29 Long Yancey
53 Big Avery Loop
57 Buckwheat Knob Loop
59 Black Mountain

Technical Playgrounds

2 Blue Clay
9 UNC Outdoor Education Center
15 Owl's Roost
19 Hobby Park
69 Fontana—Night Train Loop
Almost anything in Pisgah

Epic Rides (all day—maybe all night too)

24 South Mountain
29 Long Yancey
51 South Mills River
57 Buckwheat Knob Loop

Appendix D: Other Places to Ride and Future Rides

The trails in this book probably comprise less than half of the trails actually out there, just waiting to be rediscovered, cleaned up, and ridden. The "Other" section lists trails that I couldn't get the maps or directions right, or that I simply didn't have time to ride. It also lists a few lame gravel road rides that I, in good conscience, could not include alongside such fine singletrack. The "Future" areas either have trails in development at this time or are considering opening trails (and need your support).

Other

Beech Mountain: Excellent, fierce downhill, and some worthwhile singletrack.

Sugar Mountain: Downhill and singletrack.

Boone: Several rides around town; check at Magic Cycles for local map.

Duke Forest (Korstian and Durham divisions): Gravel roads only.

Future

North Asheville: An old landfill on the north side of town, soon to open as a city park, already has trails under construction. Eventually it could connect with a new city-wide greenway, which could link to Biltmore, which could link to Pisgah, which could link to Nantahala—the possibilities boggle the mind.

Biltmore Estate: While current rules allow riding only on guided tours, eventual plans may open the entire west side (4,000 acres) of the estate up to mountain biking.

Nantahala National Forest: Fontana Village and the Nantahala Outdoor Center are teaming up with Nantahala National Forest management to open miles of old trails and logging roads, eventually linking both resorts to Tsali, Lake Fontana, and Lake Santeela.

Shearon Harris County Park: Brand new county park (with a bike racer in the management) hopes to eventually cut trails across 1,500 acres. Fledgling trails are already open, with more being added every month.

Falls Lake Recreation Area: Ongoing talks to open existing trails (or possibly allow new trails) to mountain biking. Call and register your support.

North Carolina state parks: For all of the mountain bikers of legal voting age, I feel compelled to include a note about the fate of North Carolina's state parks. No singletrack riding, of any trail, is allowed in any state park in North Carolina. Jordan Lake State Park is 5 minutes from my house with 350 miles of shoreline. You know how much of that publicly held land I can ride? None. Not a foot. Seems sort of silly, and no one at the Park Service can give me a reasonable answer as to why. We continue to hear promising talk from Falls Lake Recreation Area, but the others are steadfastly holding the line against singletrack riders. The single exception is South Mountain State Park, which has opened a brutal, high-altitude jeep road loop to mountain bikers. Maybe, through patience and dedicated lobbying, we can help the rest to understand what we're all missing out on. Until then, it's up to the smaller parks and private landowners to join forces with the biking community in establishing trails that can be enjoyed by everyone. And these visionary managers and landowners, then, will be rewarded with the increased patronage, revenues, and public support that mountain biking brings to town.

Bandit trails: Many bandit trails are open on a don't ask/don't tell basis. No one will chase you off for riding, but they won't give actual permission to ride either, for liability reasons. Seems like every town has some of these sweet pieces of singletrack, hidden away like some crazy aunt that no one wants to talk about. These trails often provide superb riding but don't really help our cause. Ride them and take care of them. Just don't forget to push land managers for full and legal access.

Glossary

Baby heads: Small, loose, round boulders.

Bail: Attempting to abandon your bike in the middle of a dicey move. Often a precursor to a crash.

Biff: Crash; see also *bust, dump, powder, splatter, stack,* or *wrestle the dirt monkeys.*

Big ring: The largest chainring up front for going really fast. Though this one doesn't see much use on most trails, it does work well as a crampon when you're riding those really big logs.

Bomb: To ride a downhill with as little brake and abandon as possible.

Bonk: When you don't eat enough, and your brain and body run out of fuel.

Buff: Smooth, polished track that allows you to just cruise along.

Bullhorn: To snag a tree or vine with your bar-ends. Usually results in an immediate dismount.

Bunny hop: Bouncing the bike off the ground, often using some small root or rise as a launching ramp. With speed, you can sail a long distance like this and take certain trail elements completely out of play. Required technical move for clearing some sections.

Chicken heads: Fist-sized, sharp-edged rocks.

Clean: To conquer a tough section or a big move without crashing, stopping, or putting down a foot. The opposite of *dab.*

Clip/Unclip: Becoming attached or unattached to your pedals.

Contour: As a noun, a horizontal line that runs at the same elevation across the landscape. As a verb, to follow a slope's edge with little up or down.

Dab: To put a foot down in the middle of a move. As in, *I dabbed on those roots and busted my head. I'm going back to try again.*

Dialed: A rider with incredible technical skills, who seems to harmonize with his or her bike on a soul level.

Dicey: Trail section that requires very fine technical skills. Failure here usually results in some serious pain.

Ding: To hurt yourself or (gasp!) your bike.

Dive: Run brakes-free through a section. See *bomb.*

Doubletrack: And old road or path that's left two distinct tracks to choose from. Can vary from soft grassy tracks to crumbling, near-vertical jeep roads. For purposes of this book, any trail that offers you multiple lines or tracks to ride.

Dragonsteeth: Water bar made from sharp, flat stones stuck edge-first into the ground. Fall on one, and you''ll understand the name.

Endo: A crash in which you fly over the handlebars. Also known as doing a faceplant or stacking.

Faceplant: An endo that requires you to use your face as landing gear.

Fall line: The direction in which the ground slopes away. *Contouring* generally calls for you to ride across the fall line.

Granny: As in Granny gear. Your smallest (and most powerful) chainring up front. Necessary for climbing the steepest slopes.

Grinder: Long, unending climb.

Hammer: To ride a trail wide open, cranking up the climbs and bombing the downhills.

Hammerhead: He or she who likes to hammer.

Lariat: A loop with a tail on it.

Line: The clear track through an otherwise gnarly section. Often switches back and forth, or even ends suddenly, in more serious technical terrain.

Portage: Carrying your bike. Extended portages are called *hike-a-bike* sections. No fun.

Pusher: Just like the name implies: a hill you can't ride.

Rhodo: Rhododendron, as in a *rhodo tunnel*.

Roller coaster: A steep, sweeping series of curves, often running down the length of a ravine or gully.

Root drop: An erosion gully caused by water running over the lip of some trail-crossing root. The holes on the backs of these buggers are often quite deep, so best to slalom around or hop over them when possible.

Root lace: A living carpet of roots, lacing back and forth over an area, that love nothing better than to deflect or grab hold of a front wheel and bring a once-proud rider crashing to the ground.

Saddle: Long dip between two high points, usually on a ridgeline. Also, another name for your bike seat.

Singletrack: What we live for: a narrow ribbon of dirt, not much wider than your tires, that slips and dances through the woods. Good singletrack brings you as close to flying as you can get without wings.

Sketchy: Treacherous trail section, often filled with loose rocks, that threatens to chew you up and spit you out.

Superman: Landing with both arms stretched out in front of you. Good way to break both wrists, unless you are indeed the Man of Steel.

Surf: When the front wheel bobbles riding through deep sand or gravel.

Switchback: A sharp turn in the trail, generally with a steep incline either up or down. Uphill, they're as mean as they come: slow-motion, anaerobic charges that can forbid you a dozen times over. Downhill, they test your balance and courage in the face of an imminent faceplant.

Taco: To bend a wheel into a decidedly curved shape that rolls very poorly. Extremely tuned trailside wrenches can repair this problem with a single whack on the properly-sized oak tree.

Tombstone: Large, flat-faced rock sticking up out of ground. Hitting one of these head-on can earn you one with your name carved in it. Avoid or hop at all cost.

Trail toll: Some form of bloody sacrifice, as demanded by the trail gods.

Tread: The type of trail surface you're riding on.

Water bar: Any construction for diverting water from the trail to limit erosion. May be a smooth, angled mound of dirt like a big speedbump, a 6- to 8-inch log laid secured across the trail, or even a row of planted rocks. Old water bars often sport significant drops off their back sides. Most provide opportunities for some serious air time. The log varieties often offer some serious faceplant potential as well.

Waterdog: Rider known for the ability to ride his or her bike across watery stretches that normally require a pontoon boat. Accomplished waterdogs earn the title of River MacDaddy.

Whoop-dee-doos: Large dirt humps, sort of like giant water bars, generally placed to keep motorized traffic off a trail. They're usually big and nasty, and they like to travel in packs.

About the Author

As I struggled to leave the clutches of the corporate world, someone once told me, "Timm, no one's ever going to pay you to ride your bike, you know." My thanks to whoever gave me that first push.

What price do you put on nearly 2000 miles of singletrack? That's what I received for putting this book together. A priceless sum of ecstasy, of flight, of wind in my hair, bugs in my teeth, and the taste of childhood in my soul. Rolling, flying—it's all the same. Come celebrate with me some time, and let me show you my world.

In case anyone is wondering, here's what it takes, hardware-wise, to put together a book like this:

- 5 head shocks
- 3 rear shocks
- 6 wheels
- 3 computers
- 2 GPS units
- 4 micro-recorders
- 9 tires
- countless tubes
- 2 frames
- 4 rear derailleurs
- 2 front derailleurs
- 2 sets of shifters (SRAM rules!)
- countless brake pads
- 3 sets of pedals
- 2 handlebars
- 4 bar ends
- 4 sets of shoes
- lots and lots of bearing replacements
- 2 bottom brackets
- 2 cassettes
- 4 chains
- 10 sets of cables
- 3 seats
- 2 seatposts
- several pounds of flesh, and a few pints of the red stuff
- at least 5 good, permanent scars
- about 30 visits to the chiropractor
- 2 trips to the ER
- roughly 27,000 miles on my truck
- an endless supply of fine singletrack and excitable riding buds

Timm Muth is a writer, adventurer, mountain biking addict, perpetual martial arts student, tiger handler, and sometimes engineer, who is based out of Carrboro, North Carolina. He would sell his soul (or at least a large chunk of his retirement accounts) for a cabin in the heart of Pisgah Forest.

Hammerhead: He or she who likes to hammer.

Lariat: A loop with a tail on it.

Line: The clear track through an otherwise gnarly section. Often switches back and forth, or even ends suddenly, in more serious technical terrain.

Portage: Carrying your bike. Extended portages are called *hike-a-bike* sections. No fun.

Pusher: Just like the name implies: a hill you can't ride.

Rhodo: Rhododendron, as in a *rhodo tunnel.*

Roller coaster: A steep, sweeping series of curves, often running down the length of a ravine or gully.

Root drop: An erosion gully caused by water running over the lip of some trail-crossing root. The holes on the backs of these buggers are often quite deep, so best to slalom around or hop over them when possible.

Root lace: A living carpet of roots, lacing back and forth over an area, that love nothing better than to deflect or grab hold of a front wheel and bring a once-proud rider crashing to the ground.

Saddle: Long dip between two high points, usually on a ridgeline. Also, another name for your bike seat.

Singletrack: What we live for: a narrow ribbon of dirt, not much wider than your tires, that slips and dances through the woods. Good singletrack brings you as close to flying as you can get without wings.

Sketchy: Treacherous trail section, often filled with loose rocks, that threatens to chew you up and spit you out.

Superman: Landing with both arms stretched out in front of you. Good way to break both wrists, unless you are indeed the Man of Steel.

Surf: When the front wheel bobbles riding through deep sand or gravel.

Switchback: A sharp turn in the trail, generally with a steep incline either up or down. Uphill, they're as mean as they come: slow-motion, anaerobic charges that can forbid you a dozen times over. Downhill, they test your balance and courage in the face of an imminent faceplant.

Taco: To bend a wheel into a decidedly curved shape that rolls very poorly. Extremely tuned trailside wrenches can repair this problem with a single whack on the properly-sized oak tree.

Tombstone: Large, flat-faced rock sticking up out of ground. Hitting one of these head-on can earn you one with your name carved in it. Avoid or hop at all cost.

Trail toll: Some form of bloody sacrifice, as demanded by the trail gods.

Tread: The type of trail surface you're riding on.

Water bar: Any construction for diverting water from the trail to limit erosion. May be a smooth, angled mound of dirt like a big speedbump, a 6- to 8-inch log laid secured across the trail, or even a row of planted rocks. Old water bars often sport significant drops off their back sides. Most provide opportunities for some serious air time. The log varieties often offer some serious faceplant potential as well.

Waterdog: Rider known for the ability to ride his or her bike across watery stretches that normally require a pontoon boat. Accomplished waterdogs earn the title of River MacDaddy.

Whoop-dee-doos: Large dirt humps, sort of like giant water bars, generally placed to keep motorized traffic off a trail. They're usually big and nasty, and they like to travel in packs.

About the Author

As I struggled to leave the clutches of the corporate world, someone once told me, "Timm, no one's ever going to pay you to ride your bike, you know." My thanks to whoever gave me that first push.

What price do you put on nearly 2000 miles of singletrack? That's what I received for putting this book together. A priceless sum of ecstasy, of flight, of wind in my hair, bugs in my teeth, and the taste of childhood in my soul. Rolling, flying—it's all the same. Come celebrate with me some time, and let me show you my world.

In case anyone is wondering, here's what it takes, hardware-wise, to put together a book like this:

- 5 head shocks
- 3 rear shocks
- 6 wheels
- 3 computers
- 2 GPS units
- 4 micro-recorders
- 9 tires
- countless tubes
- 2 frames
- 4 rear derailleurs
- 2 front derailleurs
- 2 sets of shifters (SRAM rules!)
- countless brake pads
- 3 sets of pedals
- 2 handlebars
- 4 bar ends

- 4 sets of shoes
- lots and lots of bearing replacements
- 2 bottom brackets
- 2 cassettes
- 4 chains
- 10 sets of cables
- 3 seats
- 2 seatposts
- several pounds of flesh, and a few pints of the red stuff
- at least 5 good, permanent scars
- about 30 visits to the chiropractor
- 2 trips to the ER
- roughly 27,000 miles on my truck
- an endless supply of fine singletrack and excitable riding buds

Timm Muth is a writer, adventurer, mountain biking addict, perpetual martial arts student, tiger handler, and sometimes engineer, who is based out of Carrboro, North Carolina. He would sell his soul (or at least a large chunk of his retirement accounts) for a cabin in the heart of Pisgah Forest.